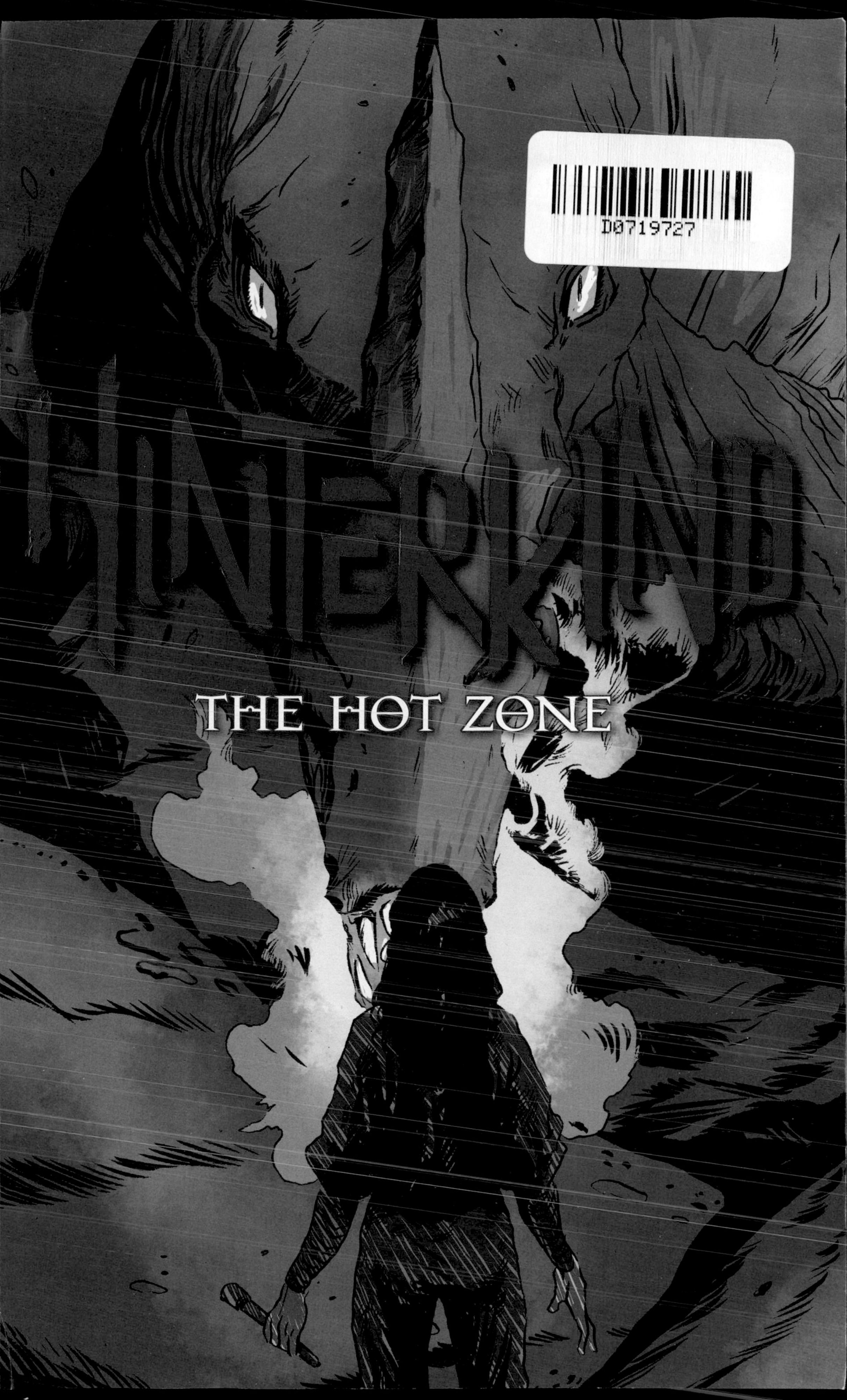
HINTERKIND
THE HOT ZONE

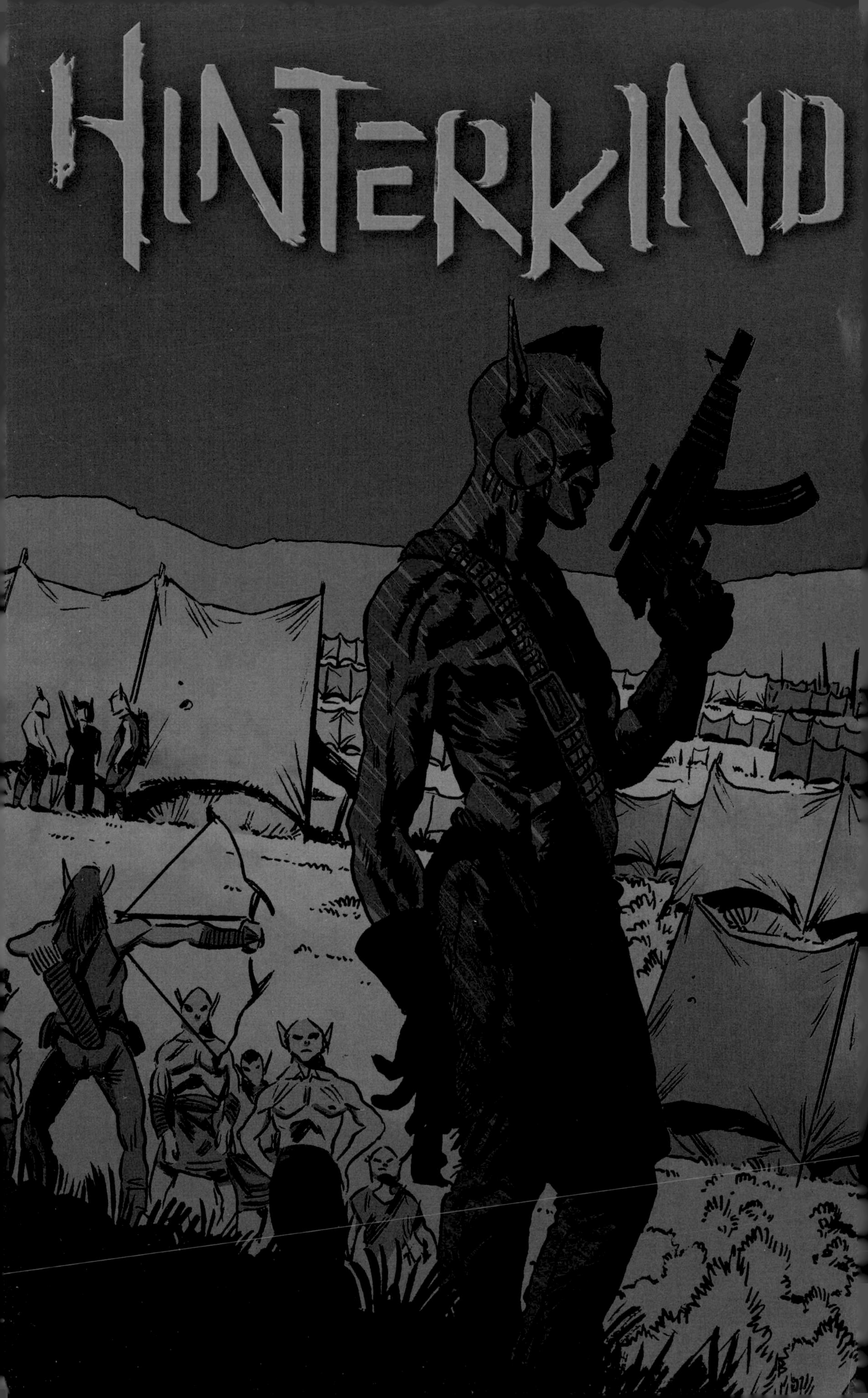
HINTERKIND

THE HOT ZONE

IAN EDGINTON
Writer

FRANCESCO TRIFOGLI
Artist

CRIS PETER
Colorist

DEZI SIENTY COREY BREEN
Letterers

MARGUERITE SAUVAGE
Cover Art and Original Series Covers

HINTERKIND *created by Ian Edginton and Francesco Trifogli*

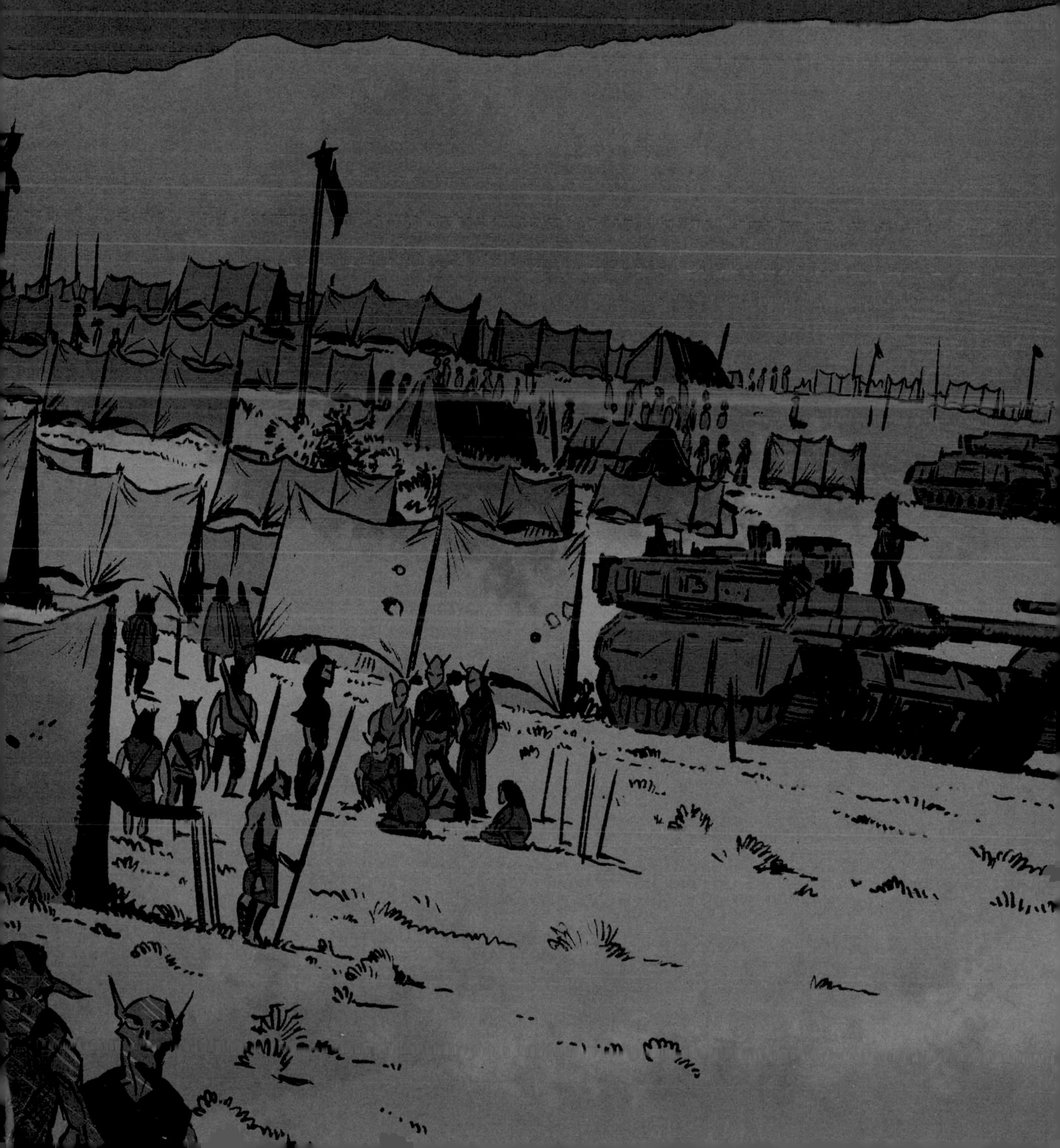

WILL DENNIS EDITOR – ORIGINAL SERIES
GREGORY LOCKARD ASSOCIATE EDITOR – ORIGINAL SERIES
SCOTT NYBAKKEN EDITOR
ROBBIN BROSTERMAN DESIGN DIRECTOR – BOOKS
CURTIS KING JR. PUBLICATION DESIGN

SHELLY BOND EXECUTIVE EDITOR – VERTIGO
HANK KANALZ SENIOR VP – VERTIGO AND INTEGRATED PUBLISHING

DIANE NELSON PRESIDENT
DAN DIDIO AND JIM LEE CO-PUBLISHERS
GEOFF JOHNS CHIEF CREATIVE OFFICER
AMIT DESAI SENIOR VP – MARKETING AND FRANCHISE MANAGEMENT
AMY GENKINS SENIOR VP – BUSINESS AND LEGAL AFFAIRS
NAIRI GARDINER SENIOR VP – FINANCE
JEFF BOISON VP – PUBLISHING PLANNING
MARK CHIARELLO VP – ART DIRECTION AND DESIGN
JOHN CUNNINGHAM VP – MARKETING
TERRI CUNNINGHAM VP – EDITORIAL ADMINISTRATION
LARRY GANEM VP – TALENT RELATIONS AND SERVICES
ALISON GILL SENIOR VP – MANUFACTURING AND OPERATIONS
JAY KOGAN VP – BUSINESS AND LEGAL AFFAIRS, PUBLISHING
JACK MAHAN VP – BUSINESS AFFAIRS, TALENT
NICK NAPOLITANO VP – MANUFACTURING ADMINISTRATION
SUE POHJA VP – BOOK SALES
FRED RUIZ VP – MANUFACTURING OPERATIONS
COURTNEY SIMMONS SENIOR VP – PUBLICITY
BOB WAYNE SENIOR VP – SALES

HINTERKIND: THE HOT ZONE

Published by DC Comics. Copyright © 2015 Ian Edginton and
Francesco Trifogli. All Rights Reserved.

Originally published in single magazine form as HINTERKIND
13-18. Copyright © 2015 Ian Edginton and Francesco Trifogli.
All Rights Reserved. All characters, their distinctive likenesses
and related elements featured in this publication are
trademarks of DC Comics. VERTIGO is a trademark of DC Comics.
The stories, characters and incidents featured in this
publication are entirely fictional. DC Comics does not read
or accept unsolicited submissions of ideas, stories or artwork.

DC Comics, 4000 Warner Blvd., Burbank, CA 91522
A Warner Bros. Entertainment Company
Printed in the USA. First Printing.
ISBN: 978-1-4012-5435-3

Library of Congress Cataloging-in-Publication Data

Edginton, Ian, author.
  Hinterkind. Volume 3, The Hot Zone / Ian Edginton ; illustrated by Francesco Trifogli.
    pages cm
  ISBN 978-1-4012-5435-3 (paperback)
  1. Graphic novels. I. Trifogli, Francesco, illustrator. II. Title. III. Title: The Hot Zone
PN6737.E34H56 2014
  741.5'942—dc23

                                                2013049813

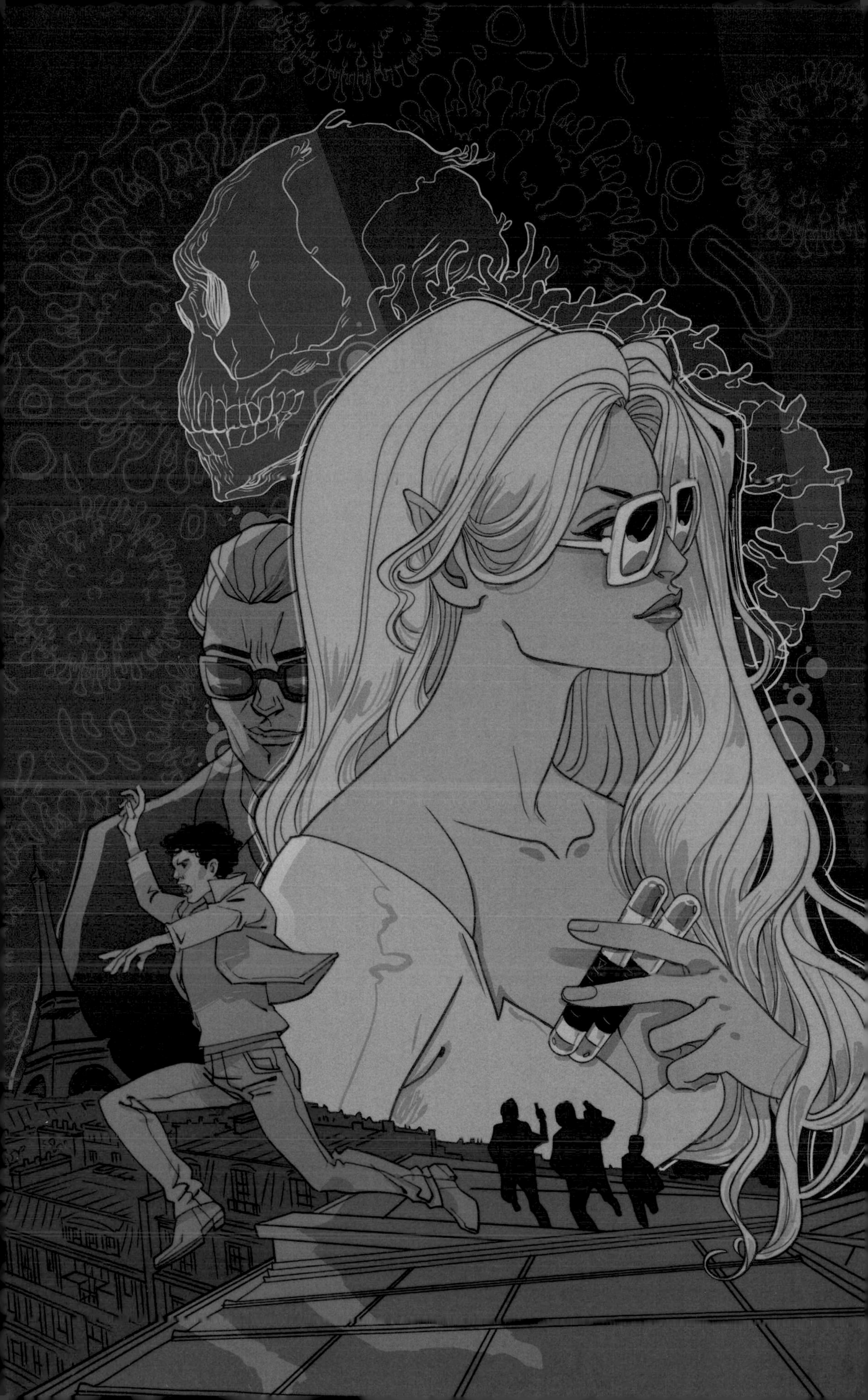

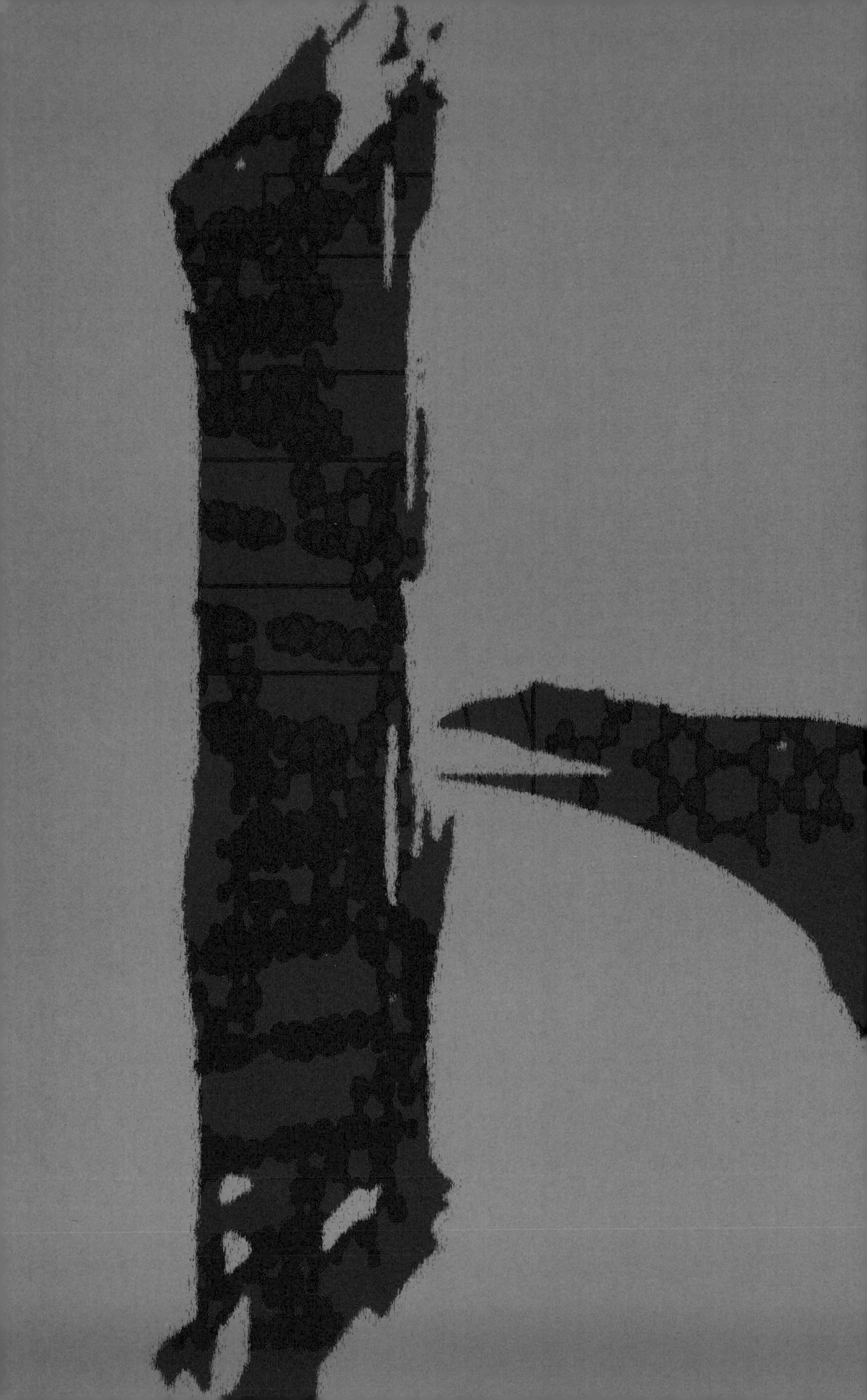

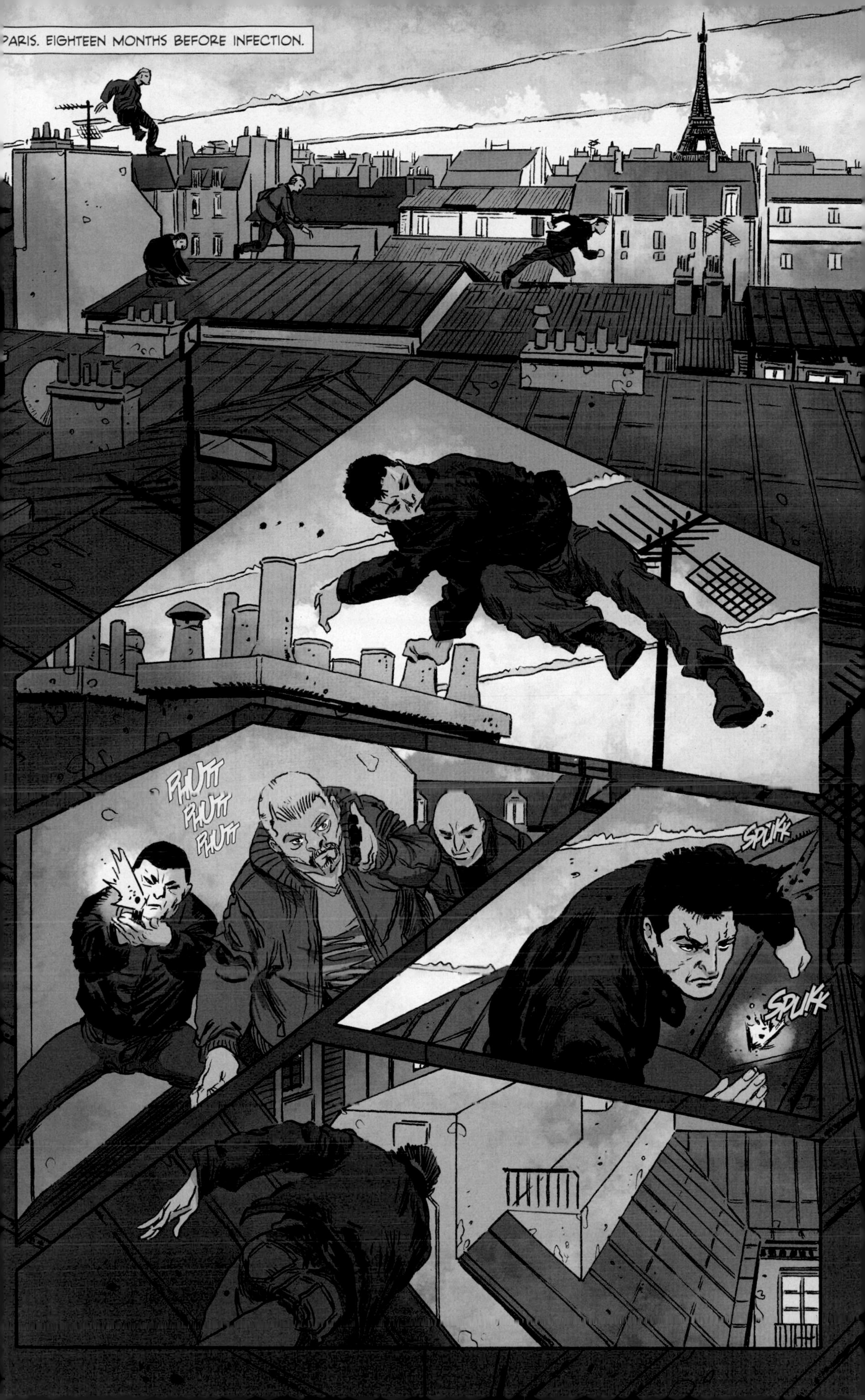
PARIS. EIGHTEEN MONTHS BEFORE INFECTION.
PHUTT PHUTT PHUTT
SPLIKK
SPLIKK

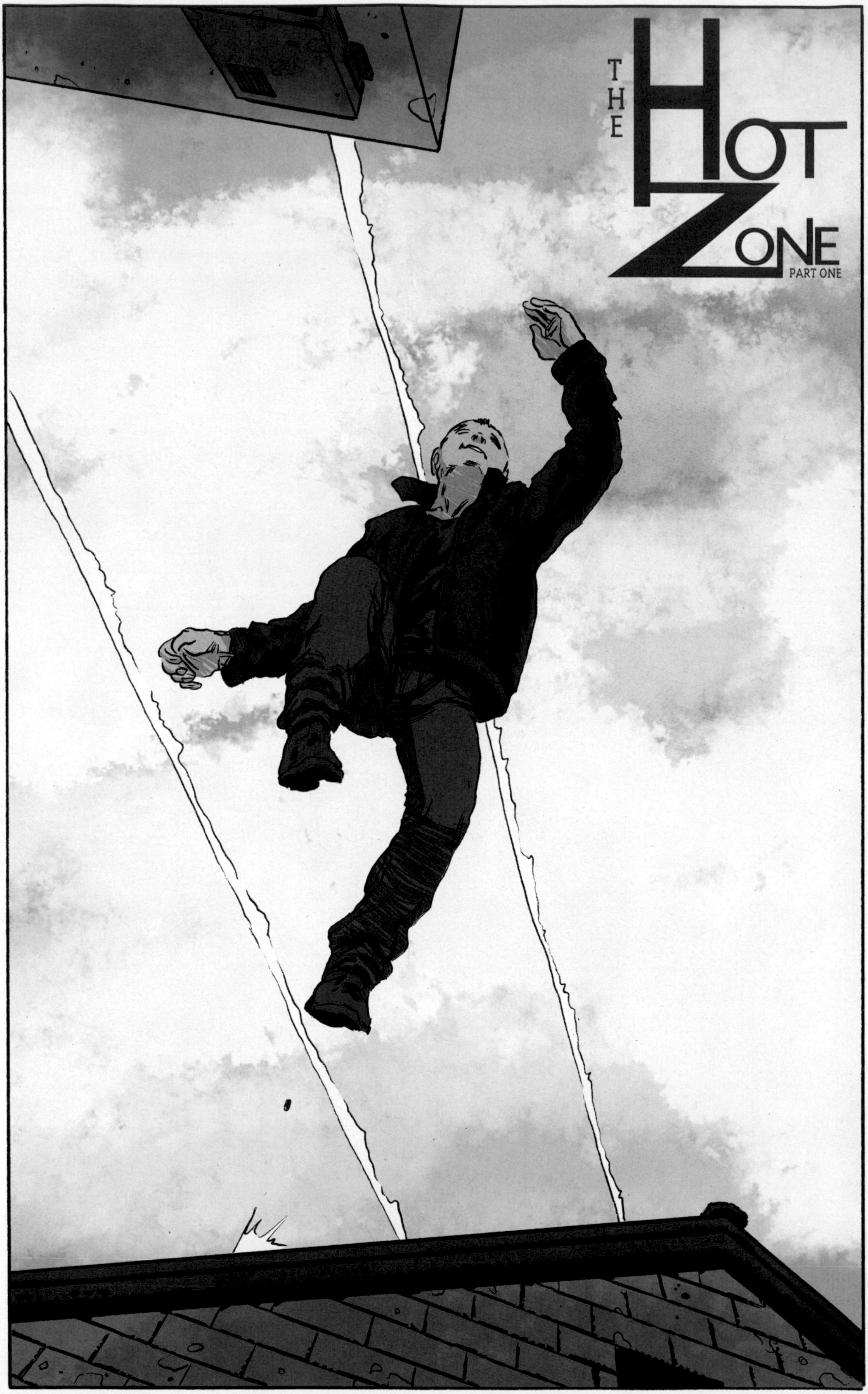
THE HOT ZONE
PART ONE

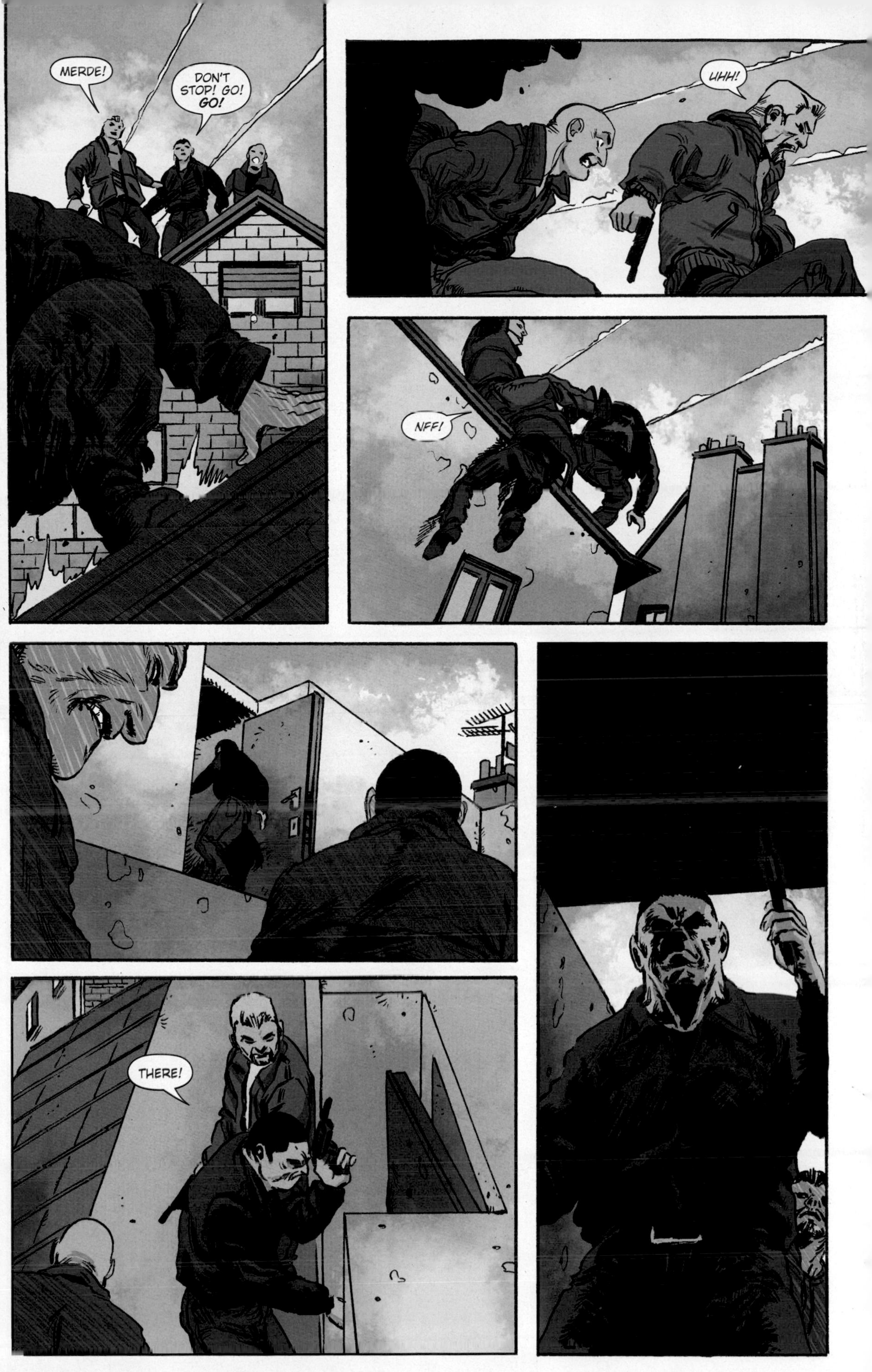
MERDE!
DON'T STOP! GO! GO!
UHH!
NFF!
THERE!

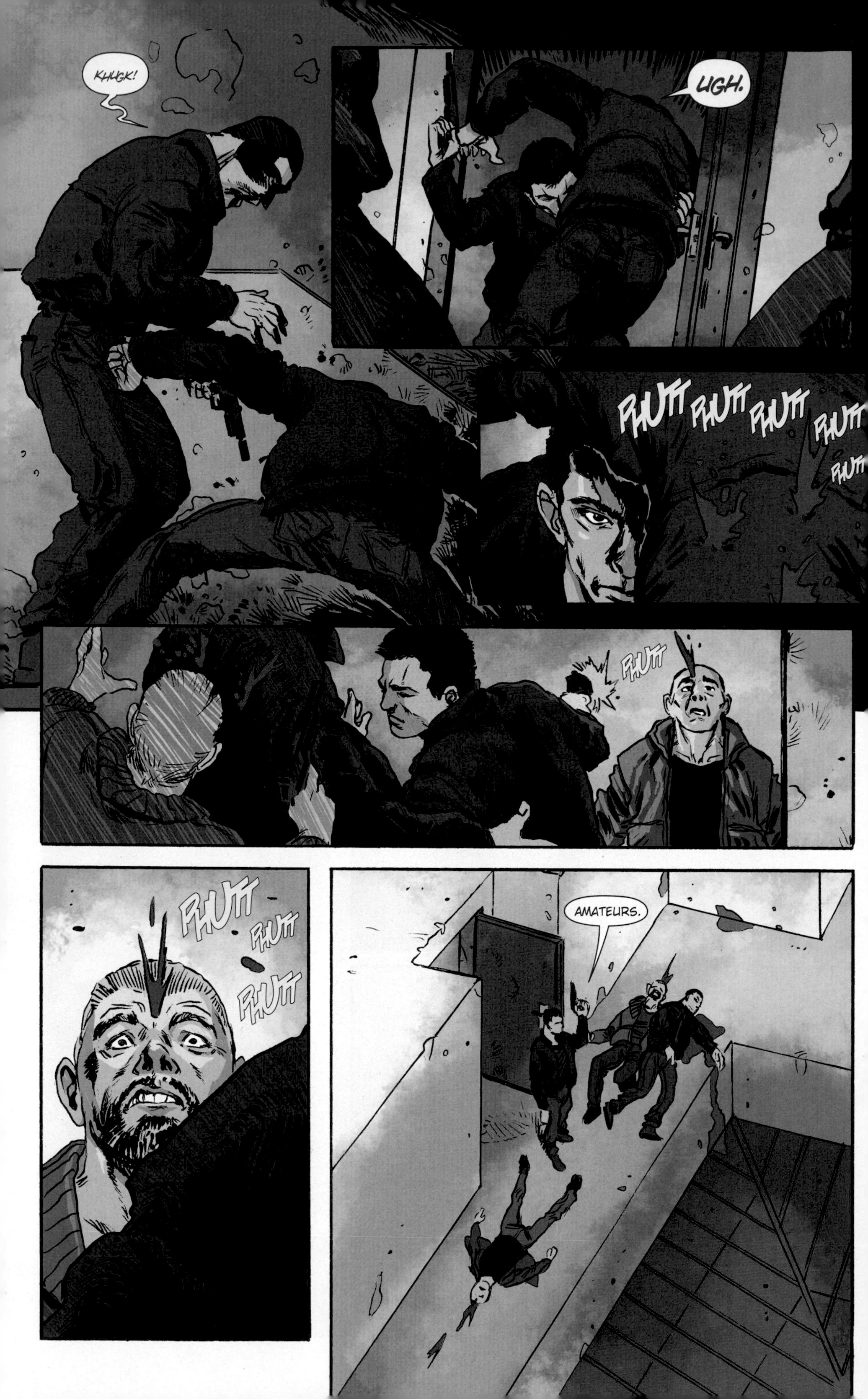
KHUGK!
UGH.
PHUTT PHUTT PHUTT PHUTT PHUTT
PHUTT
PHUTT PHUTT PHUTT
AMATEURS.

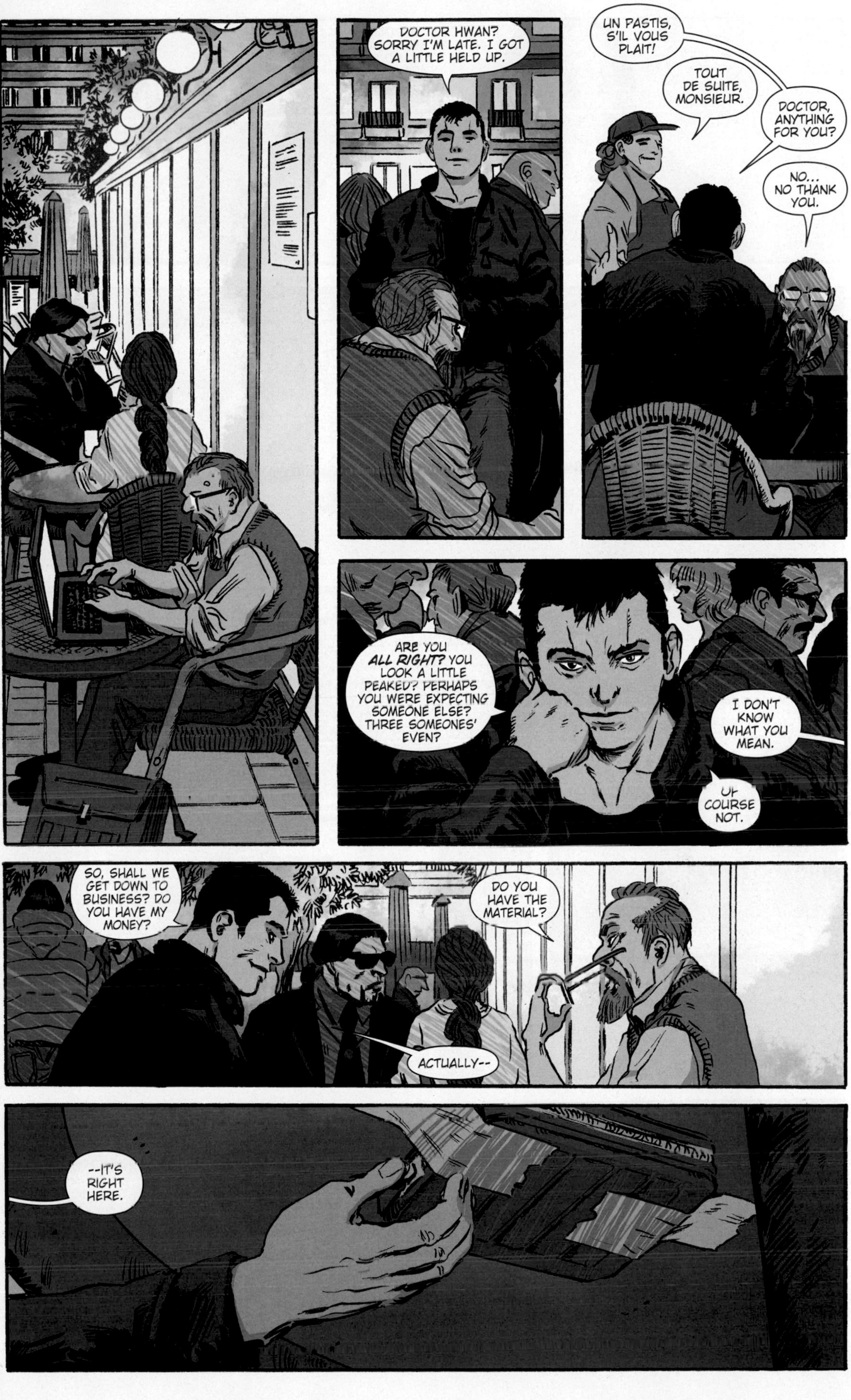
DOCTOR HWAN? SORRY I'M LATE. I GOT A LITTLE HELD UP.
UN PASTIS, S'IL VOUS PLAIT!
TOUT DE SUITE, MONSIEUR.
DOCTOR, ANYTHING FOR YOU?
NO... NO THANK YOU.
ARE YOU **ALL RIGHT?** YOU LOOK A LITTLE PEAKED? PERHAPS YOU WERE EXPECTING SOMEONE ELSE? THREE SOMEONES' EVEN?
I DON'T KNOW WHAT YOU MEAN.
OF COURSE NOT.
SO, SHALL WE GET DOWN TO BUSINESS? DO YOU HAVE MY MONEY?
DO YOU HAVE THE MATERIAL?
ACTUALLY--
--IT'S RIGHT HERE.

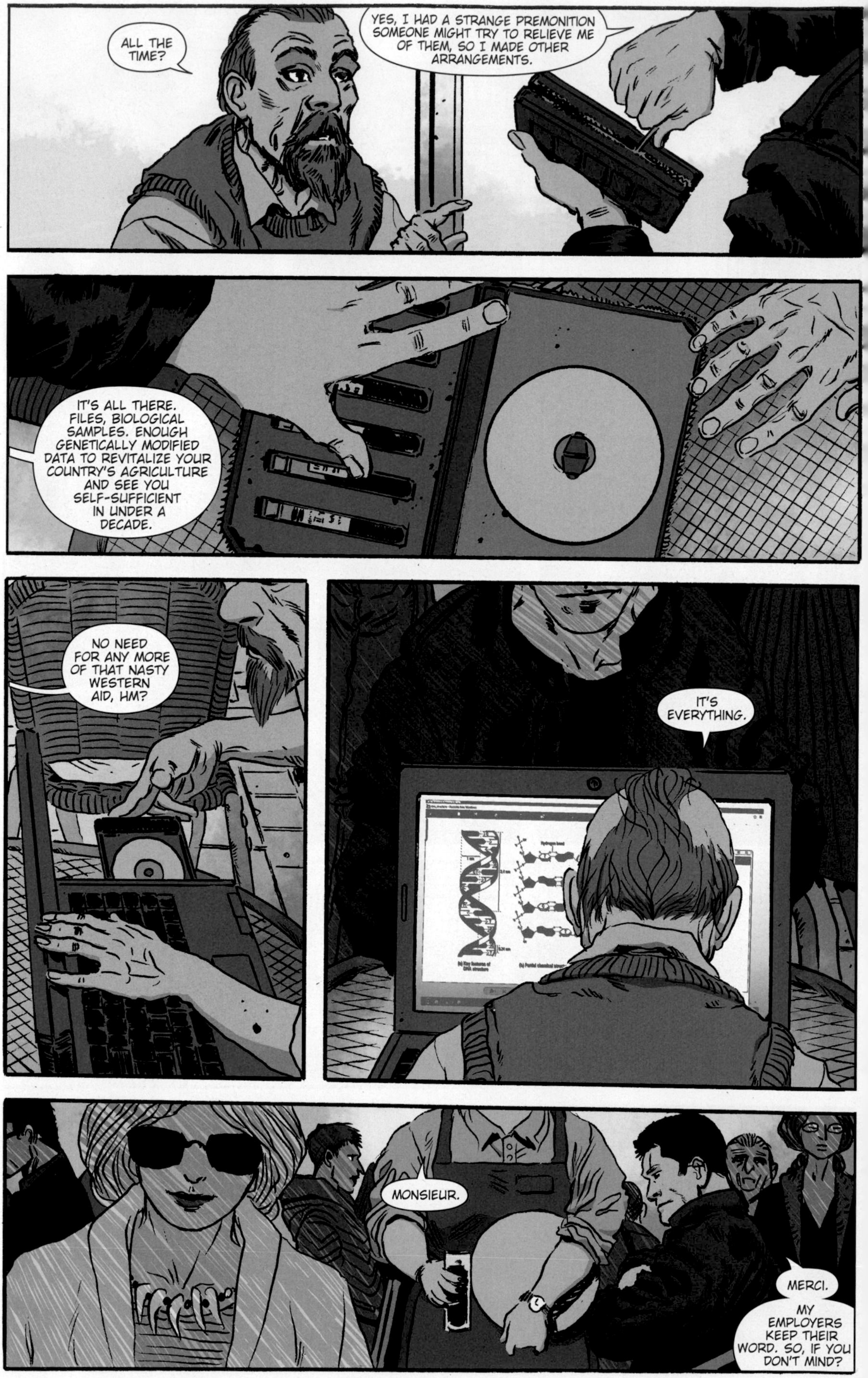
ALL THE TIME?
YES, I HAD A STRANGE PREMONITION SOMEONE MIGHT TRY TO RELIEVE ME OF THEM, SO I MADE OTHER ARRANGEMENTS.
IT'S ALL THERE. FILES, BIOLOGICAL SAMPLES. ENOUGH GENETICALLY MODIFIED DATA TO REVITALIZE YOUR COUNTRY'S AGRICULTURE AND SEE YOU SELF-SUFFICIENT IN UNDER A DECADE.
NO NEED FOR ANY MORE OF THAT NASTY WESTERN AID, HM?
IT'S EVERYTHING.
MONSIEUR.
MERCI.
MY EMPLOYERS KEEP THEIR WORD. SO, IF YOU DON'T MIND?

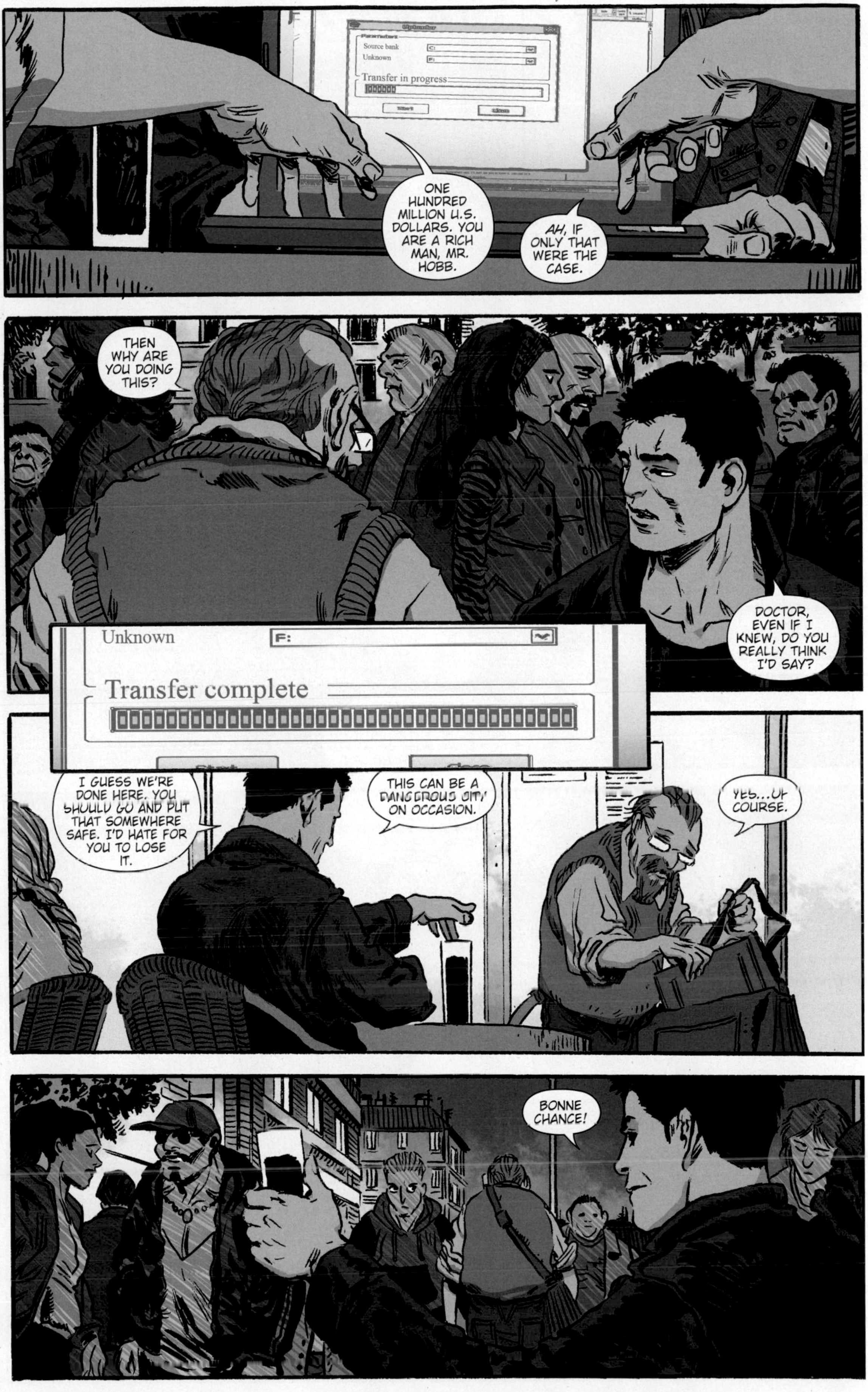
Source bank
Unknown
Transfer in progress
ONE HUNDRED MILLION U.S. DOLLARS. YOU ARE A RICH MAN, MR. HOBB.
AH, IF ONLY THAT WERE THE CASE.
THEN WHY ARE YOU DOING THIS?
DOCTOR, EVEN IF I KNEW, DO YOU REALLY THINK I'D SAY?
Unknown
F:
Transfer complete
I GUESS WE'RE DONE HERE. YOU SHOULD GO AND PUT THAT SOMEWHERE SAFE. I'D HATE FOR YOU TO LOSE IT.
THIS CAN BE A DANGEROUS CITY ON OCCASION.
YES...OF COURSE.
BONNE CHANCE!

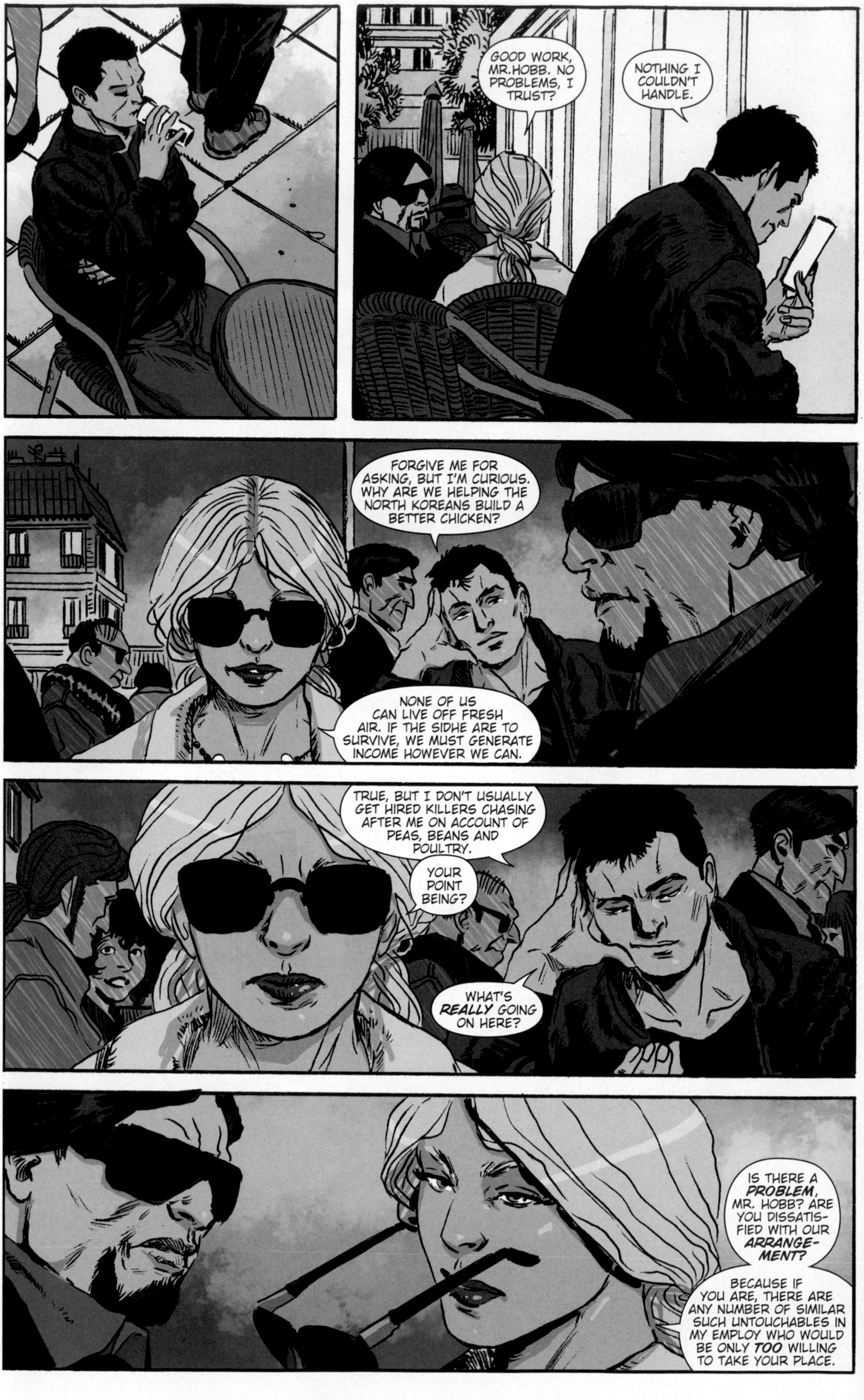
GOOD WORK, MR.HOBB. NO PROBLEMS, I TRUST?
NOTHING I COULDN'T HANDLE.
FORGIVE ME FOR ASKING, BUT I'M CURIOUS. WHY ARE WE HELPING THE NORTH KOREANS BUILD A BETTER CHICKEN?
NONE OF US CAN LIVE OFF FRESH AIR. IF THE SIDHE ARE TO SURVIVE, WE MUST GENERATE INCOME HOWEVER WE CAN.
TRUE, BUT I DON'T USUALLY GET HIRED KILLERS CHASING AFTER ME ON ACCOUNT OF PEAS, BEANS AND POULTRY.
YOUR POINT BEING?
WHAT'S REALLY GOING ON HERE?
IS THERE A PROBLEM, MR. HOBB? ARE YOU DISSATIS-FIED WITH OUR ARRANGE-MENT?
BECAUSE IF YOU ARE, THERE ARE ANY NUMBER OF SIMILAR SUCH UNTOUCHABLES IN MY EMPLOY WHO WOULD BE ONLY TOO WILLING TO TAKE YOUR PLACE.

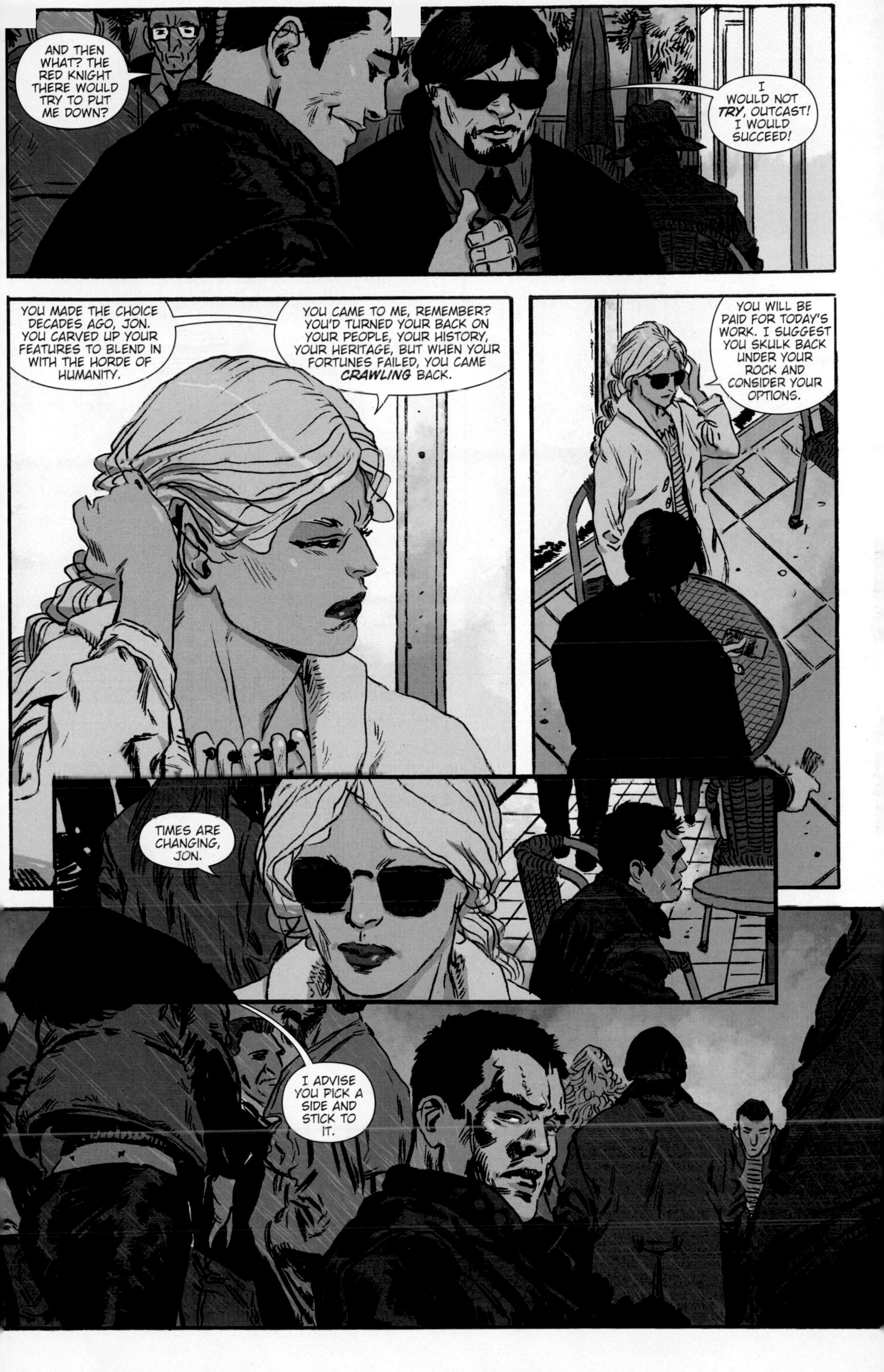
AND THEN WHAT? THE RED KNIGHT THERE WOULD TRY TO PUT ME DOWN?
I WOULD NOT TRY, OUTCAST! I WOULD SUCCEED!
YOU MADE THE CHOICE DECADES AGO, JON. YOU CARVED UP YOUR FEATURES TO BLEND IN WITH THE HORDE OF HUMANITY.
YOU CAME TO ME, REMEMBER? YOU'D TURNED YOUR BACK ON YOUR PEOPLE, YOUR HISTORY, YOUR HERITAGE, BUT WHEN YOUR FORTUNES FAILED, YOU CAME CRAWLING BACK.
YOU WILL BE PAID FOR TODAY'S WORK. I SUGGEST YOU SKULK BACK UNDER YOUR ROCK AND CONSIDER YOUR OPTIONS.
TIMES ARE CHANGING, JON.
I ADVISE YOU PICK A SIDE AND STICK TO IT.

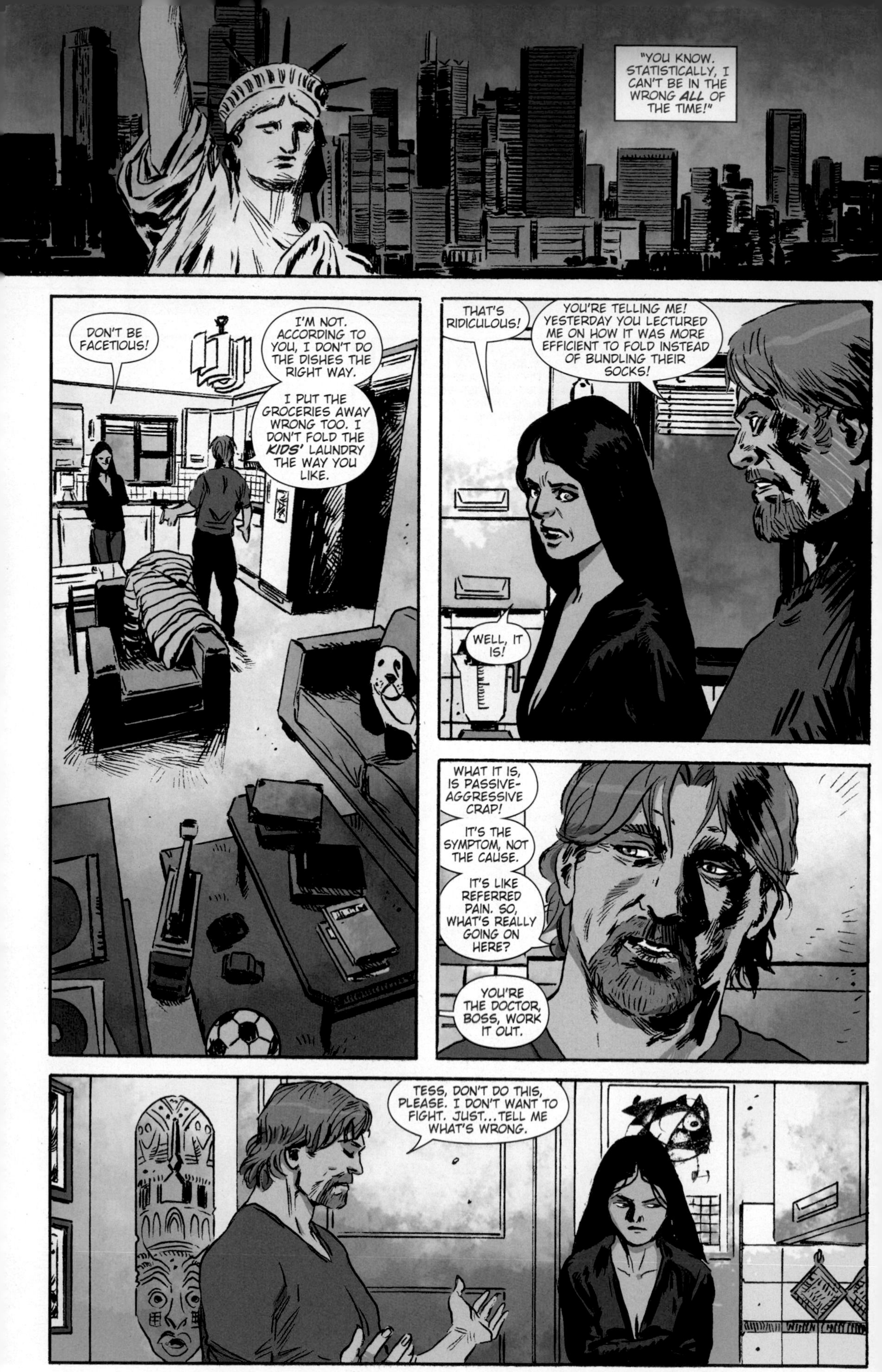
"YOU KNOW. STATISTICALLY, I CAN'T BE IN THE WRONG ALL OF THE TIME!"
DON'T BE FACETIOUS!
I'M NOT. ACCORDING TO YOU, I DON'T DO THE DISHES THE RIGHT WAY.
I PUT THE GROCERIES AWAY WRONG TOO. I DON'T FOLD THE KIDS' LAUNDRY THE WAY YOU LIKE.
THAT'S RIDICULOUS!
YOU'RE TELLING ME! YESTERDAY YOU LECTURED ME ON HOW IT WAS MORE EFFICIENT TO FOLD INSTEAD OF BUNDLING THEIR SOCKS!
WELL, IT IS!
WHAT IT IS, IS PASSIVE-AGGRESSIVE CRAP!
IT'S THE SYMPTOM, NOT THE CAUSE.
IT'S LIKE REFERRED PAIN. SO, WHAT'S REALLY GOING ON HERE?
YOU'RE THE DOCTOR, BOSS, WORK IT OUT.
TESS, DON'T DO THIS, PLEASE. I DON'T WANT TO FIGHT. JUST...TELL ME WHAT'S WRONG.

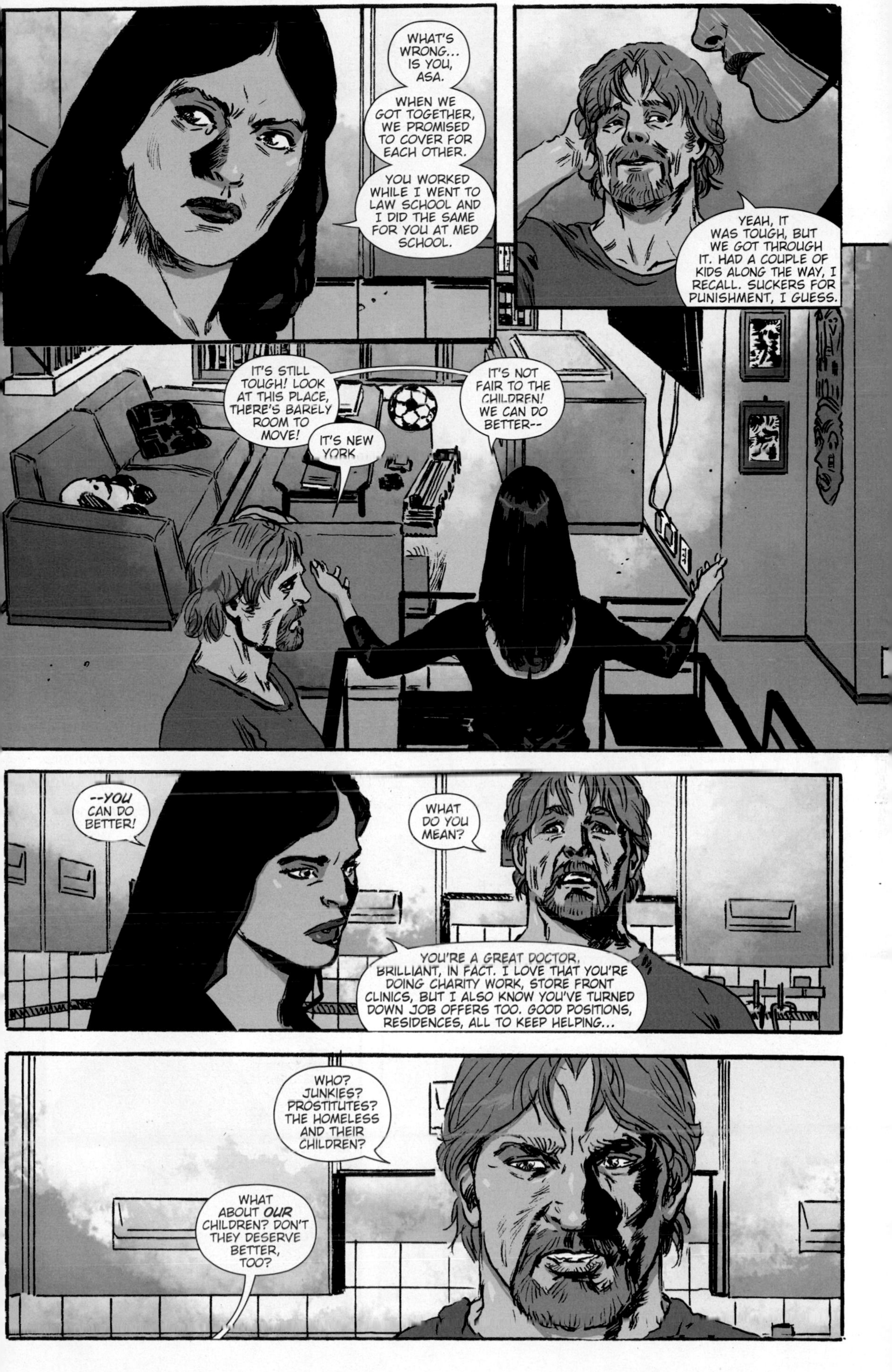
WHAT'S WRONG... IS YOU, ASA.
WHEN WE GOT TOGETHER, WE PROMISED TO COVER FOR EACH OTHER.
YOU WORKED WHILE I WENT TO LAW SCHOOL AND I DID THE SAME FOR YOU AT MED SCHOOL.
YEAH, IT WAS TOUGH, BUT WE GOT THROUGH IT. HAD A COUPLE OF KIDS ALONG THE WAY, I RECALL. SUCKERS FOR PUNISHMENT, I GUESS.
IT'S STILL TOUGH! LOOK AT THIS PLACE, THERE'S BARELY ROOM TO MOVE!
IT'S NOT FAIR TO THE CHILDREN! WE CAN DO BETTER--
IT'S NEW YORK
--YOU CAN DO BETTER!
WHAT DO YOU MEAN?
YOU'RE A GREAT DOCTOR, BRILLIANT, IN FACT. I LOVE THAT YOU'RE DOING CHARITY WORK, STORE FRONT CLINICS, BUT I ALSO KNOW YOU'VE TURNED DOWN JOB OFFERS TOO. GOOD POSITIONS, RESIDENCES, ALL TO KEEP HELPING...
WHO? JUNKIES? PROSTITUTES? THE HOMELESS AND THEIR CHILDREN?
WHAT ABOUT OUR CHILDREN? DON'T THEY DESERVE BETTER, TOO?

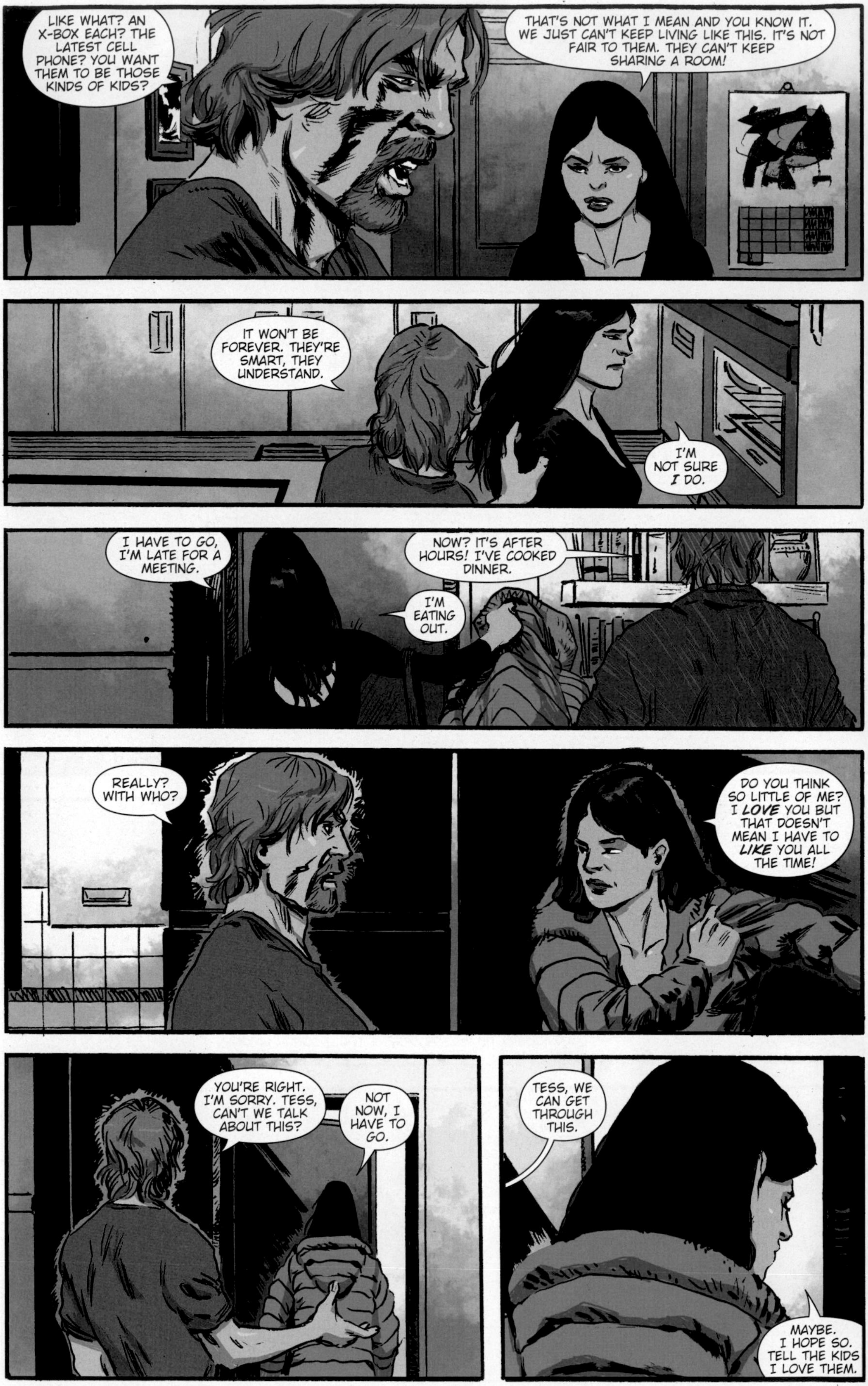
LIKE WHAT? AN X-BOX EACH? THE LATEST CELL PHONE? YOU WANT THEM TO BE THOSE KINDS OF KIDS?
THAT'S NOT WHAT I MEAN AND YOU KNOW IT. WE JUST CAN'T KEEP LIVING LIKE THIS. IT'S NOT FAIR TO THEM. THEY CAN'T KEEP SHARING A ROOM!
IT WON'T BE FOREVER. THEY'RE SMART, THEY UNDERSTAND.
I'M NOT SURE *I* DO.
I HAVE TO GO, I'M LATE FOR A MEETING.
NOW? IT'S AFTER HOURS! I'VE COOKED DINNER.
I'M EATING OUT.
REALLY? WITH WHO?
DO YOU THINK SO LITTLE OF ME? I ***LOVE*** YOU BUT THAT DOESN'T MEAN I HAVE TO ***LIKE*** YOU ALL THE TIME!
YOU'RE RIGHT. I'M SORRY. TESS, CAN'T WE TALK ABOUT THIS?
NOT NOW, I HAVE TO GO.
TESS, WE CAN GET THROUGH THIS.
MAYBE. I HOPE SO. TELL THE KIDS I LOVE THEM.

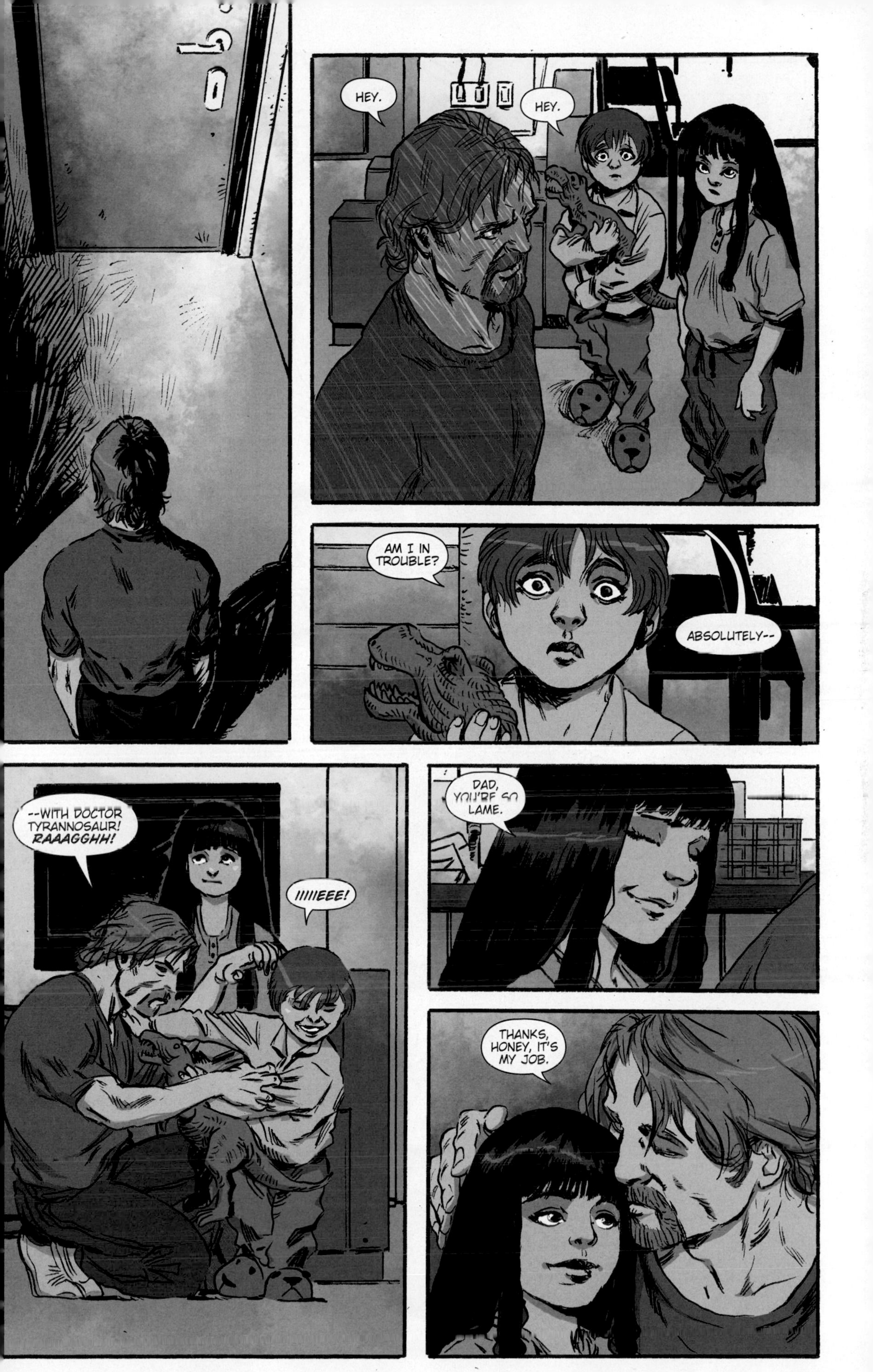
HEY.
HEY.
AM I IN TROUBLE?
ABSOLUTELY--
--WITH DOCTOR TYRANNOSAUR! *RAAAGGHH!*
IIIIIEEE!
DAD, YOU'RE SO LAME.
THANKS, HONEY, IT'S MY JOB.

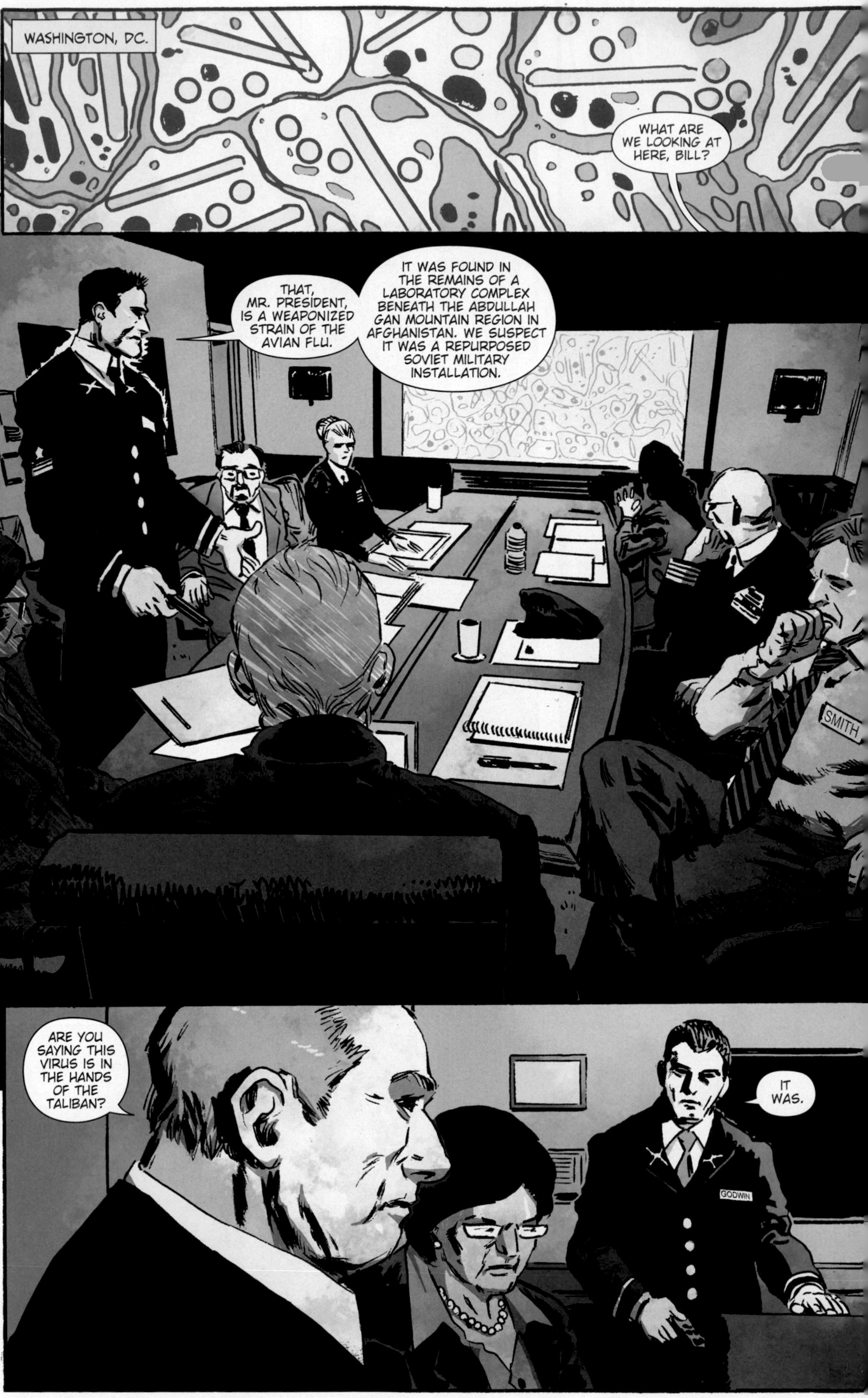
WASHINGTON, DC.
WHAT ARE WE LOOKING AT HERE, BILL?
THAT, MR. PRESIDENT, IS A WEAPONIZED STRAIN OF THE AVIAN FLU.
IT WAS FOUND IN THE REMAINS OF A LABORATORY COMPLEX BENEATH THE ABDULLAH GAN MOUNTAIN REGION IN AFGHANISTAN. WE SUSPECT IT WAS A REPURPOSED SOVIET MILITARY INSTALLATION.
SMITH
ARE YOU SAYING THIS VIRUS IS IN THE HANDS OF THE TALIBAN?
IT WAS.
GODWIN

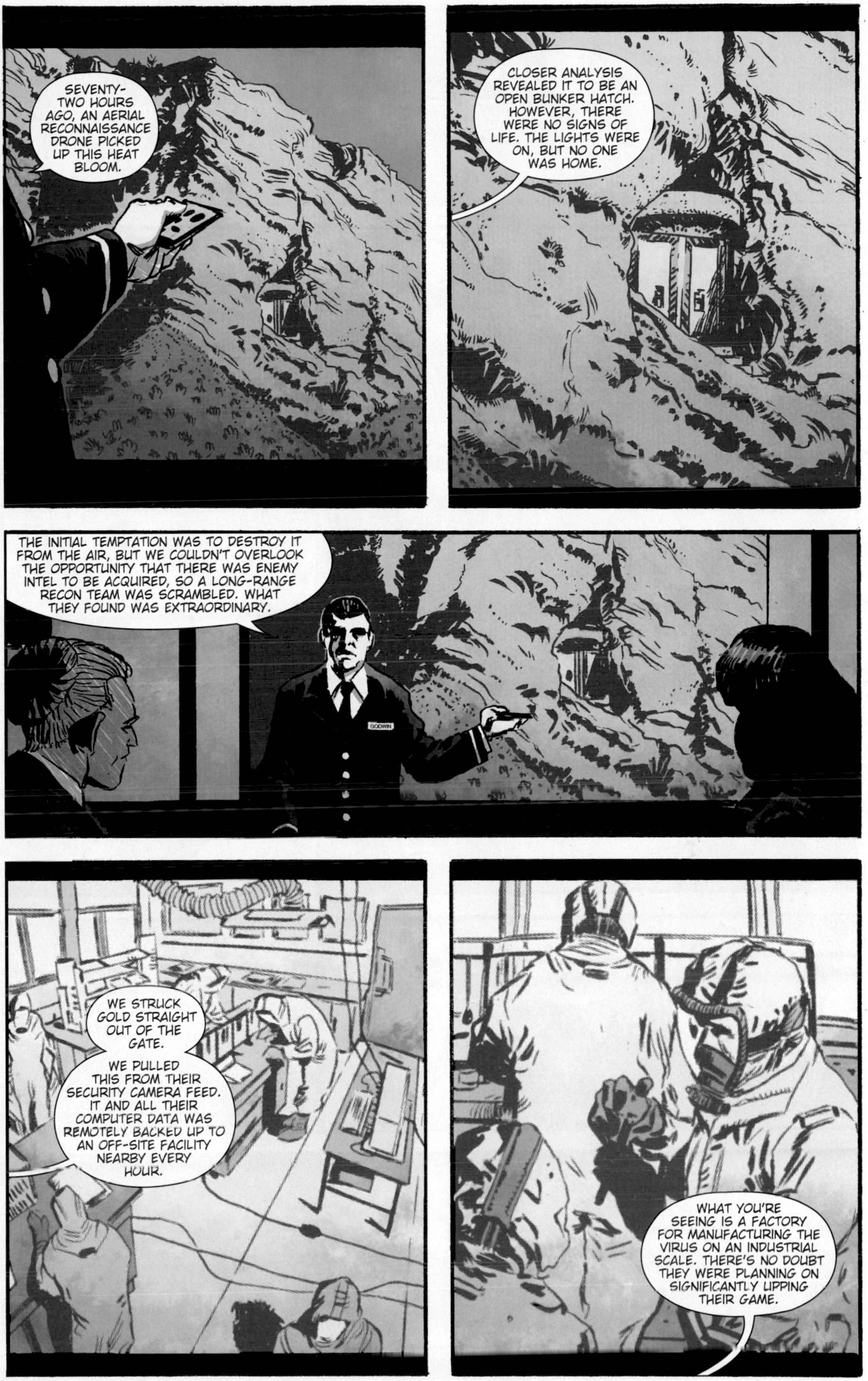
SEVENTY-TWO HOURS AGO, AN AERIAL RECONNAISSANCE DRONE PICKED UP THIS HEAT BLOOM.
CLOSER ANALYSIS REVEALED IT TO BE AN OPEN BUNKER HATCH. HOWEVER, THERE WERE NO SIGNS OF LIFE. THE LIGHTS WERE ON, BUT NO ONE WAS HOME.
THE INITIAL TEMPTATION WAS TO DESTROY IT FROM THE AIR, BUT WE COULDN'T OVERLOOK THE OPPORTUNITY THAT THERE WAS ENEMY INTEL TO BE ACQUIRED, SO A LONG-RANGE RECON TEAM WAS SCRAMBLED. WHAT THEY FOUND WAS EXTRAORDINARY.
GODWIN
WE STRUCK GOLD STRAIGHT OUT OF THE GATE.
WE PULLED THIS FROM THEIR SECURITY CAMERA FEED. IT AND ALL THEIR COMPUTER DATA WAS REMOTELY BACKED UP TO AN OFF-SITE FACILITY NEARBY EVERY HOUR.
WHAT YOU'RE SEEING IS A FACTORY FOR MANUFACTURING THE VIRUS ON AN INDUSTRIAL SCALE. THERE'S NO DOUBT THEY WERE PLANNING ON SIGNIFICANTLY UPPING THEIR GAME.

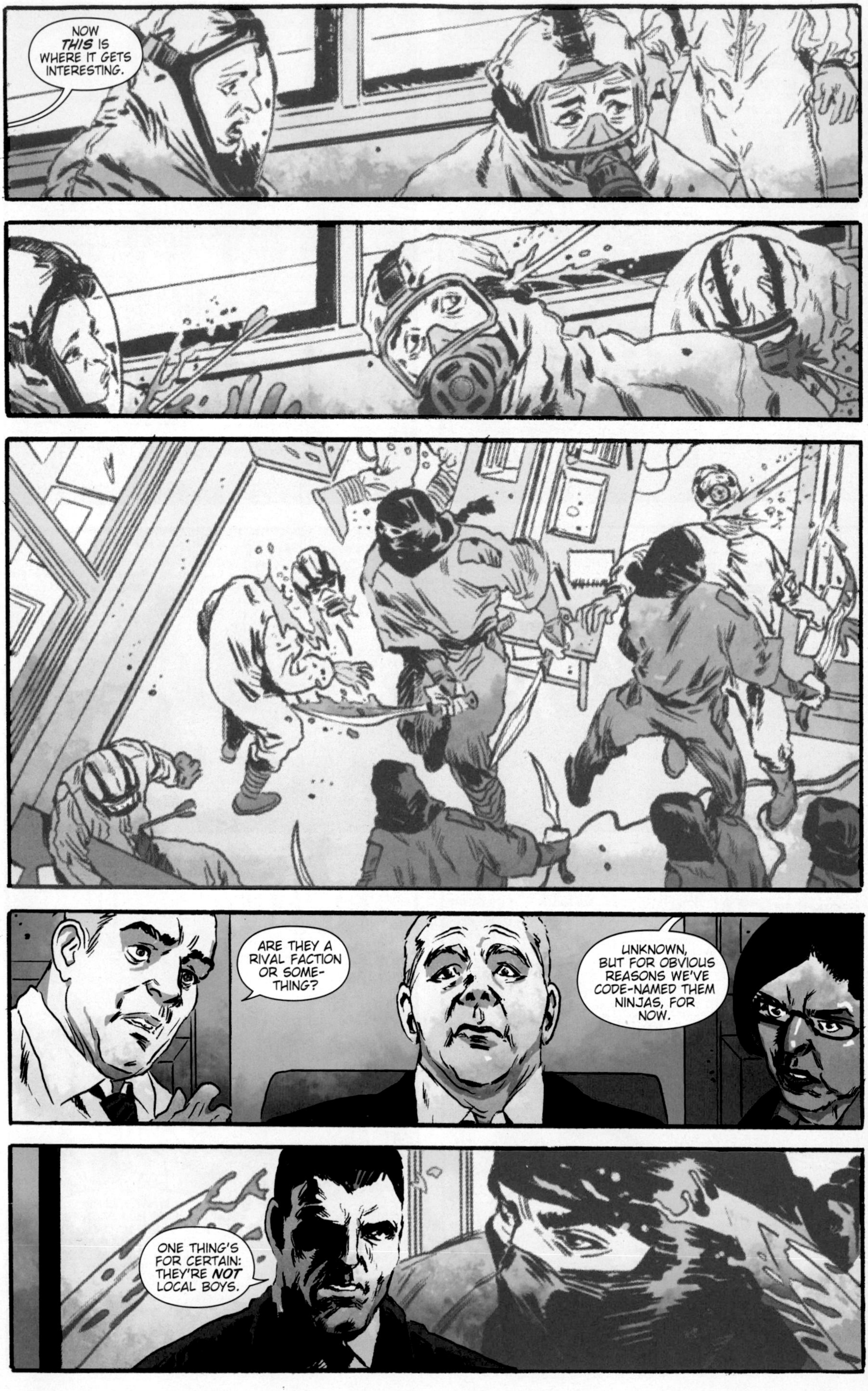
NOW THIS IS WHERE IT GETS INTERESTING.
ARE THEY A RIVAL FACTION OR SOME-THING?
UNKNOWN, BUT FOR OBVIOUS REASONS WE'VE CODE-NAMED THEM NINJAS, FOR NOW.
ONE THING'S FOR CERTAIN: THEY'RE NOT LOCAL BOYS.

FROM THE COMPUTER DATA, IT SEEMS THE DOORS WERE OPENED AND SECURITY COUNTERMEASURES TO THE MAIN APPROACH DELIBERATELY DEACTIVATED.

SOMEONE LET THEM IN. IT WAS AN INSIDE JOB.

SO YOU'RE TELLING ME WE HAVE AN UNKNOWN AGENCY ON THE LOOSE AND IN POSSESSION OF A LETHAL PATHOGEN THAT THEY COULD USE ANYWHERE, ANY TIME?

YES, BUT I DO HAVE A FEW THREADS OF A THEORY, FOR WHAT IT'S WORTH.

WHEN THEY BREACHED THE CLEAN ROOM, THE NINJAS WEREN'T WEARING ANY PROTECTIVE CLOTHING. EITHER THEY DIDN'T KNOW TO OR DIDN'T CARE, WHICH I FIND UNLIKELY.

I SUGGEST, THEREFORE, THEY WERE EITHER INOCULATED OR IMMUNE TO THE VIRUS.

IMMUNE, HOW?

A CURSORY EXAMINATION OF THE SAMPLES WE FOUND SHOWED IT TAGGED WITH HUMAN DNA MARKERS.

SMITH

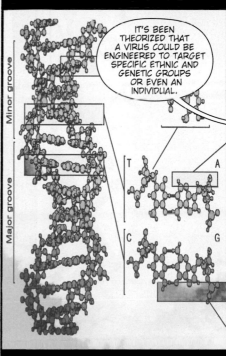

IT'S BEEN THEORIZED THAT A VIRUS COULD BE ENGINEERED TO TARGET SPECIFIC ETHNIC AND GENETIC GROUPS OR EVEN AN INDIVIDUAL.

Minor groove

Major groove

T

A

C

G

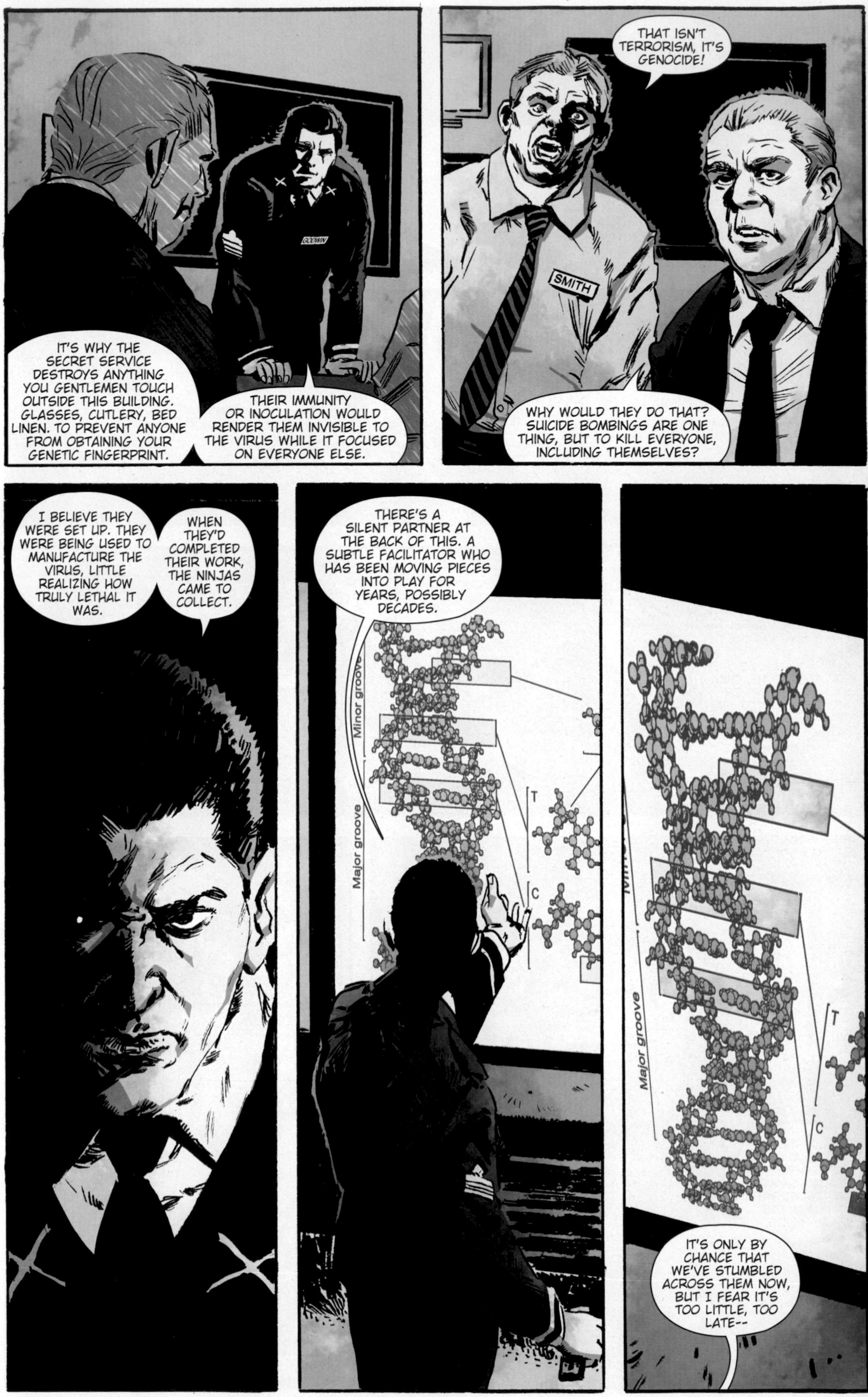
GODWIN
IT'S WHY THE SECRET SERVICE DESTROYS ANYTHING YOU GENTLEMEN TOUCH OUTSIDE THIS BUILDING. GLASSES, CUTLERY, BED LINEN. TO PREVENT ANYONE FROM OBTAINING YOUR GENETIC FINGERPRINT.
THEIR IMMUNITY OR INOCULATION WOULD RENDER THEM INVISIBLE TO THE VIRUS WHILE IT FOCUSED ON EVERYONE ELSE.
THAT ISN'T TERRORISM, IT'S GENOCIDE!
SMITH
WHY WOULD THEY DO THAT? SUICIDE BOMBINGS ARE ONE THING, BUT TO KILL EVERYONE, INCLUDING THEMSELVES?
I BELIEVE THEY WERE SET UP. THEY WERE BEING USED TO MANUFACTURE THE VIRUS, LITTLE REALIZING HOW TRULY LETHAL IT WAS.
WHEN THEY'D COMPLETED THEIR WORK, THE NINJAS CAME TO COLLECT.
THERE'S A SILENT PARTNER AT THE BACK OF THIS. A SUBTLE FACILITATOR WHO HAS BEEN MOVING PIECES INTO PLAY FOR YEARS, POSSIBLY DECADES.
Minor groove
Major groove
T
C
Major groove
T
C
IT'S ONLY BY CHANCE THAT WE'VE STUMBLED ACROSS THEM NOW, BUT I FEAR IT'S TOO LITTLE, TOO LATE--

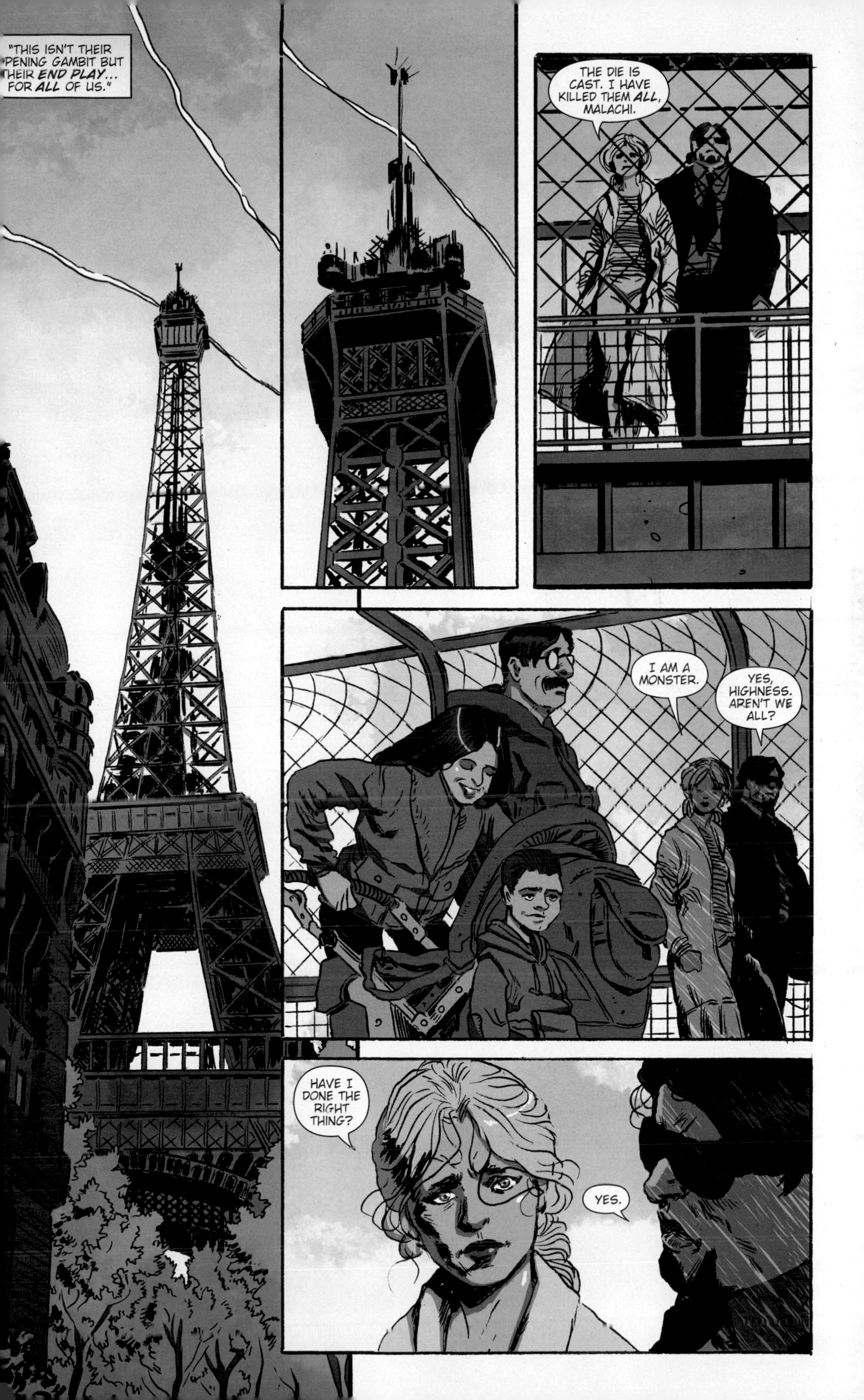
"THIS ISN'T THEIR
OPENING GAMBIT BUT
THEIR **END PLAY**...
FOR **ALL** OF US."
THE DIE IS CAST. I HAVE KILLED THEM **ALL**, MALACHI.
I AM A MONSTER.
YES, HIGHNESS. AREN'T WE ALL?
HAVE I DONE THE RIGHT THING?
YES.

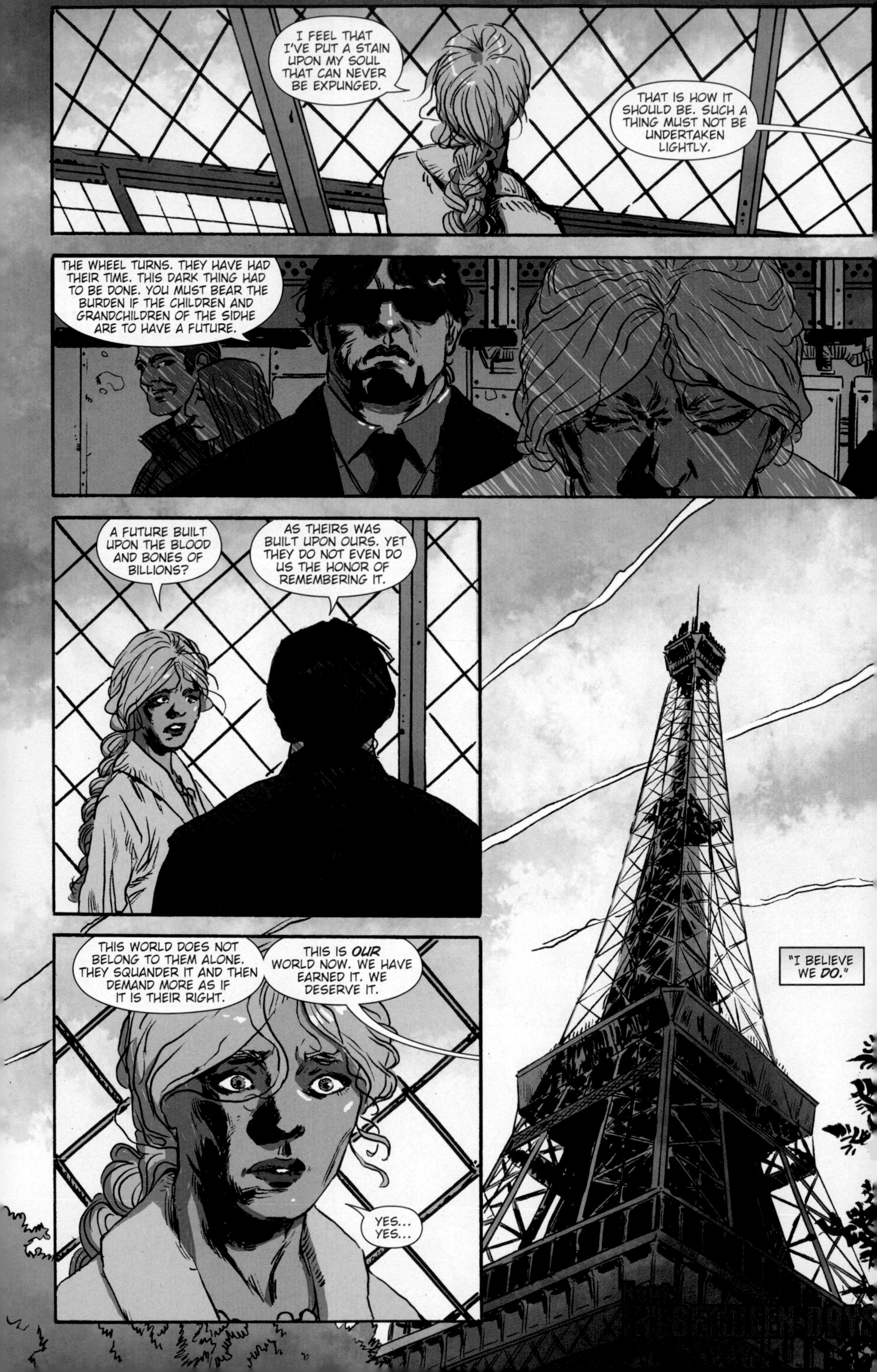
I FEEL THAT I'VE PUT A STAIN UPON MY SOUL THAT CAN NEVER BE EXPUNGED.
THAT IS HOW IT SHOULD BE. SUCH A THING MUST NOT BE UNDERTAKEN LIGHTLY.
THE WHEEL TURNS. THEY HAVE HAD THEIR TIME. THIS DARK THING HAD TO BE DONE. YOU MUST BEAR THE BURDEN IF THE CHILDREN AND GRANDCHILDREN OF THE SIDHE ARE TO HAVE A FUTURE.
A FUTURE BUILT UPON THE BLOOD AND BONES OF BILLIONS?
AS THEIRS WAS BUILT UPON OURS. YET THEY DO NOT EVEN DO US THE HONOR OF REMEMBERING IT.
THIS WORLD DOES NOT BELONG TO THEM ALONE. THEY SQUANDER IT AND THEN DEMAND MORE AS IF IT IS THEIR RIGHT.
THIS IS OUR WORLD NOW. WE HAVE EARNED IT. WE DESERVE IT.
YES... YES...
"I BELIEVE WE DO."

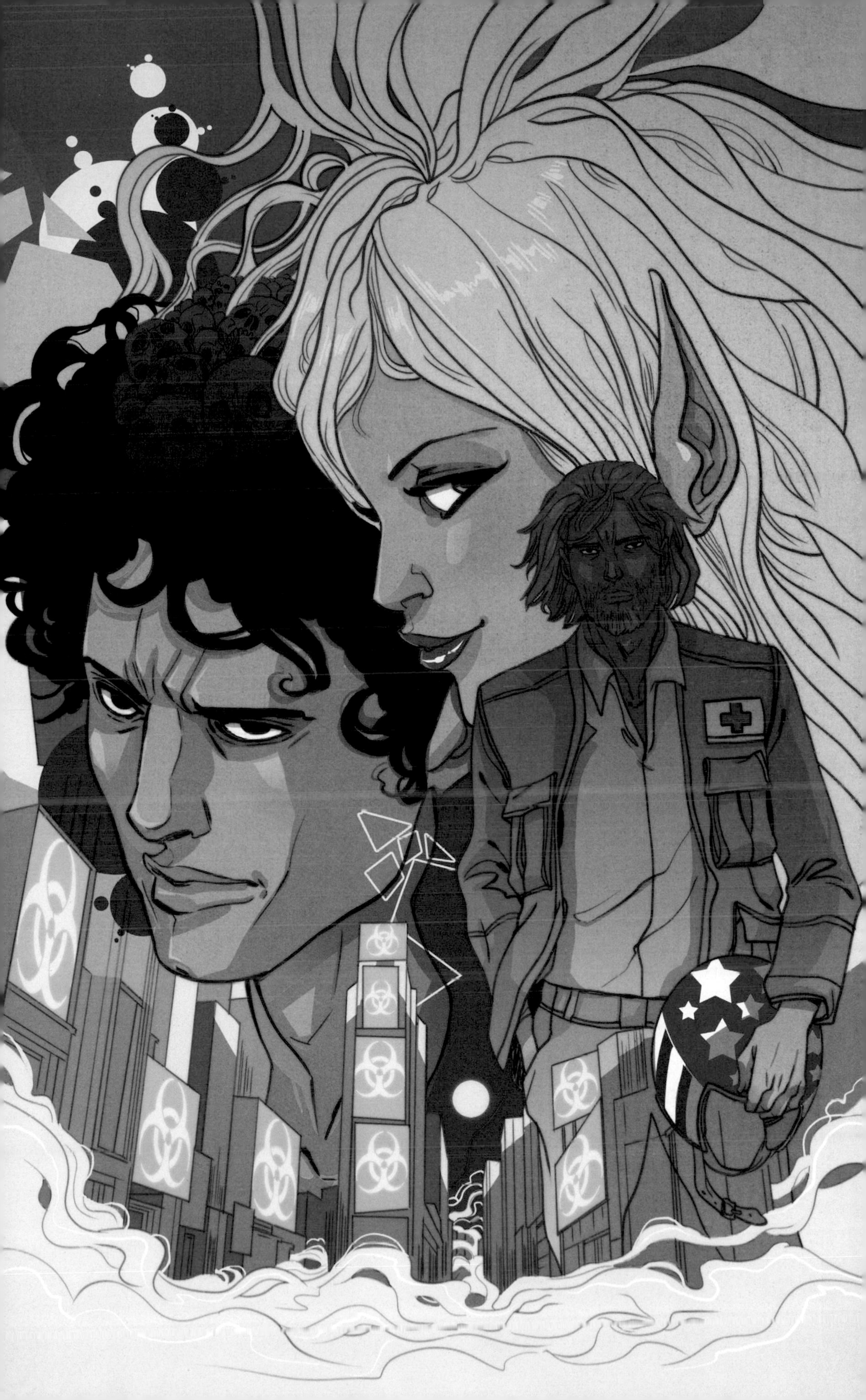

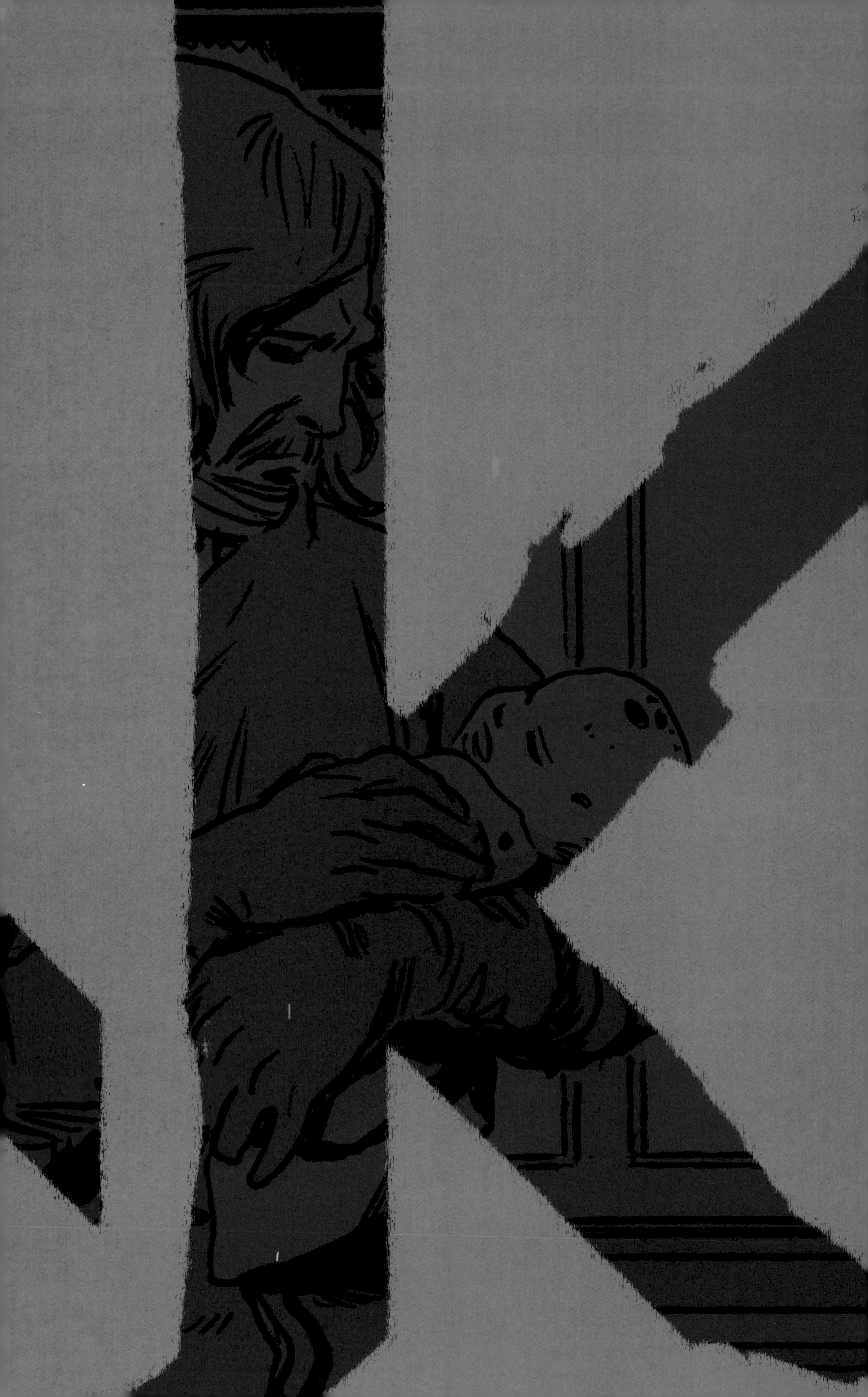

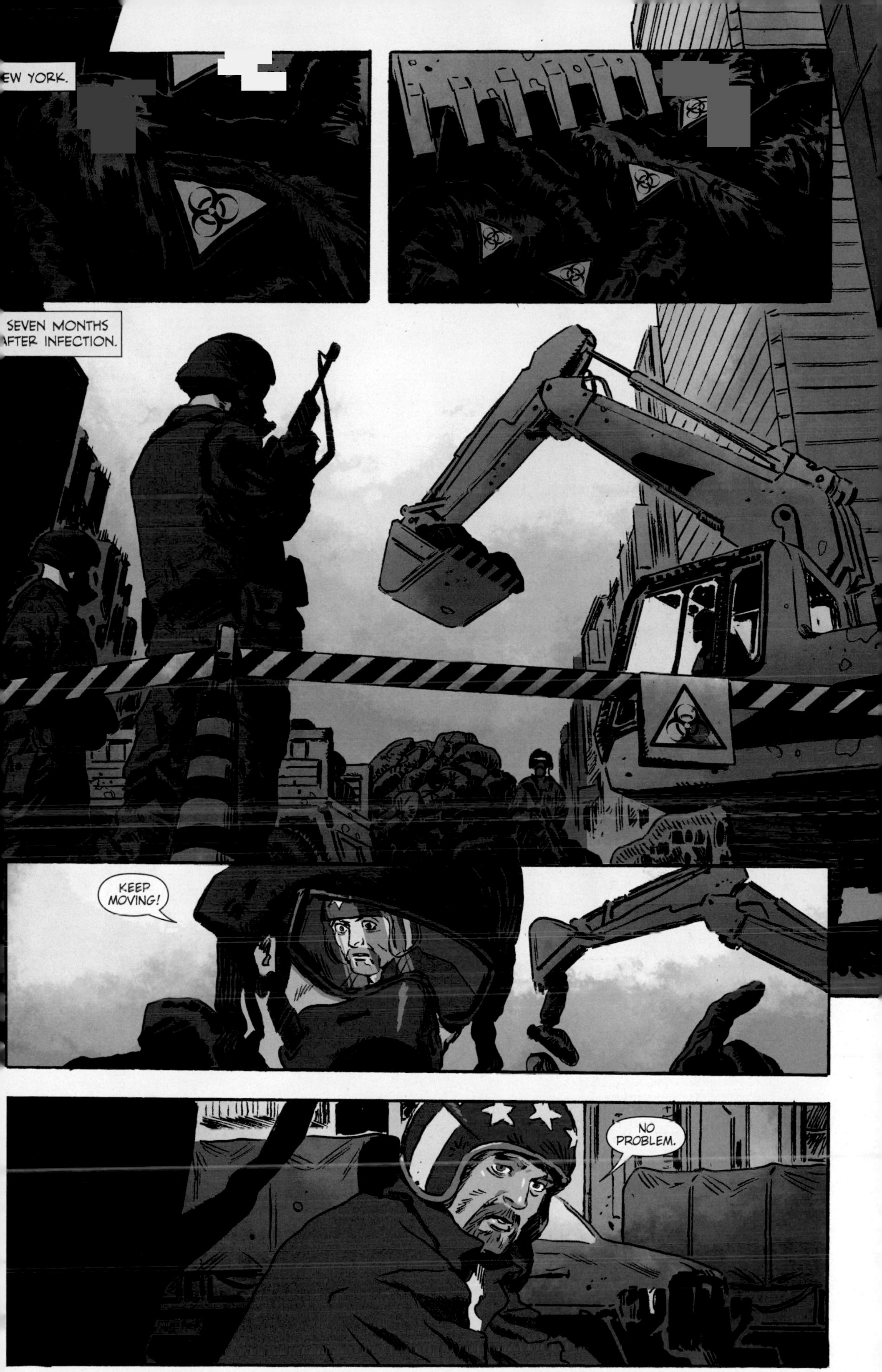
EW YORK.
SEVEN MONTHS AFTER INFECTION.
KEEP MOVING!
NO PROBLEM.

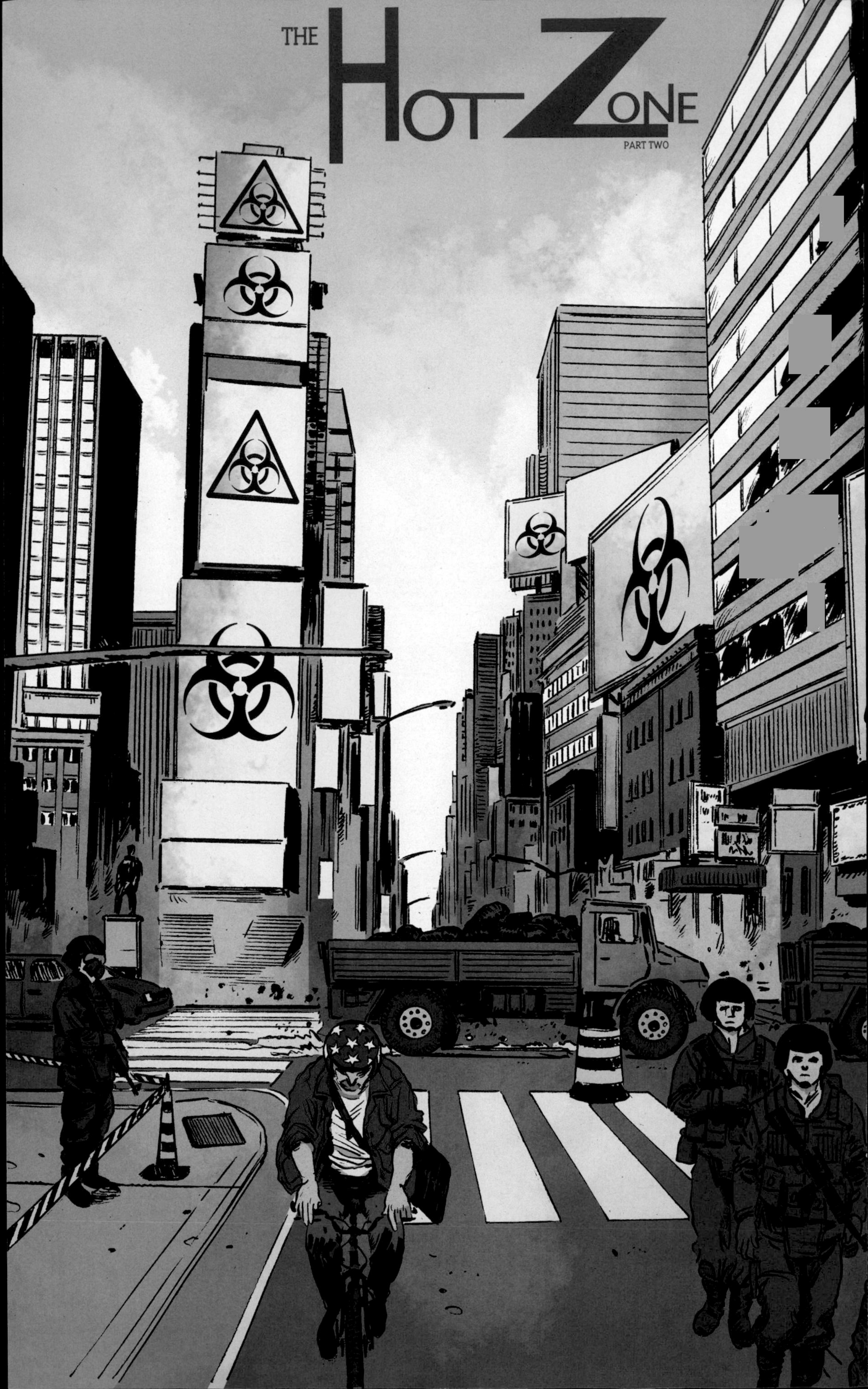
THE HOT ZONE
PART TWO

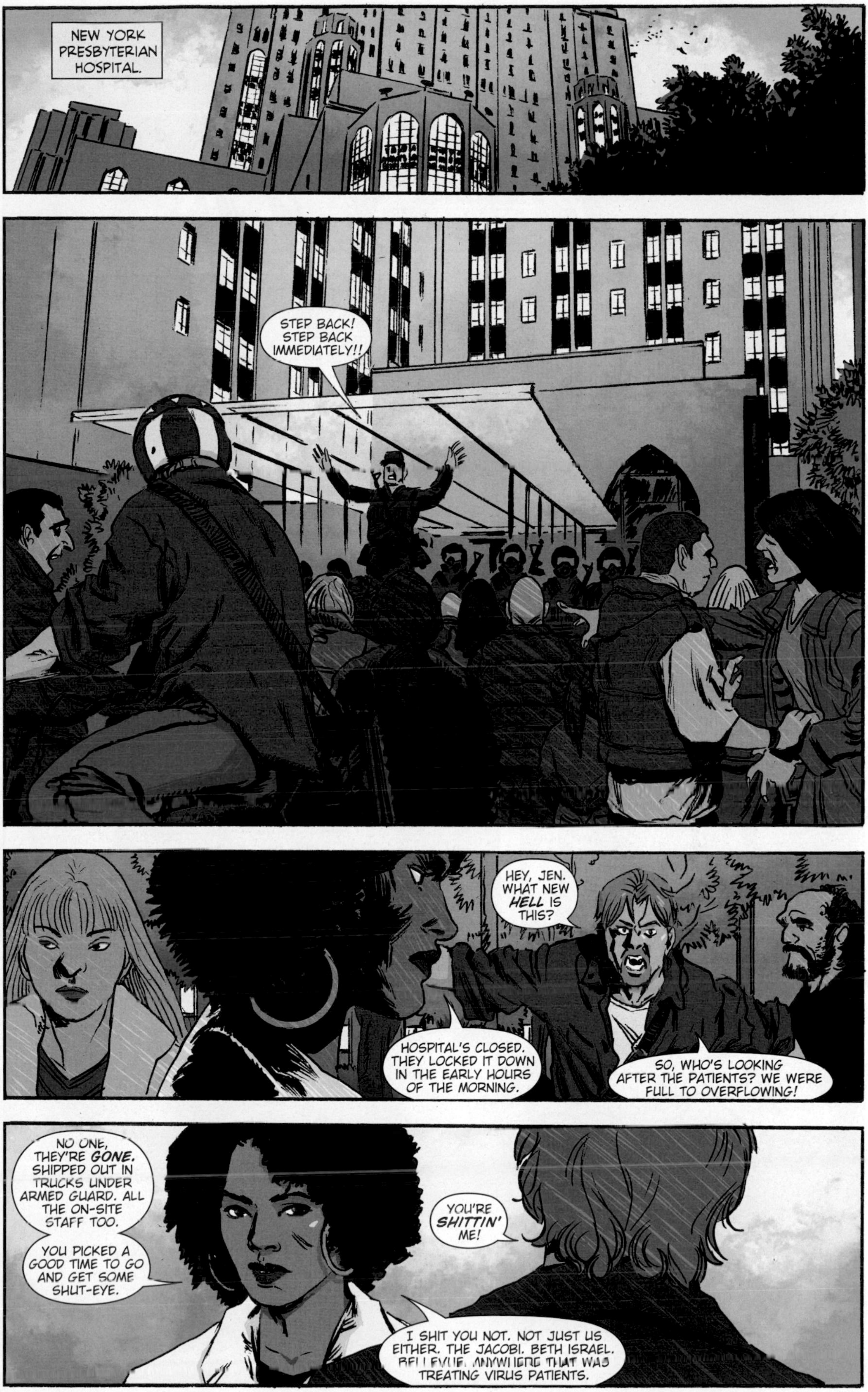
NEW YORK PRESBYTERIAN HOSPITAL.
STEP BACK! STEP BACK IMMEDIATELY!!
HEY, JEN. WHAT NEW HELL IS THIS?
HOSPITAL'S CLOSED. THEY LOCKED IT DOWN IN THE EARLY HOURS OF THE MORNING.
SO, WHO'S LOOKING AFTER THE PATIENTS? WE WERE FULL TO OVERFLOWING!
NO ONE, THEY'RE GONE. SHIPPED OUT IN TRUCKS UNDER ARMED GUARD. ALL THE ON-SITE STAFF TOO.
YOU PICKED A GOOD TIME TO GO AND GET SOME SHUT-EYE.
YOU'RE SHITTIN' ME!
I SHIT YOU NOT. NOT JUST US EITHER. THE JACOBI. BETH ISRAEL. BELLEVUE. ANYWHERE THAT WAS TREATING VIRUS PATIENTS.

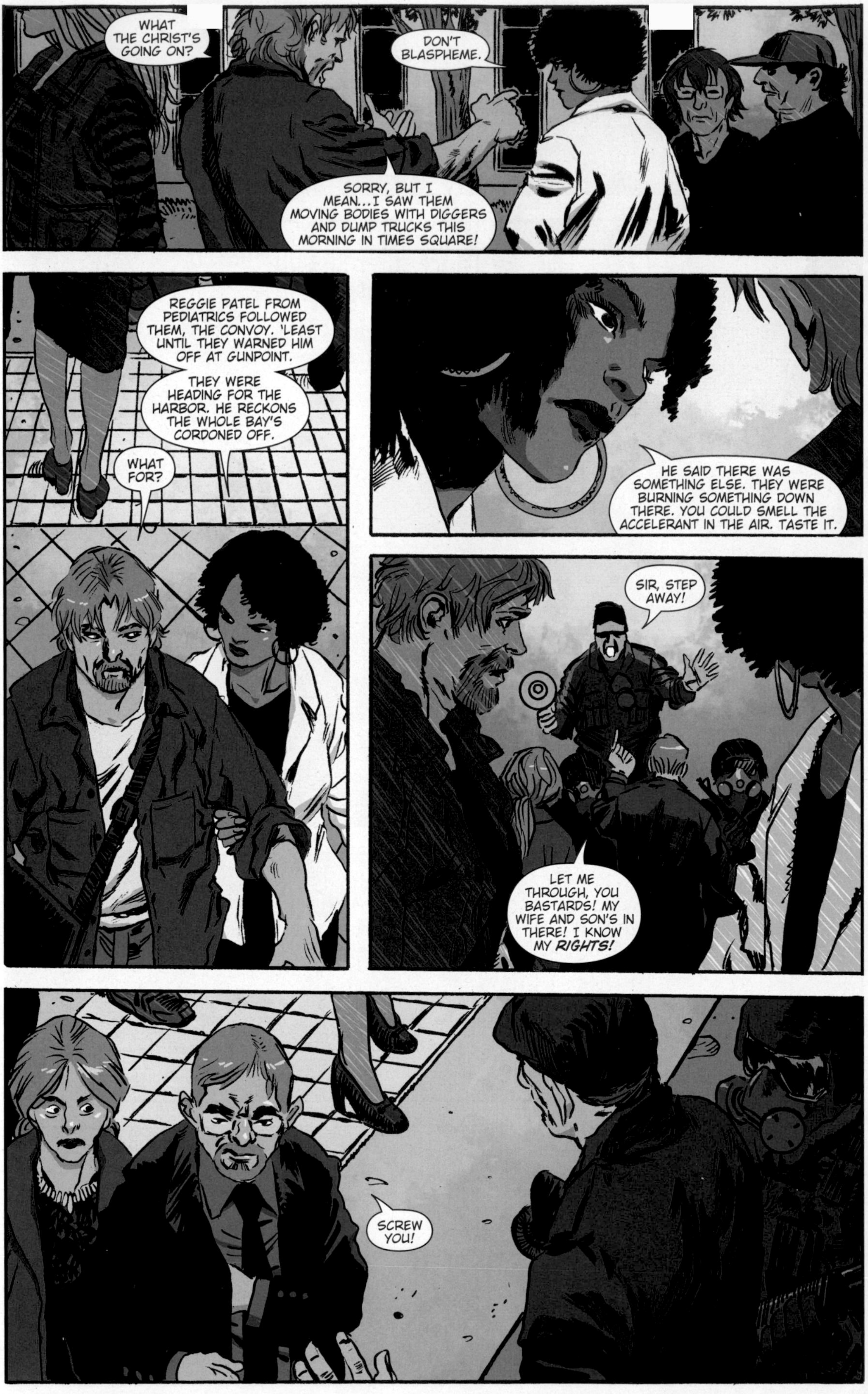
WHAT THE CHRIST'S GOING ON?
DON'T BLASPHEME.
SORRY, BUT I MEAN...I SAW THEM MOVING BODIES WITH DIGGERS AND DUMP TRUCKS THIS MORNING IN TIMES SQUARE!
REGGIE PATEL FROM PEDIATRICS FOLLOWED THEM, THE CONVOY. 'LEAST UNTIL THEY WARNED HIM OFF AT GUNPOINT.
THEY WERE HEADING FOR THE HARBOR. HE RECKONS THE WHOLE BAY'S CORDONED OFF.
WHAT FOR?
HE SAID THERE WAS SOMETHING ELSE. THEY WERE BURNING SOMETHING DOWN THERE. YOU COULD SMELL THE ACCELERANT IN THE AIR. TASTE IT.
SIR, STEP AWAY!
LET ME THROUGH, YOU BASTARDS! MY WIFE AND SON'S IN THERE! I KNOW MY *RIGHTS!*
SCREW YOU!

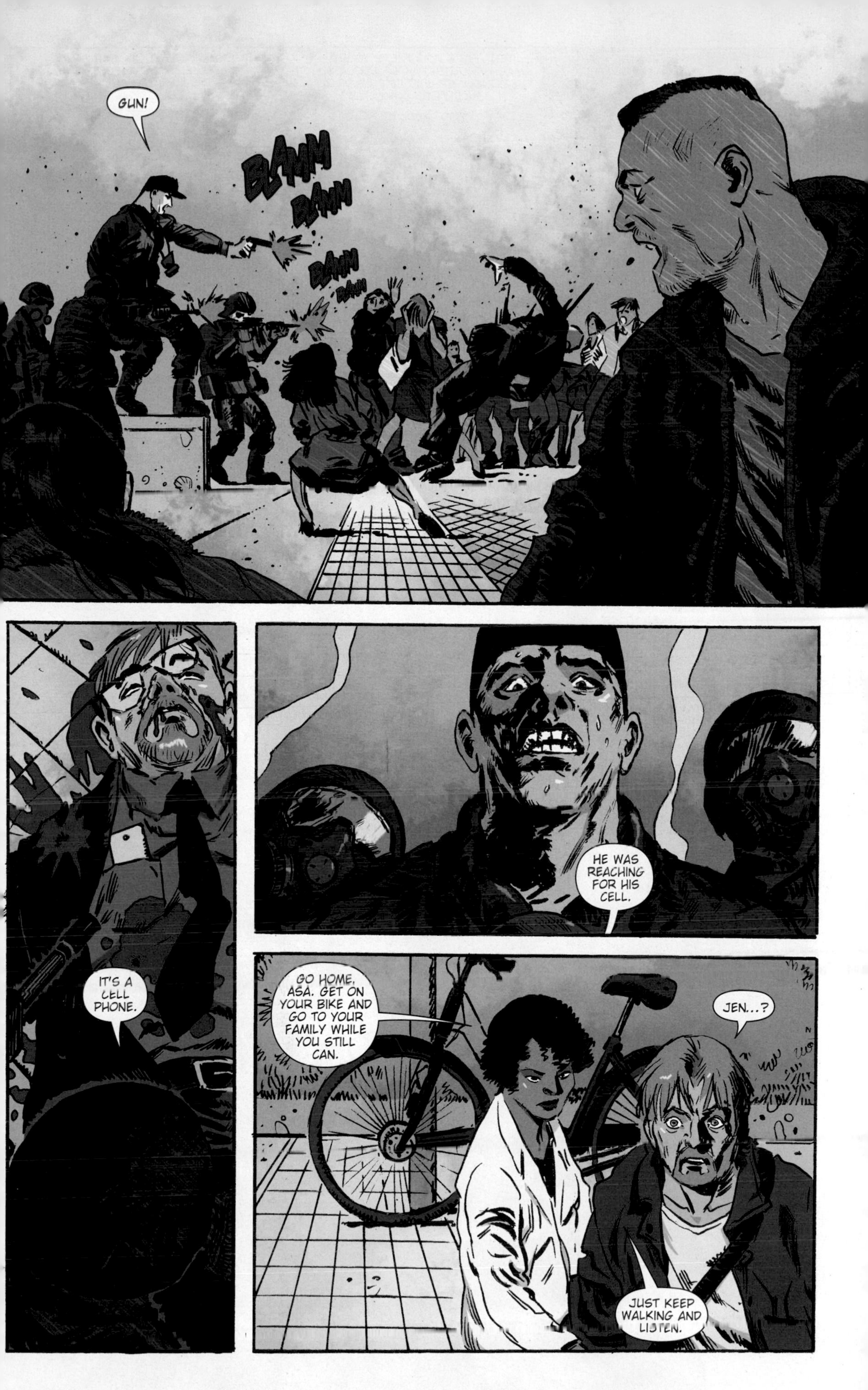
GUN!
BLAMM BLAMM
BLAMM BLAMM
IT'S A CELL PHONE.
HE WAS REACHING FOR HIS CELL.
GO HOME, ASA. GET ON YOUR BIKE AND GO TO YOUR FAMILY WHILE YOU STILL CAN.
JEN...?
JUST KEEP WALKING AND LISTEN.

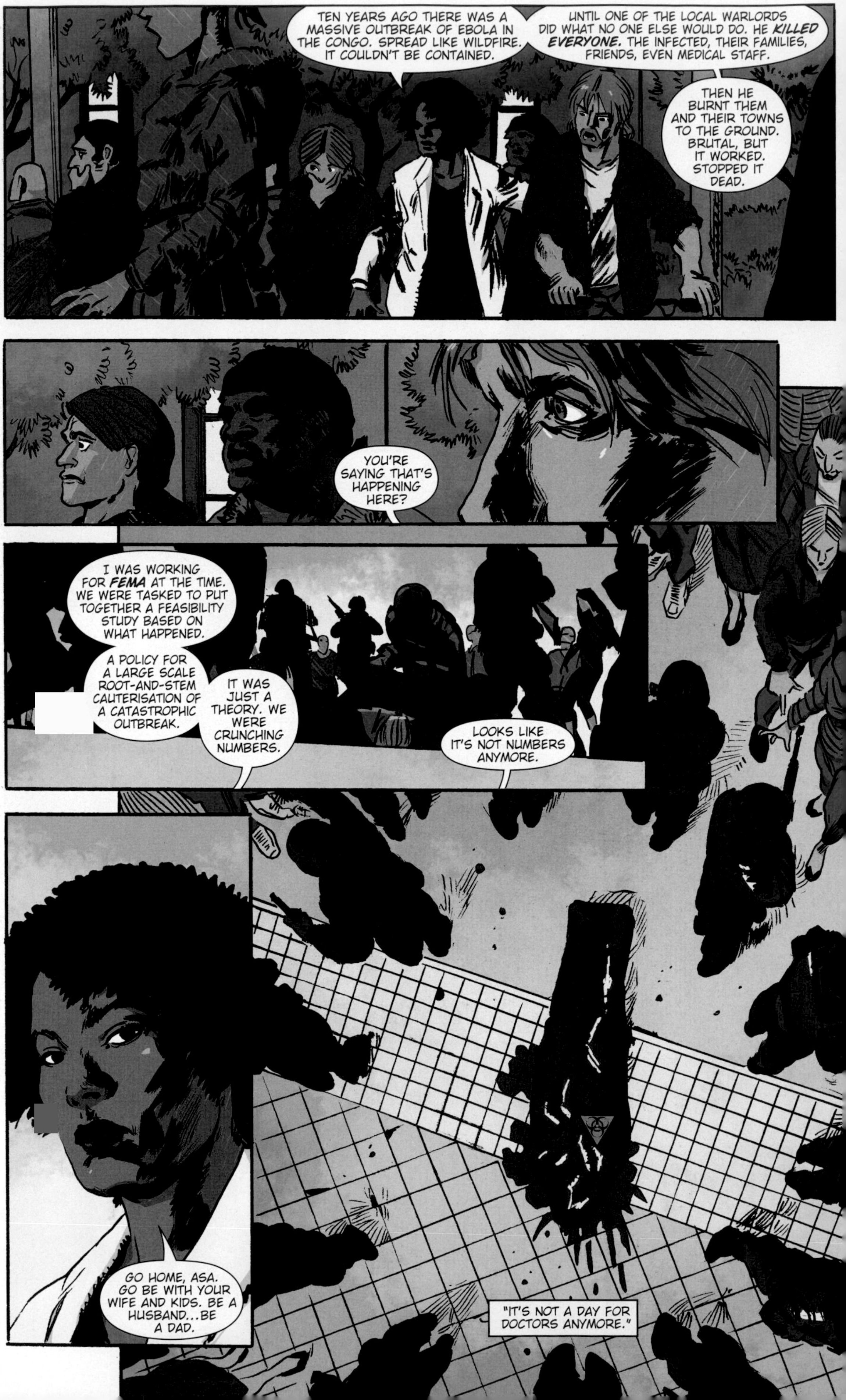

TEN YEARS AGO THERE WAS A MASSIVE OUTBREAK OF EBOLA IN THE CONGO. SPREAD LIKE WILDFIRE. IT COULDN'T BE CONTAINED.
UNTIL ONE OF THE LOCAL WARLORDS DID WHAT NO ONE ELSE WOULD DO. HE *KILLED EVERYONE.* THE INFECTED, THEIR FAMILIES, FRIENDS, EVEN MEDICAL STAFF.
THEN HE BURNT THEM AND THEIR TOWNS TO THE GROUND. BRUTAL, BUT IT WORKED. STOPPED IT DEAD.
YOU'RE SAYING THAT'S HAPPENING HERE?
I WAS WORKING FOR *FEMA* AT THE TIME. WE WERE TASKED TO PUT TOGETHER A FEASIBILITY STUDY BASED ON WHAT HAPPENED.
A POLICY FOR A LARGE SCALE ROOT-AND-STEM CAUTERISATION OF A CATASTROPHIC OUTBREAK.
IT WAS JUST A THEORY. WE WERE CRUNCHING NUMBERS.
LOOKS LIKE IT'S NOT NUMBERS ANYMORE.
GO HOME, ASA. GO BE WITH YOUR WIFE AND KIDS. BE A HUSBAND...BE A DAD.
"IT'S NOT A DAY FOR DOCTORS ANYMORE."

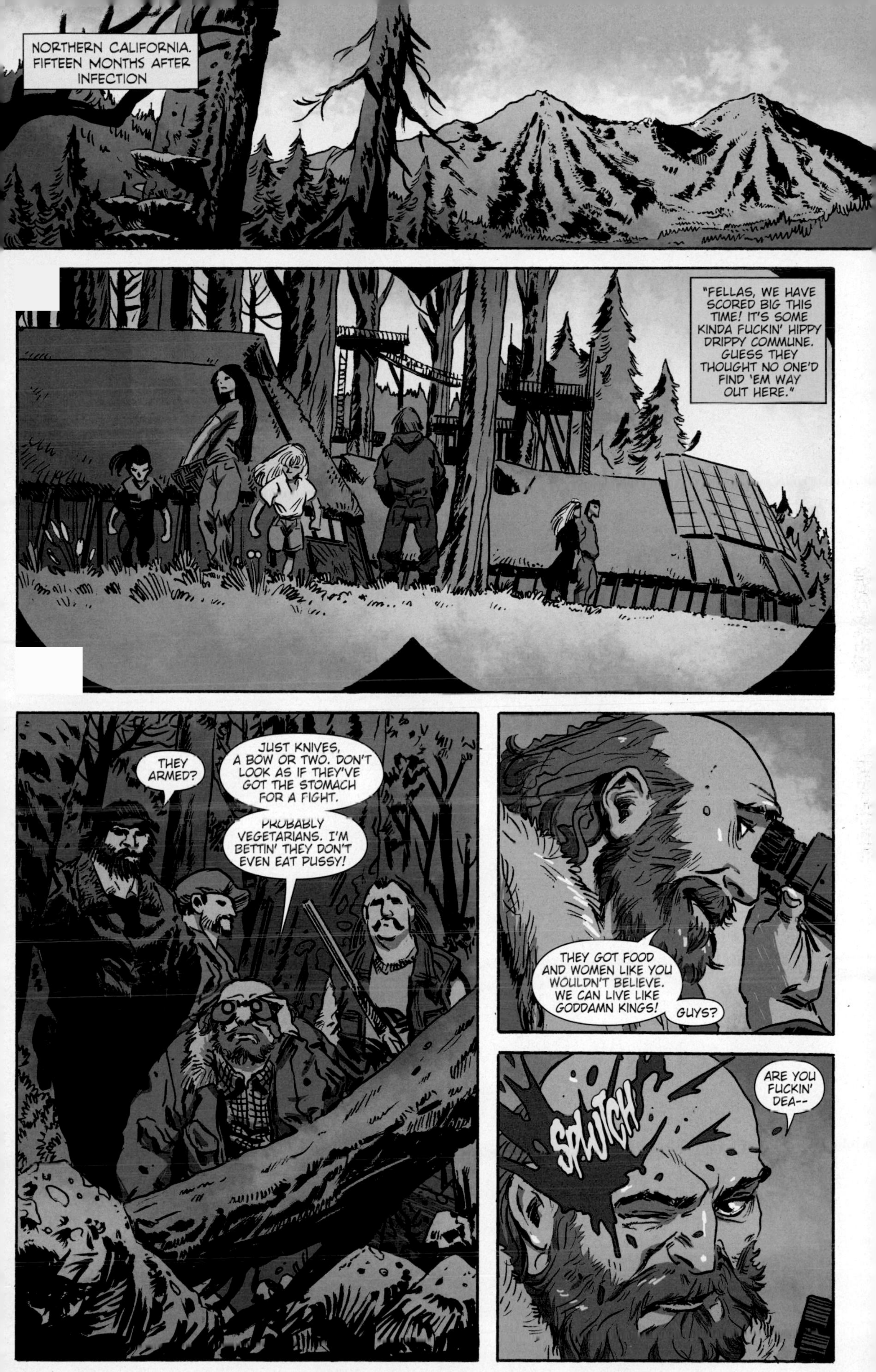
NORTHERN CALIFORNIA. FIFTEEN MONTHS AFTER INFECTION
"FELLAS, WE HAVE SCORED BIG THIS TIME! IT'S SOME KINDA FUCKIN' HIPPY DRIPPY COMMUNE. GUESS THEY THOUGHT NO ONE'D FIND 'EM WAY OUT HERE."
THEY ARMED?
JUST KNIVES, A BOW OR TWO. DON'T LOOK AS IF THEY'VE GOT THE STOMACH FOR A FIGHT.
PROBABLY VEGETARIANS. I'M BETTIN' THEY DON'T EVEN EAT PUSSY!
THEY GOT FOOD AND WOMEN LIKE YOU WOULDN'T BELIEVE. WE CAN LIVE LIKE GODDAMN KINGS!
GUYS?
SPLUTCH
ARE YOU FUCKIN' DEA--

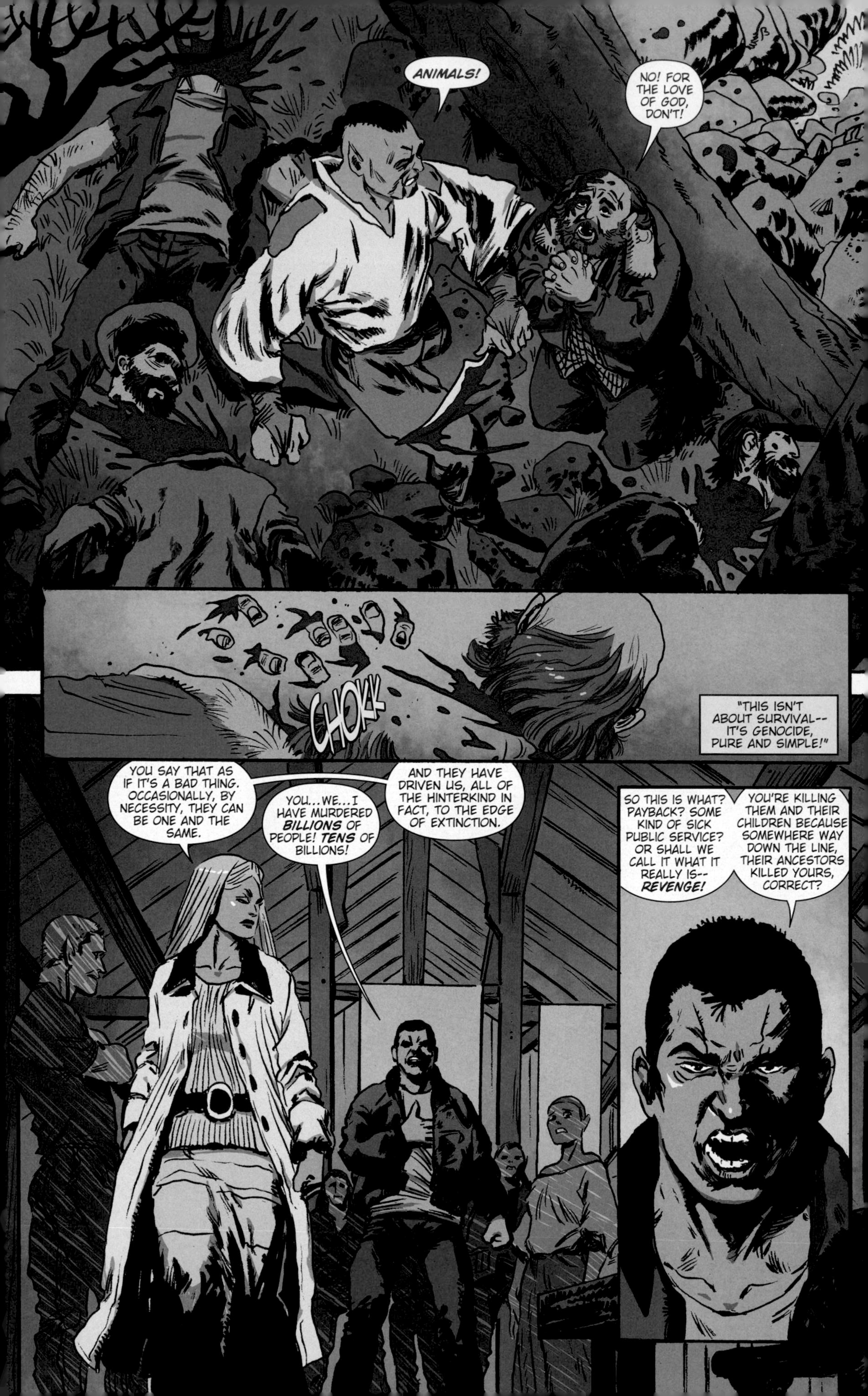
ANIMALS!
NO! FOR THE LOVE OF GOD, DON'T!
CHOKK
"THIS ISN'T ABOUT SURVIVAL-- IT'S GENOCIDE, PURE AND SIMPLE!"
YOU SAY THAT AS IF IT'S A BAD THING. OCCASIONALLY, BY NECESSITY, THEY CAN BE ONE AND THE SAME.
AND THEY HAVE DRIVEN US, ALL OF THE HINTERKIND IN FACT, TO THE EDGE OF EXTINCTION.
YOU...WE...I HAVE MURDERED BILLIONS OF PEOPLE! TENS OF BILLIONS!
SO THIS IS WHAT? PAYBACK? SOME KIND OF SICK PUBLIC SERVICE? OR SHALL WE CALL IT WHAT IT REALLY IS-- REVENGE!
YOU'RE KILLING THEM AND THEIR CHILDREN BECAUSE SOMEWHERE WAY DOWN THE LINE, THEIR ANCESTORS KILLED YOURS, CORRECT?

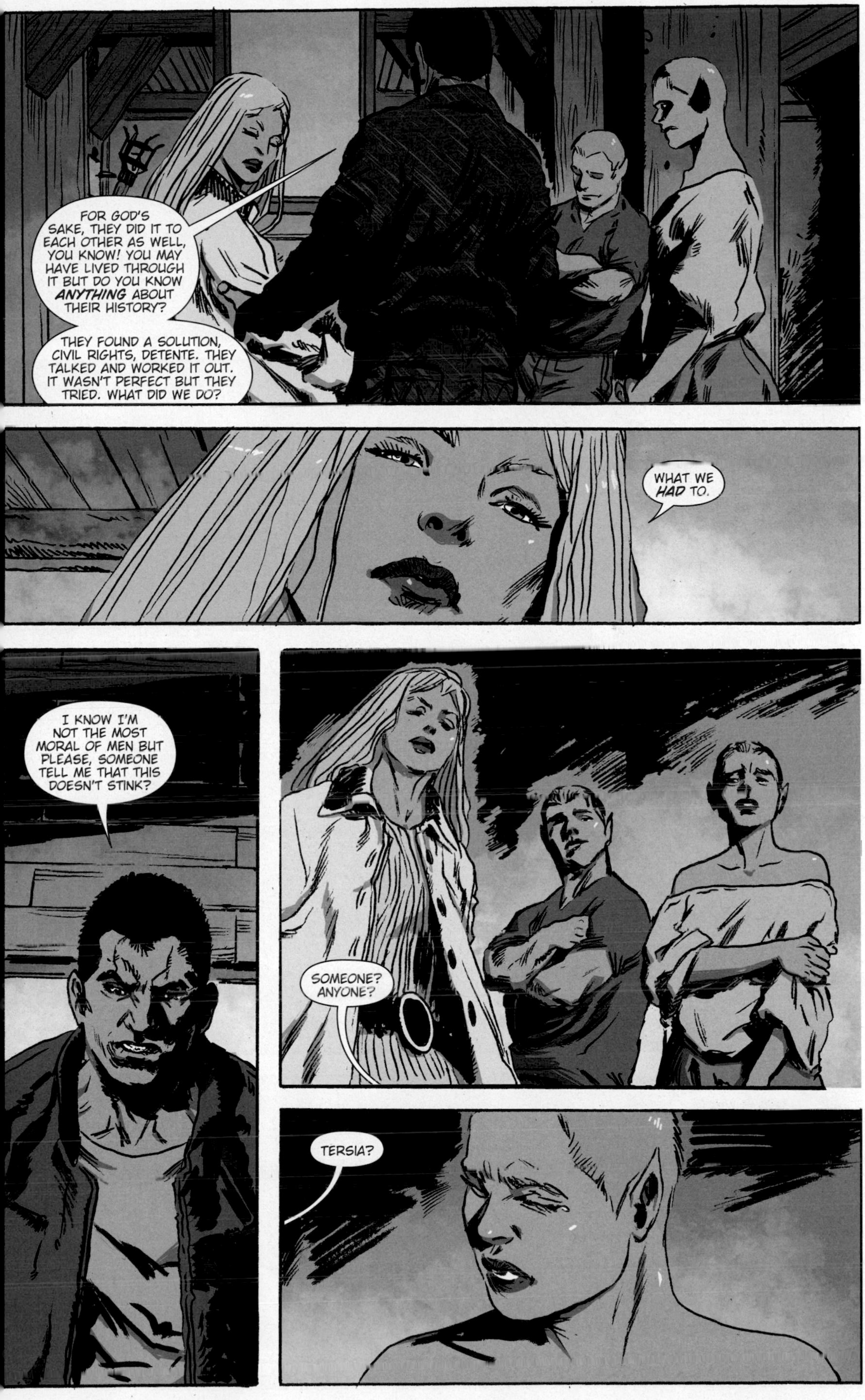
FOR GOD'S SAKE, THEY DID IT TO EACH OTHER AS WELL, YOU KNOW! YOU MAY HAVE LIVED THROUGH IT BUT DO YOU KNOW ANYTHING ABOUT THEIR HISTORY?
THEY FOUND A SOLUTION, CIVIL RIGHTS, DETENTE. THEY TALKED AND WORKED IT OUT. IT WASN'T PERFECT BUT THEY TRIED. WHAT DID WE DO?
WHAT WE HAD TO.
I KNOW I'M NOT THE MOST MORAL OF MEN BUT PLEASE, SOMEONE TELL ME THAT THIS DOESN'T STINK?
SOMEONE? ANYONE?
TERSIA?

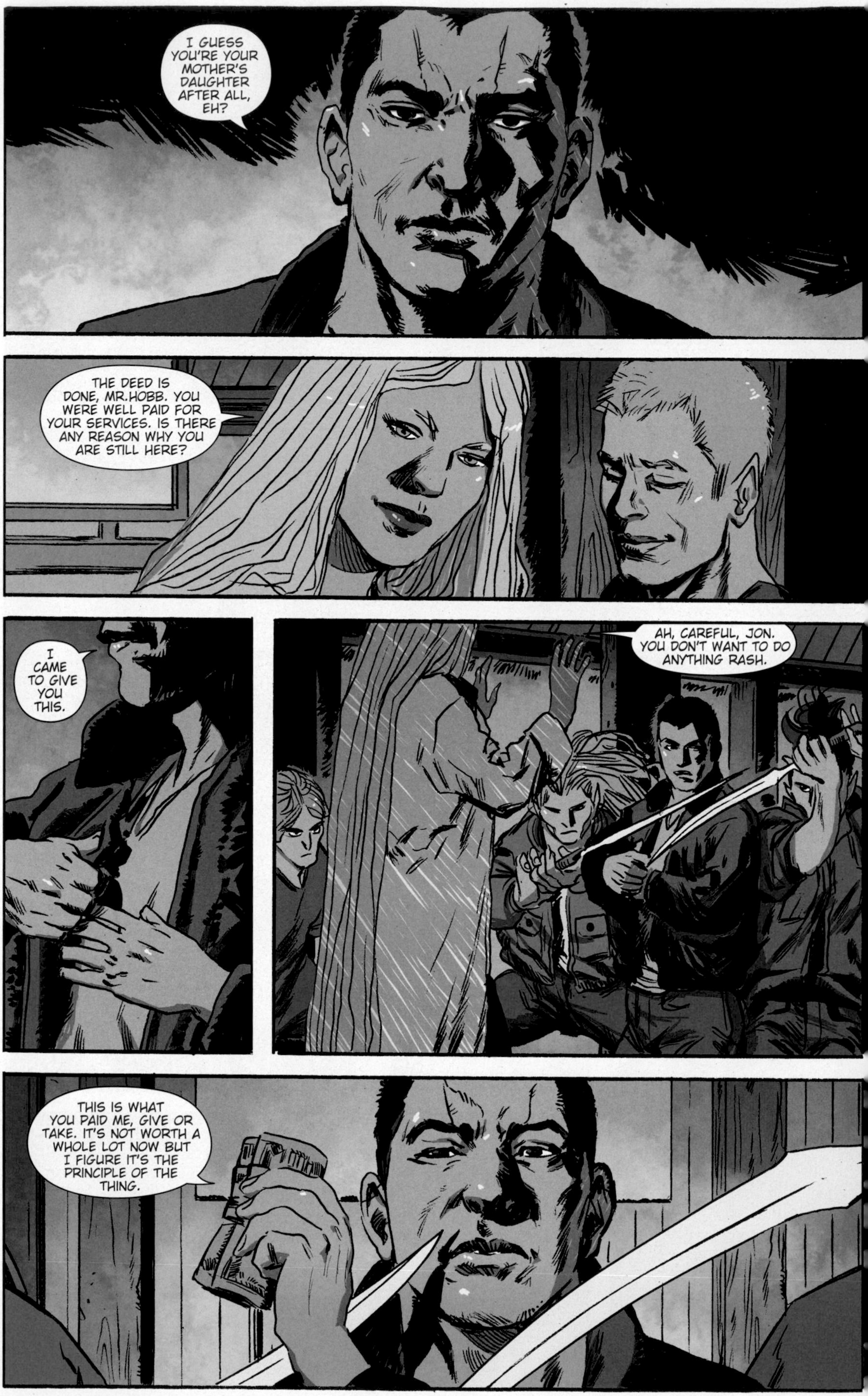
I GUESS YOU'RE YOUR MOTHER'S DAUGHTER AFTER ALL, EH?
THE DEED IS DONE, MR.HOBB. YOU WERE WELL PAID FOR YOUR SERVICES. IS THERE ANY REASON WHY YOU ARE STILL HERE?
I CAME TO GIVE YOU THIS.
AH, CAREFUL, JON. YOU DON'T WANT TO DO ANYTHING RASH.
THIS IS WHAT YOU PAID ME, GIVE OR TAKE. IT'S NOT WORTH A WHOLE LOT NOW BUT I FIGURE IT'S THE PRINCIPLE OF THE THING.

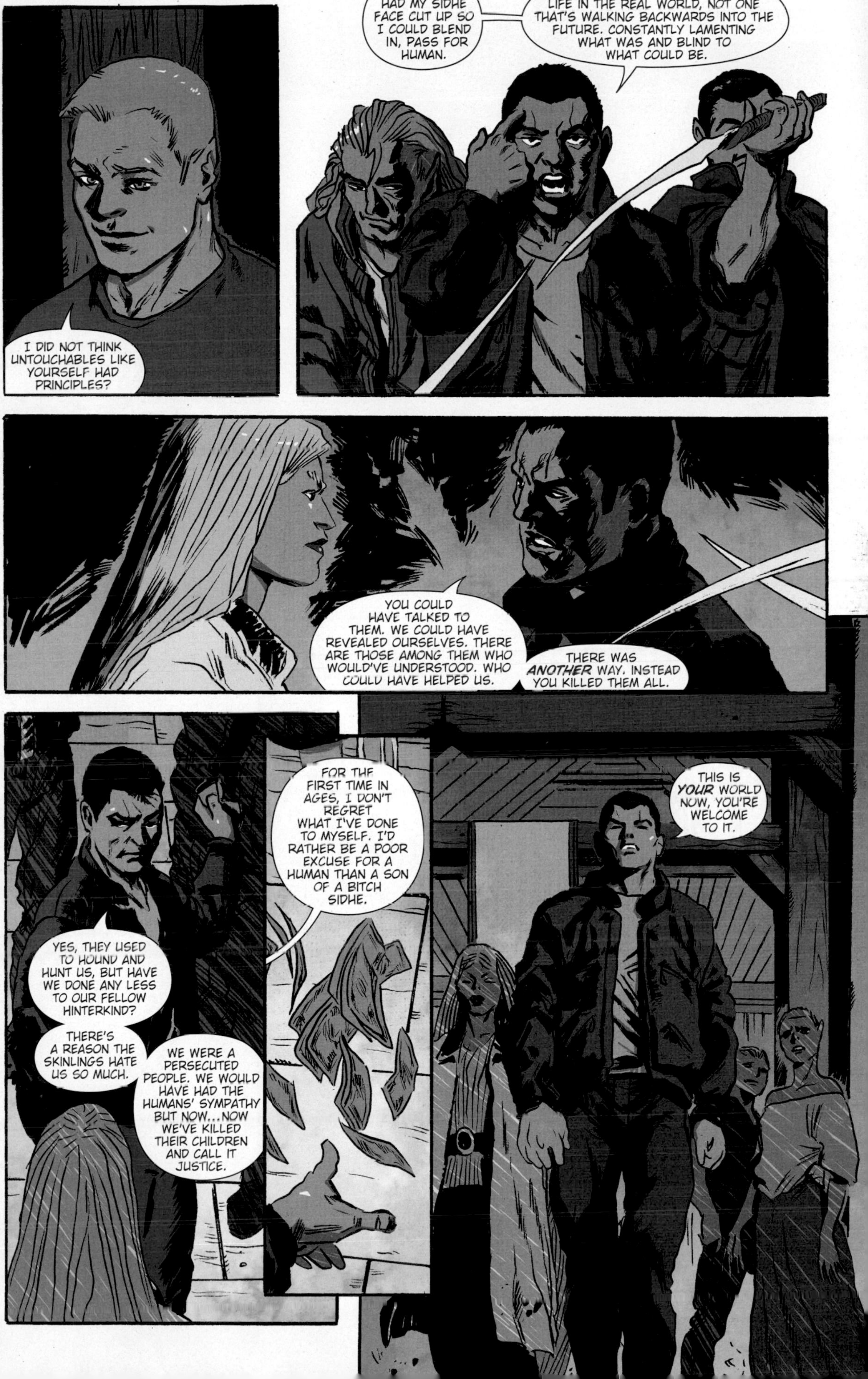
I DID NOT THINK UNTOUCHABLES LIKE YOURSELF HAD PRINCIPLES?
I DID THIS... HAD MY SIDHE FACE CUT UP SO I COULD BLEND IN, PASS FOR HUMAN.
I DID IT BECAUSE I WANTED A LIFE IN THE REAL WORLD, NOT ONE THAT'S WALKING BACKWARDS INTO THE FUTURE. CONSTANTLY LAMENTING WHAT WAS AND BLIND TO WHAT COULD BE.
YOU COULD HAVE TALKED TO THEM. WE COULD HAVE REVEALED OURSELVES. THERE ARE THOSE AMONG THEM WHO WOULD'VE UNDERSTOOD. WHO COULD HAVE HELPED US.
THERE WAS ANOTHER WAY. INSTEAD YOU KILLED THEM ALL.
YES, THEY USED TO HOUND AND HUNT US, BUT HAVE WE DONE ANY LESS TO OUR FELLOW HINTERKIND?
THERE'S A REASON THE SKINLINGS HATE US SO MUCH.
WE WERE A PERSECUTED PEOPLE. WE WOULD HAVE HAD THE HUMANS' SYMPATHY BUT NOW...NOW WE'VE KILLED THEIR CHILDREN AND CALL IT JUSTICE.
FOR THE FIRST TIME IN AGES, I DON'T REGRET WHAT I'VE DONE TO MYSELF. I'D RATHER BE A POOR EXCUSE FOR A HUMAN THAN A SON OF A BITCH SIDHE.
THIS IS YOUR WORLD NOW, YOU'RE WELCOME TO IT.

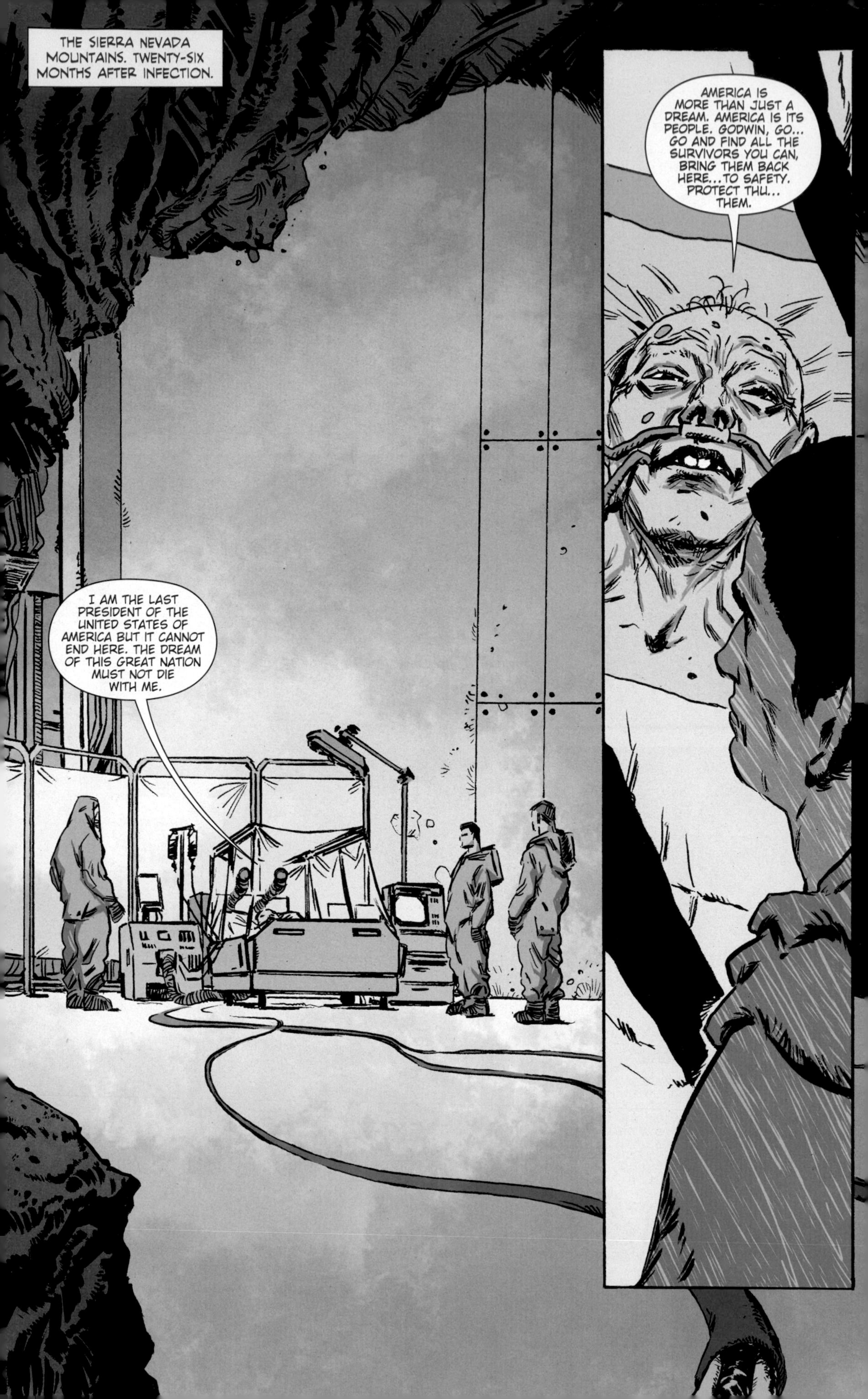
THE SIERRA NEVADA MOUNTAINS. TWENTY-SIX MONTHS AFTER INFECTION.
I AM THE LAST PRESIDENT OF THE UNITED STATES OF AMERICA BUT IT CANNOT END HERE. THE DREAM OF THIS GREAT NATION MUST NOT DIE WITH ME.
AMERICA IS MORE THAN JUST A DREAM. AMERICA IS ITS PEOPLE. GODWIN, GO... GO AND FIND ALL THE SURVIVORS YOU CAN, BRING THEM BACK HERE...TO SAFETY. PROTECT THU... THEM.

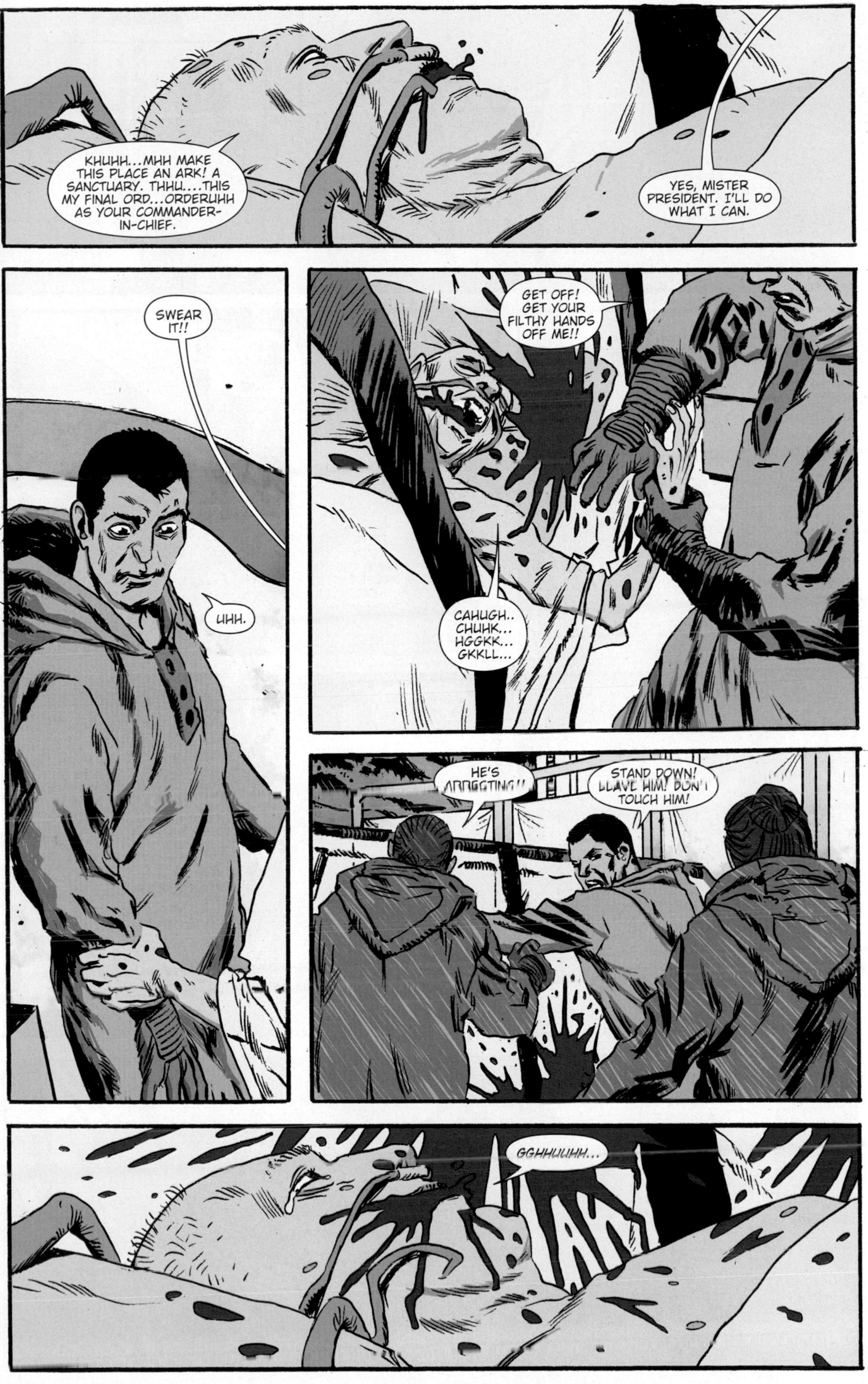
KHUHH...MHH MAKE THIS PLACE AN ARK! A SANCTUARY. THHU....THIS MY FINAL ORD...ORDERUHH AS YOUR COMMANDER-IN-CHIEF.
YES, MISTER PRESIDENT. I'LL DO WHAT I CAN.
SWEAR IT!!
UHH.
GET OFF! GET YOUR FILTHY HANDS OFF ME!!
CAHUGH.. CHUHK.. HGGKK... GKKLL...
HE'S ARRESTING!!
STAND DOWN! LEAVE HIM! DON'T TOUCH HIM!
GGHHUUHH...

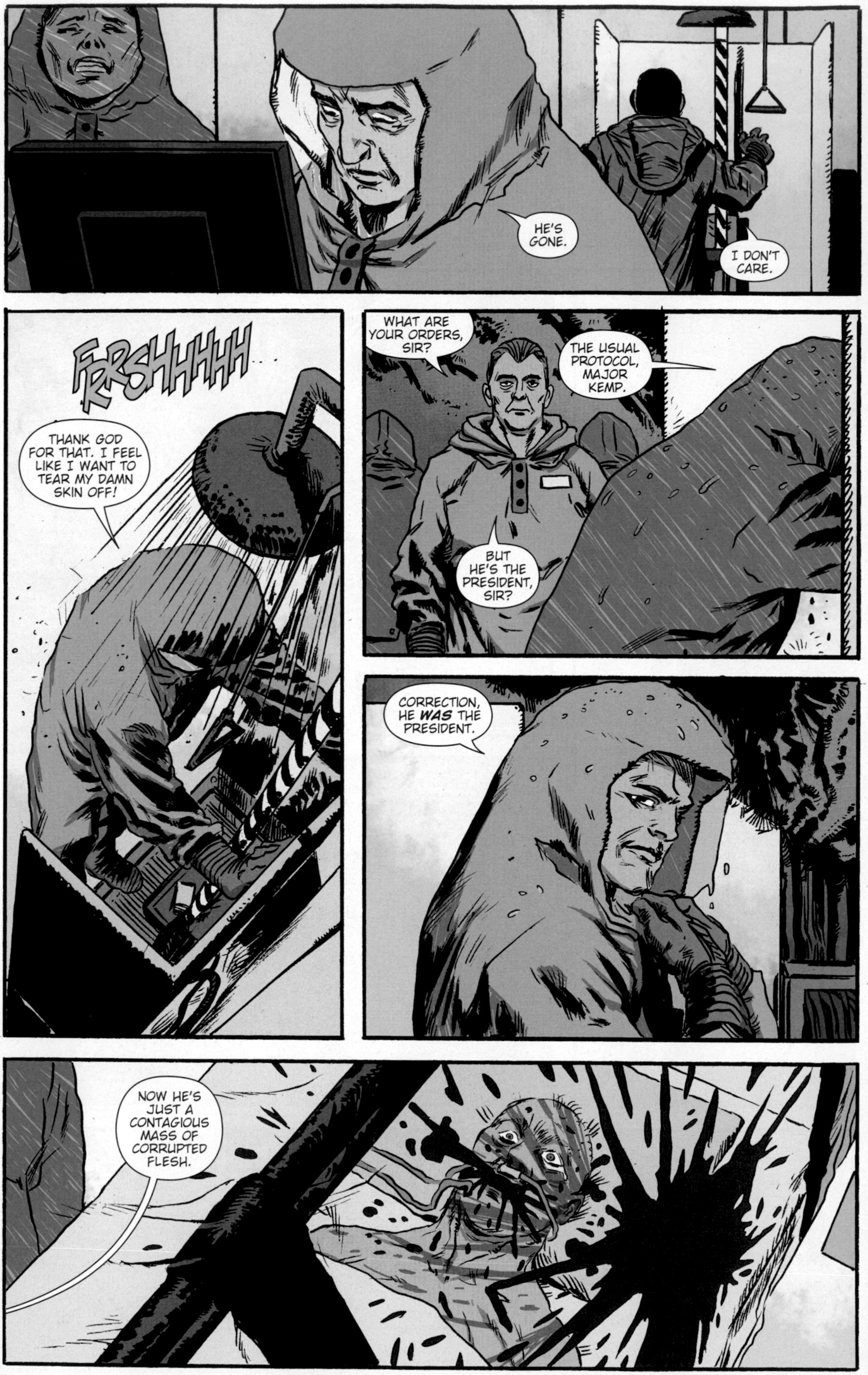
HE'S GONE.
I DON'T CARE.
FRRSHHHHH
THANK GOD FOR THAT. I FEEL LIKE I WANT TO TEAR MY DAMN SKIN OFF!
WHAT ARE YOUR ORDERS, SIR?
THE USUAL PROTOCOL, MAJOR KEMP.
BUT HE'S THE PRESIDENT, SIR?
CORRECTION, HE **WAS** THE PRESIDENT.
NOW HE'S JUST A CONTAGIOUS MASS OF CORRUPTED FLESH.

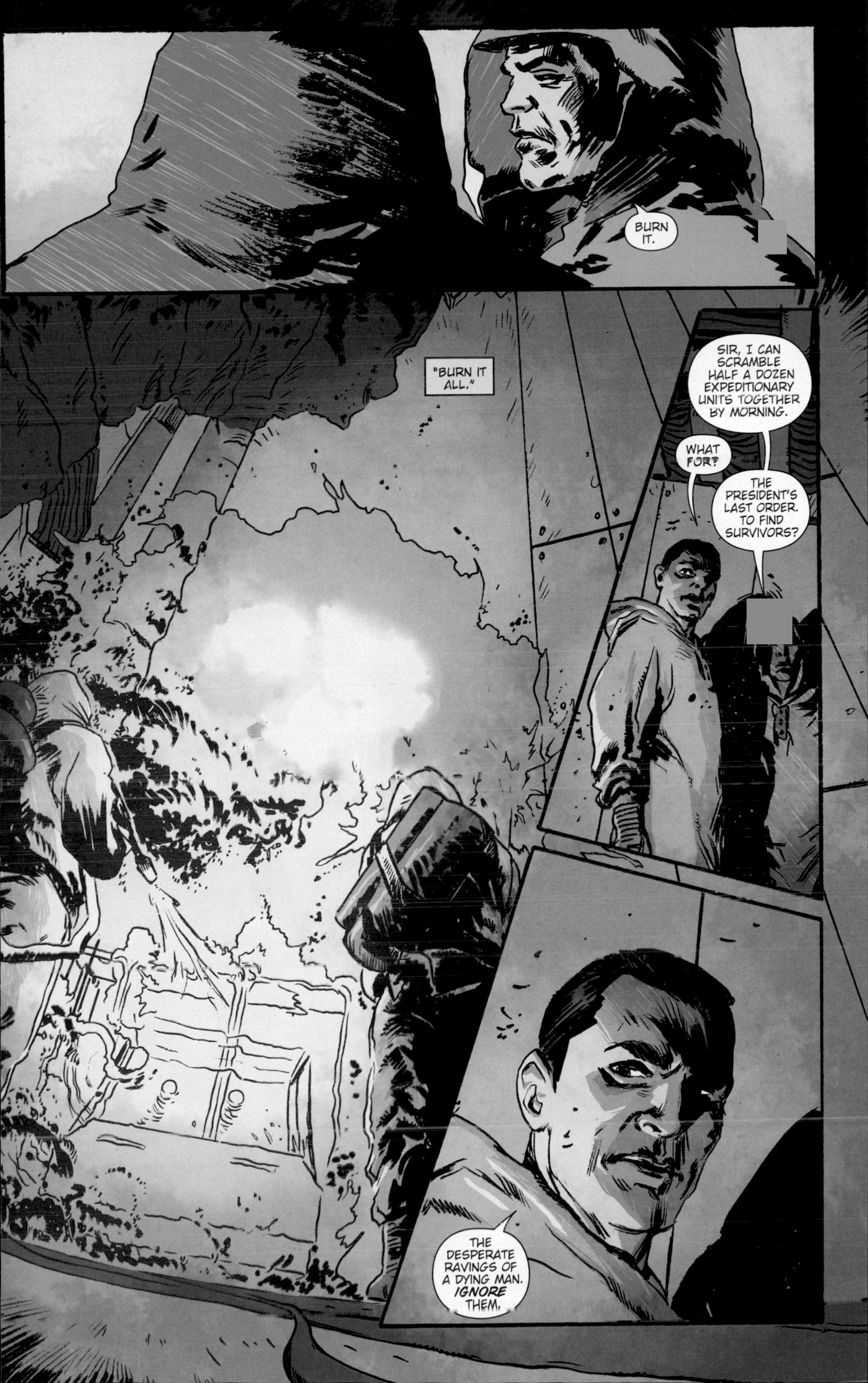
BURN IT.
"BURN IT ALL."
SIR, I CAN SCRAMBLE HALF A DOZEN EXPEDITIONARY UNITS TOGETHER BY MORNING.
WHAT FOR?
THE PRESIDENT'S LAST ORDER. TO FIND SURVIVORS?
THE DESPERATE RAVINGS OF A DYING MAN. **IGNORE** THEM.

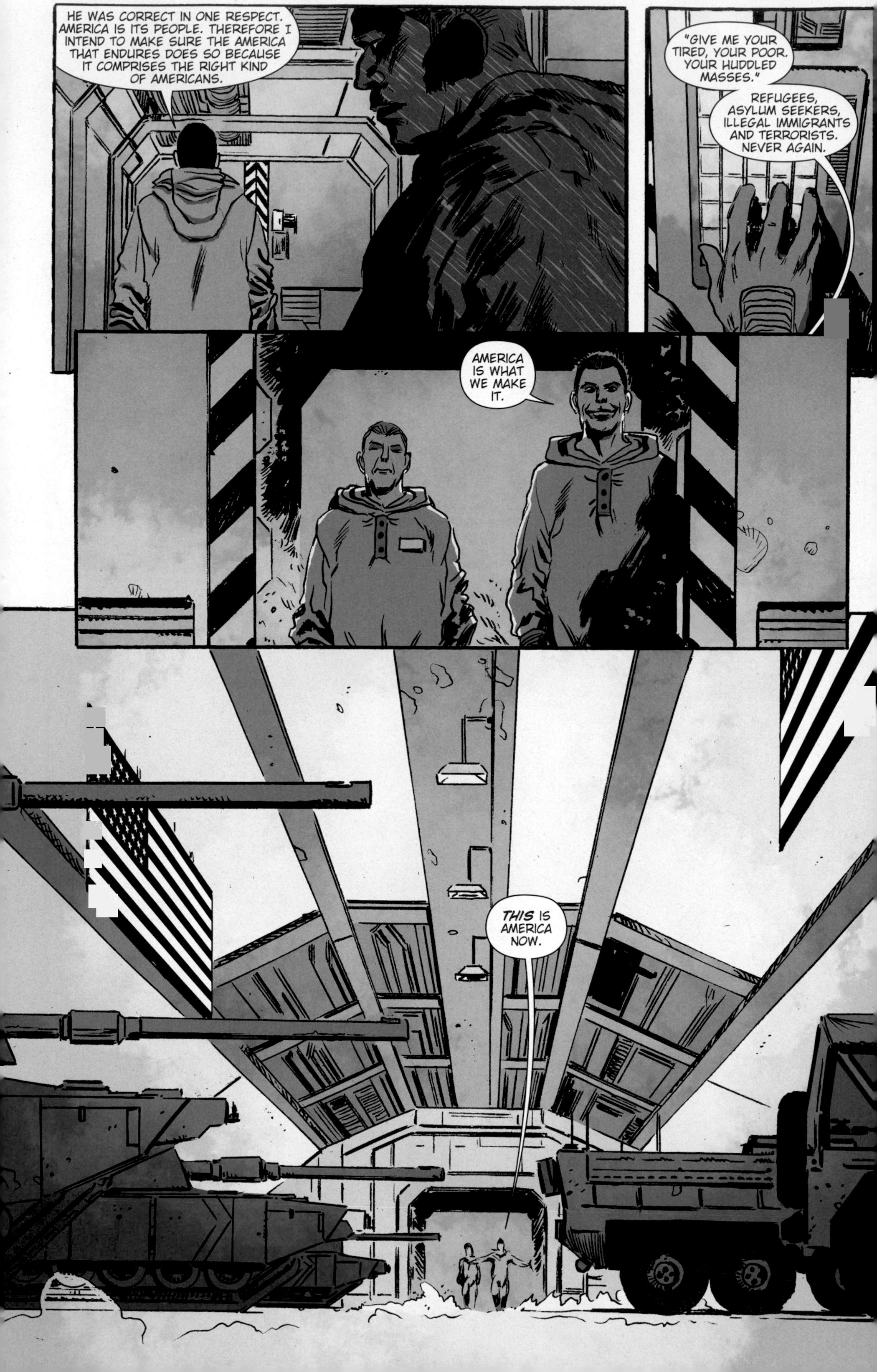
HE WAS CORRECT IN ONE RESPECT. AMERICA IS ITS PEOPLE. THEREFORE I INTEND TO MAKE SURE THE AMERICA THAT ENDURES DOES SO BECAUSE IT COMPRISES THE RIGHT KIND OF AMERICANS.
"GIVE ME YOUR TIRED, YOUR POOR. YOUR HUDDLED MASSES."
REFUGEES, ASYLUM SEEKERS, ILLEGAL IMMIGRANTS AND TERRORISTS. NEVER AGAIN.
AMERICA IS WHAT WE MAKE IT.
THIS IS AMERICA NOW.

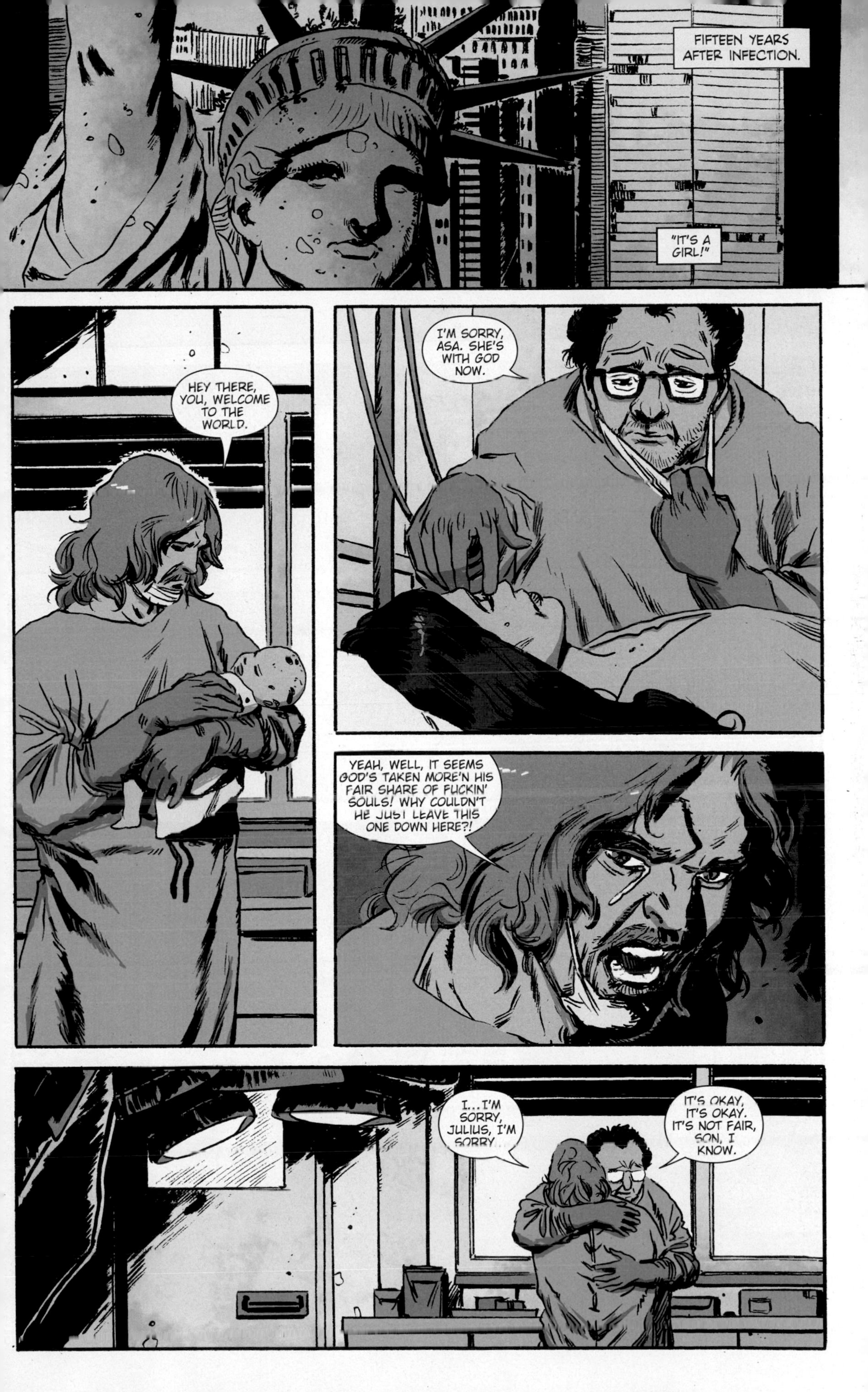
FIFTEEN YEARS AFTER INFECTION.
"IT'S A GIRL!"
HEY THERE, YOU, WELCOME TO THE WORLD.
I'M SORRY, ASA. SHE'S WITH GOD NOW.
YEAH, WELL, IT SEEMS GOD'S TAKEN MORE'N HIS FAIR SHARE OF FUCKIN' SOULS! WHY COULDN'T HE JUST LEAVE THIS ONE DOWN HERE?!
I...I'M SORRY, JULIUS, I'M SORRY...
IT'S OKAY, IT'S OKAY. IT'S NOT FAIR, SON, I KNOW.

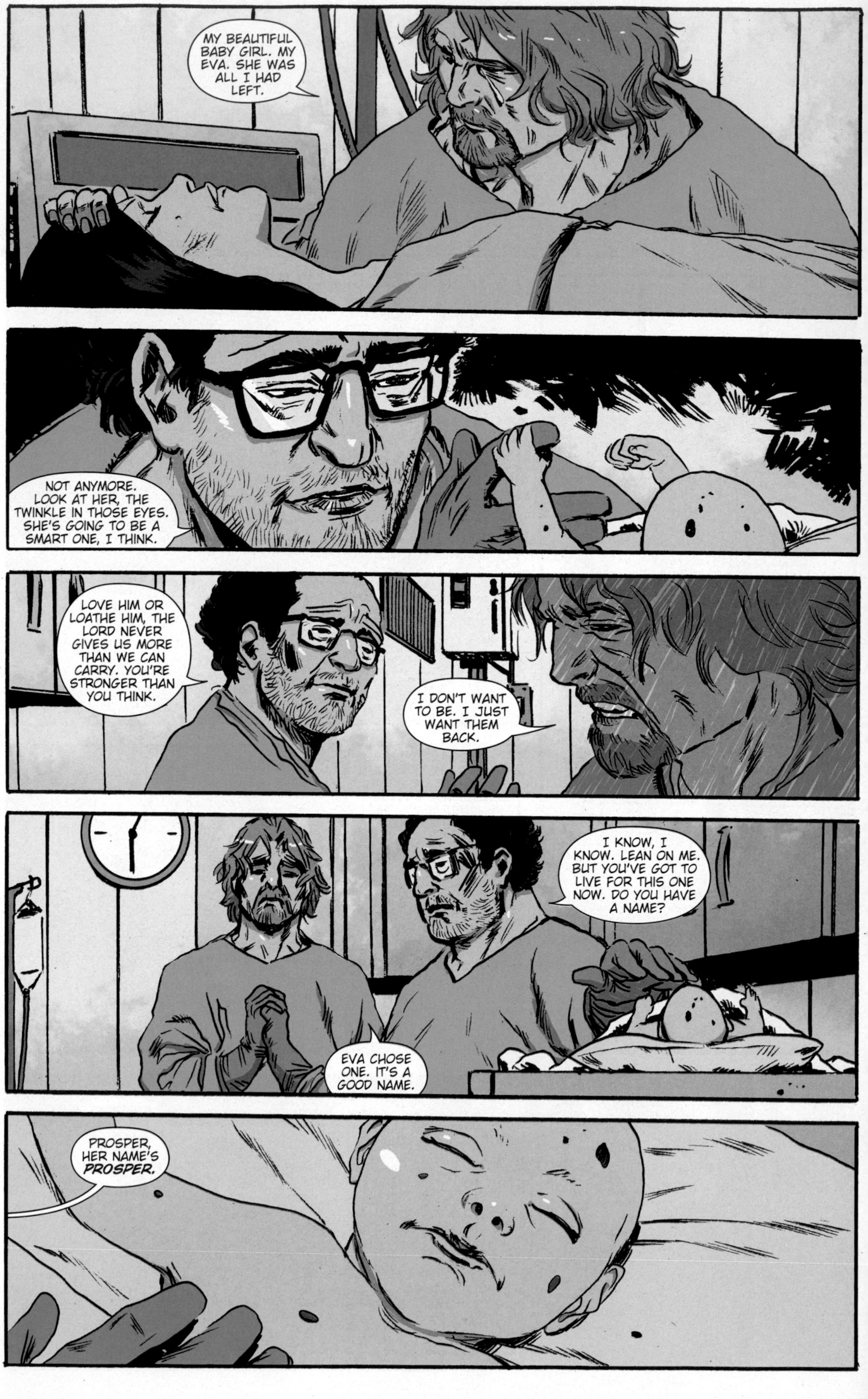
MY BEAUTIFUL BABY GIRL. MY EVA. SHE WAS ALL I HAD LEFT.
NOT ANYMORE. LOOK AT HER, THE TWINKLE IN THOSE EYES. SHE'S GOING TO BE A SMART ONE, I THINK.
LOVE HIM OR LOATHE HIM, THE LORD NEVER GIVES US MORE THAN WE CAN CARRY. YOU'RE STRONGER THAN YOU THINK.
I DON'T WANT TO BE. I JUST WANT THEM BACK.
I KNOW, I KNOW. LEAN ON ME. BUT YOU'VE GOT TO LIVE FOR THIS ONE NOW. DO YOU HAVE A NAME?
EVA CHOSE ONE. IT'S A GOOD NAME.
PROSPER, HER NAME'S ***PROSPER.***

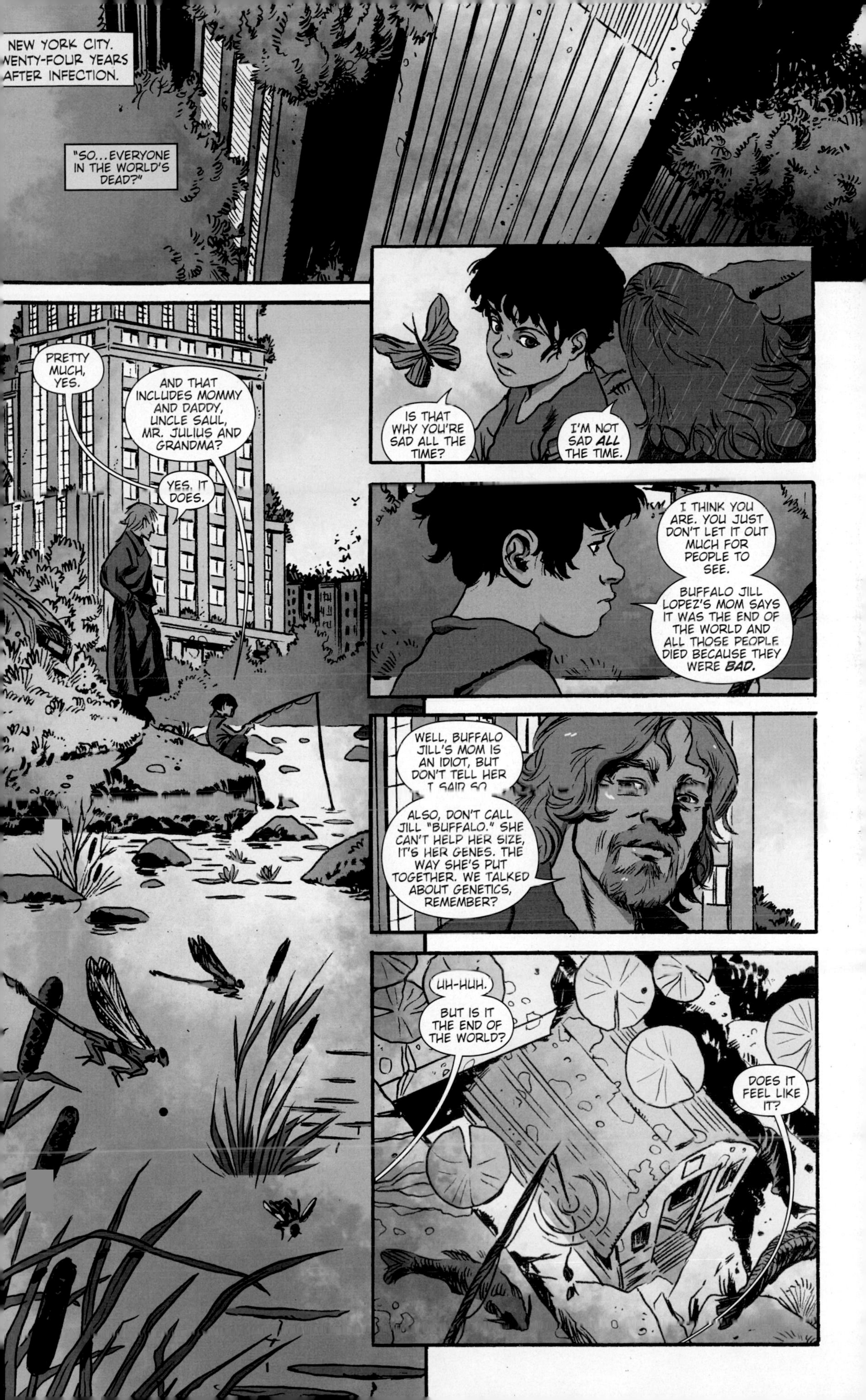
NEW YORK CITY. WENTY-FOUR YEARS AFTER INFECTION.
"SO...EVERYONE IN THE WORLD'S DEAD?"
PRETTY MUCH, YES.
AND THAT INCLUDES MOMMY AND DADDY, UNCLE SAUL, MR. JULIUS AND GRANDMA?
YES, IT DOES.
IS THAT WHY YOU'RE SAD ALL THE TIME?
I'M NOT SAD ALL THE TIME.
I THINK YOU ARE. YOU JUST DON'T LET IT OUT MUCH FOR PEOPLE TO SEE.
BUFFALO JILL LOPEZ'S MOM SAYS IT WAS THE END OF THE WORLD AND ALL THOSE PEOPLE DIED BECAUSE THEY WERE BAD.
WELL, BUFFALO JILL'S MOM IS AN IDIOT, BUT DON'T TELL HER I SAID SO.
ALSO, DON'T CALL JILL "BUFFALO." SHE CAN'T HELP HER SIZE, IT'S HER GENES. THE WAY SHE'S PUT TOGETHER. WE TALKED ABOUT GENETICS, REMEMBER?
UH-HUH.
BUT IS IT THE END OF THE WORLD?
DOES IT FEEL LIKE IT?

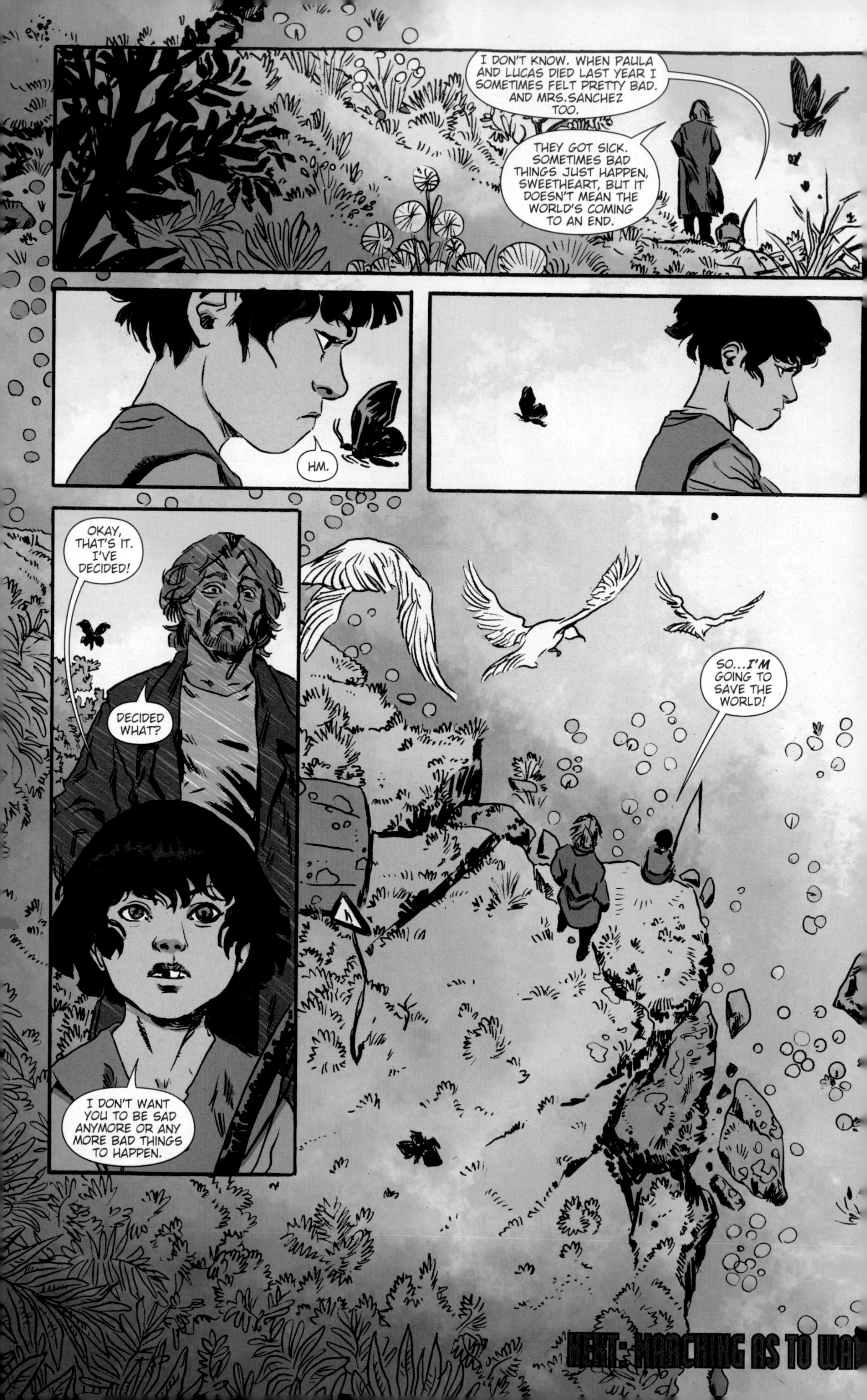

I DON'T KNOW. WHEN PAULA AND LUCAS DIED LAST YEAR I SOMETIMES FELT PRETTY BAD. AND MRS.SANCHEZ TOO.
THEY GOT SICK. SOMETIMES BAD THINGS JUST HAPPEN, SWEETHEART, BUT IT DOESN'T MEAN THE WORLD'S COMING TO AN END.
HM.
OKAY, THAT'S IT. I'VE DECIDED!
DECIDED WHAT?
I DON'T WANT YOU TO BE SAD ANYMORE OR ANY MORE BAD THINGS TO HAPPEN.
SO...*I'M* GOING TO SAVE THE WORLD!
NEXT: MARCHING AS TO WA

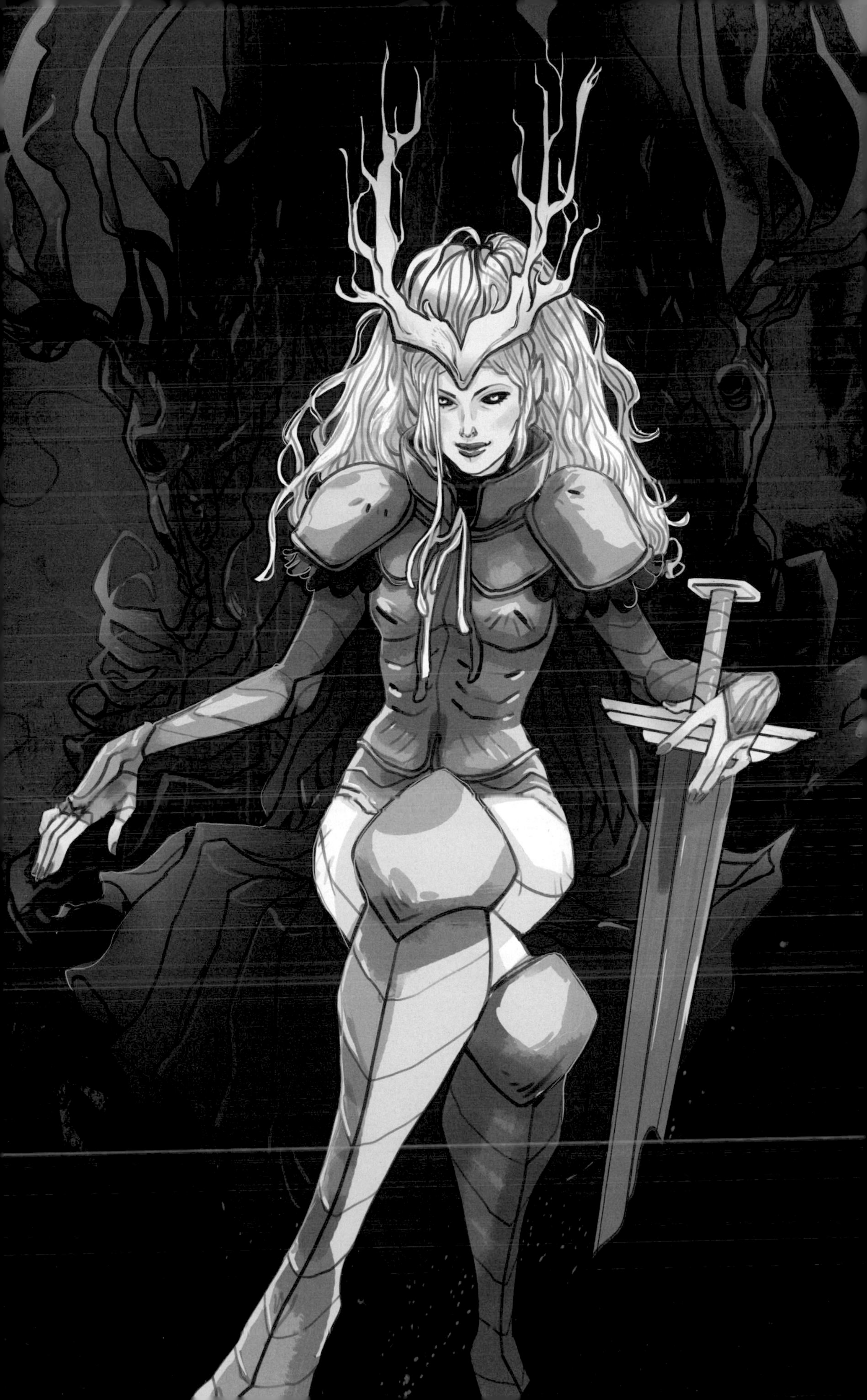

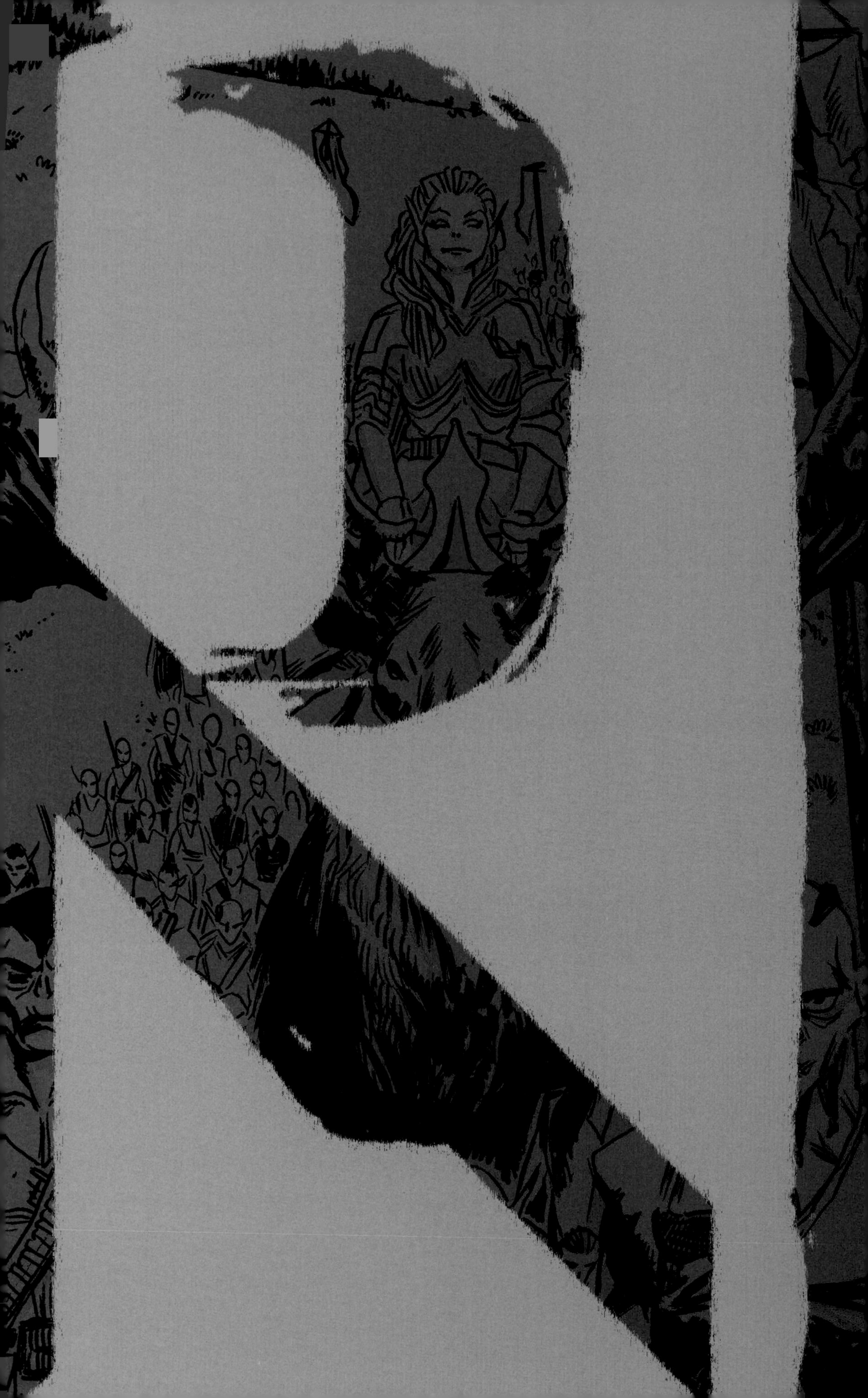

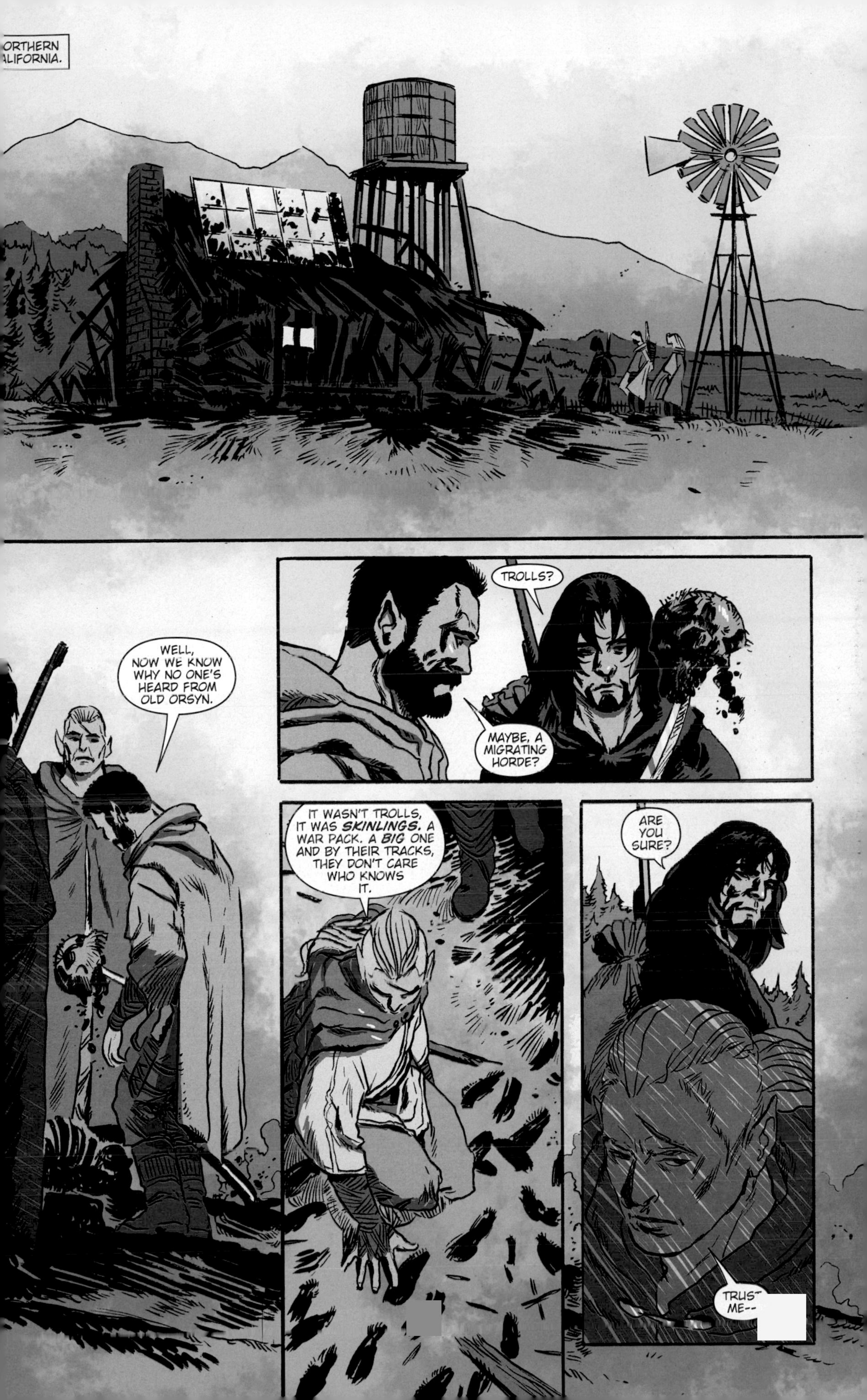
ORTHERN ALIFORNIA.
WELL, NOW WE KNOW WHY NO ONE'S HEARD FROM OLD ORSYN.
TROLLS?
MAYBE, A MIGRATING HORDE?
IT WASN'T TROLLS, IT WAS *SKINLINGS.* A WAR PACK. A *BIG* ONE AND BY THEIR TRACKS, THEY DON'T CARE WHO KNOWS IT.
ARE YOU SURE?
TRUST ME--

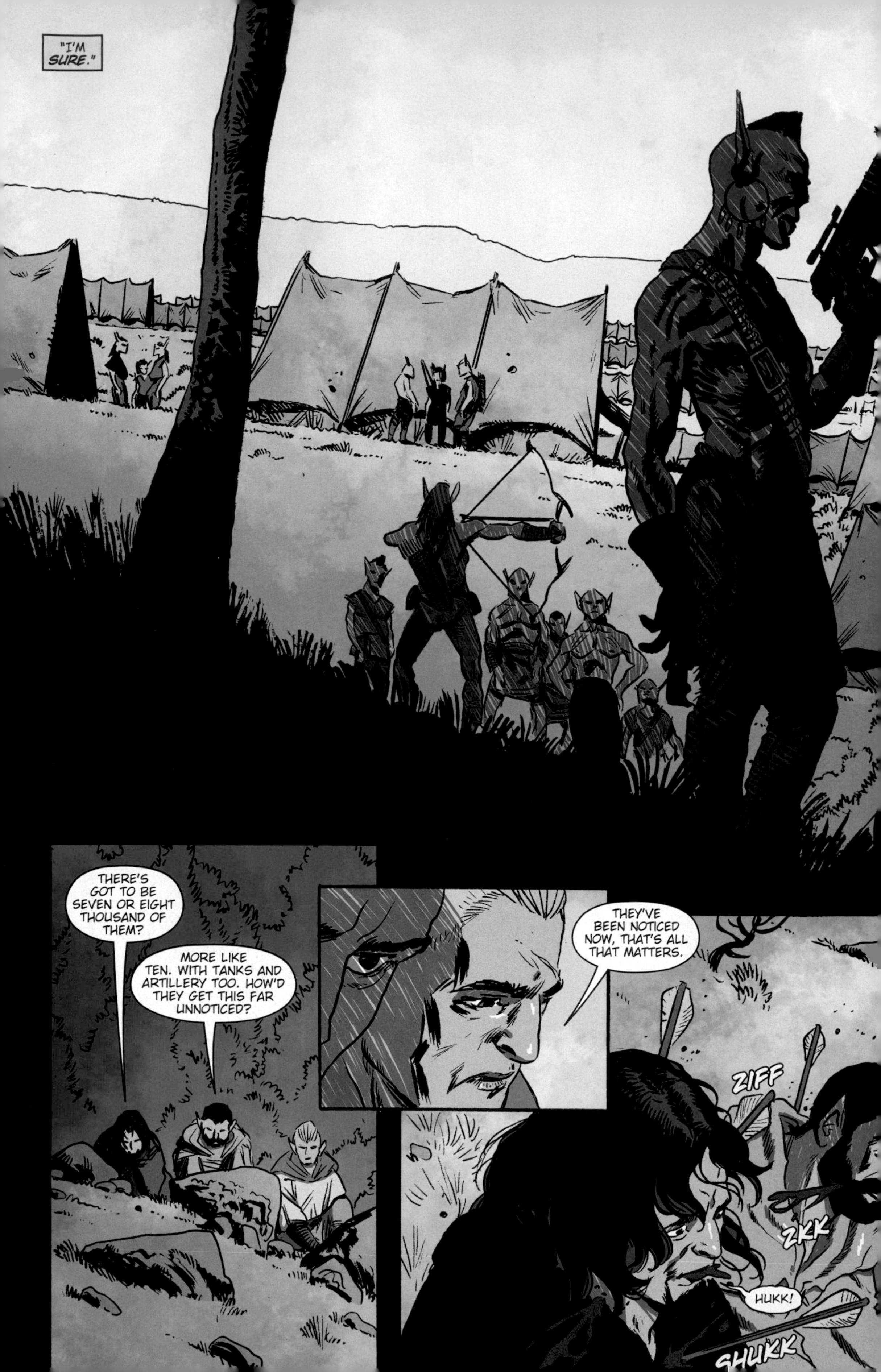
"I'M SURE."
THERE'S GOT TO BE SEVEN OR EIGHT THOUSAND OF THEM?
MORE LIKE TEN. WITH TANKS AND ARTILLERY TOO. HOW'D THEY GET THIS FAR UNNOTICED?
THEY'VE BEEN NOTICED NOW, THAT'S ALL THAT MATTERS.
ZIFF
ZKK
HUKK!
SHUKK

Falls the Shadow

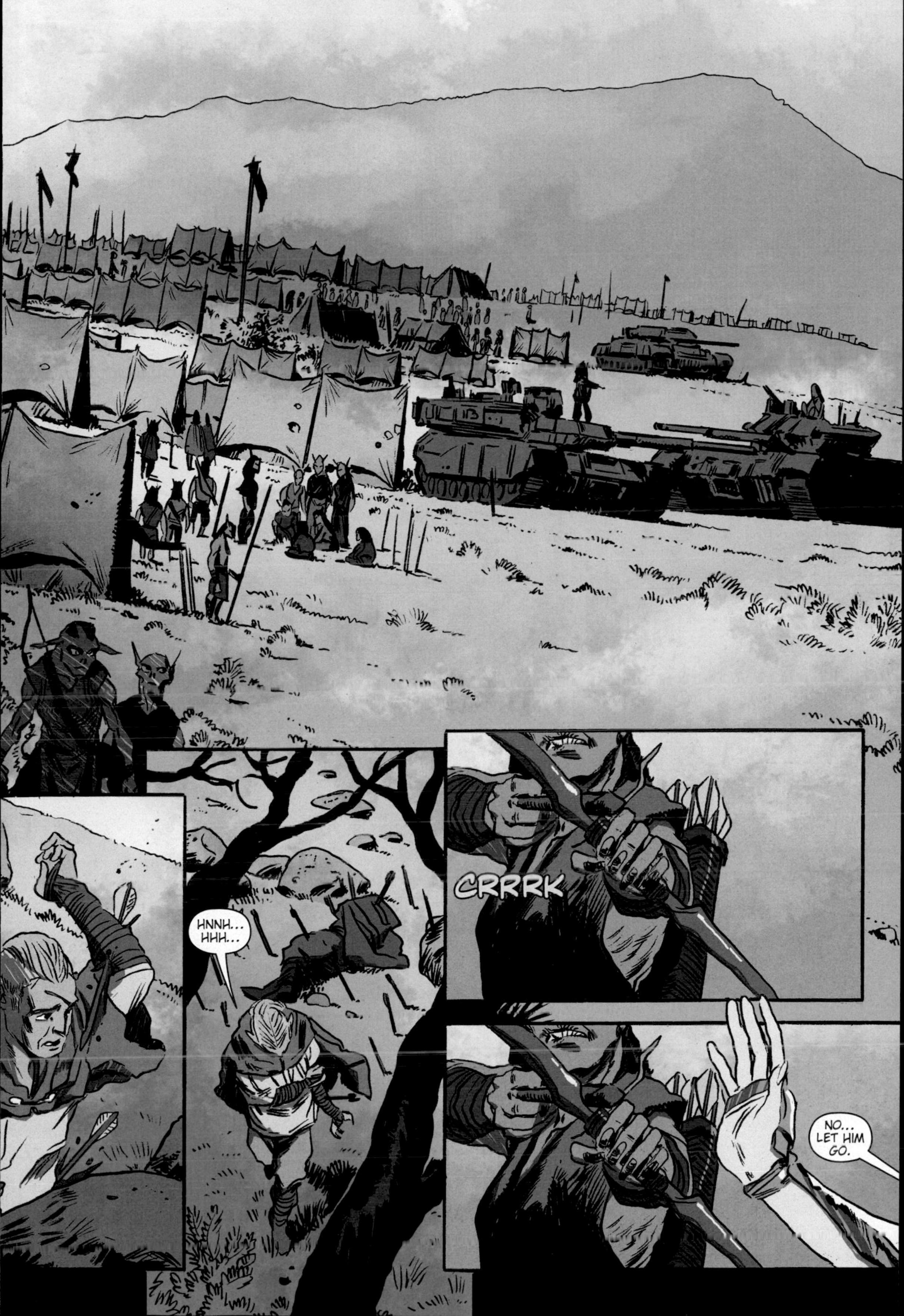
HNNH... HHH...
CRRRK
NO... LET HIM GO.

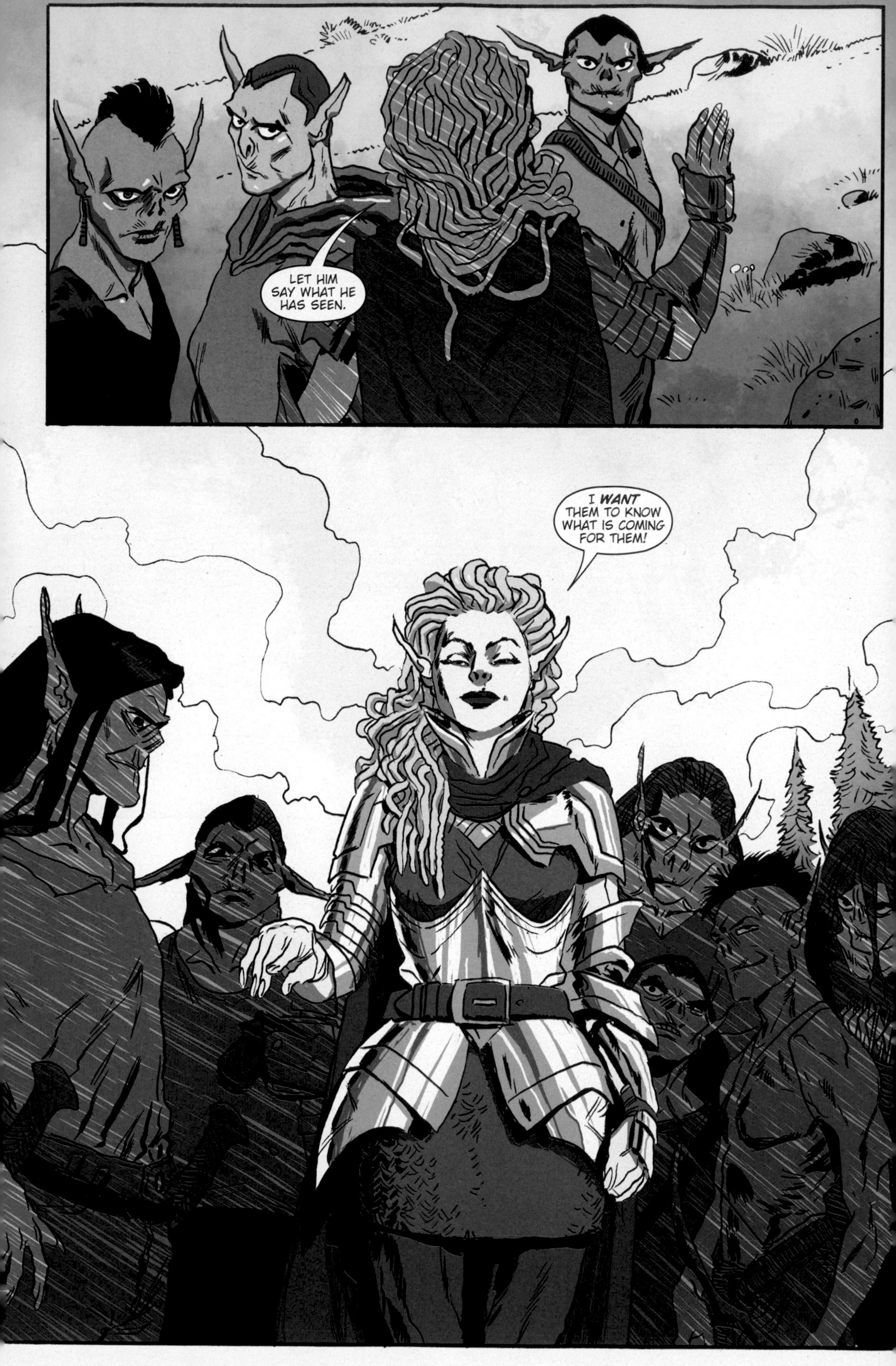
LET HIM SAY WHAT HE HAS SEEN.
I *WANT* THEM TO KNOW WHAT IS COMING FOR THEM!

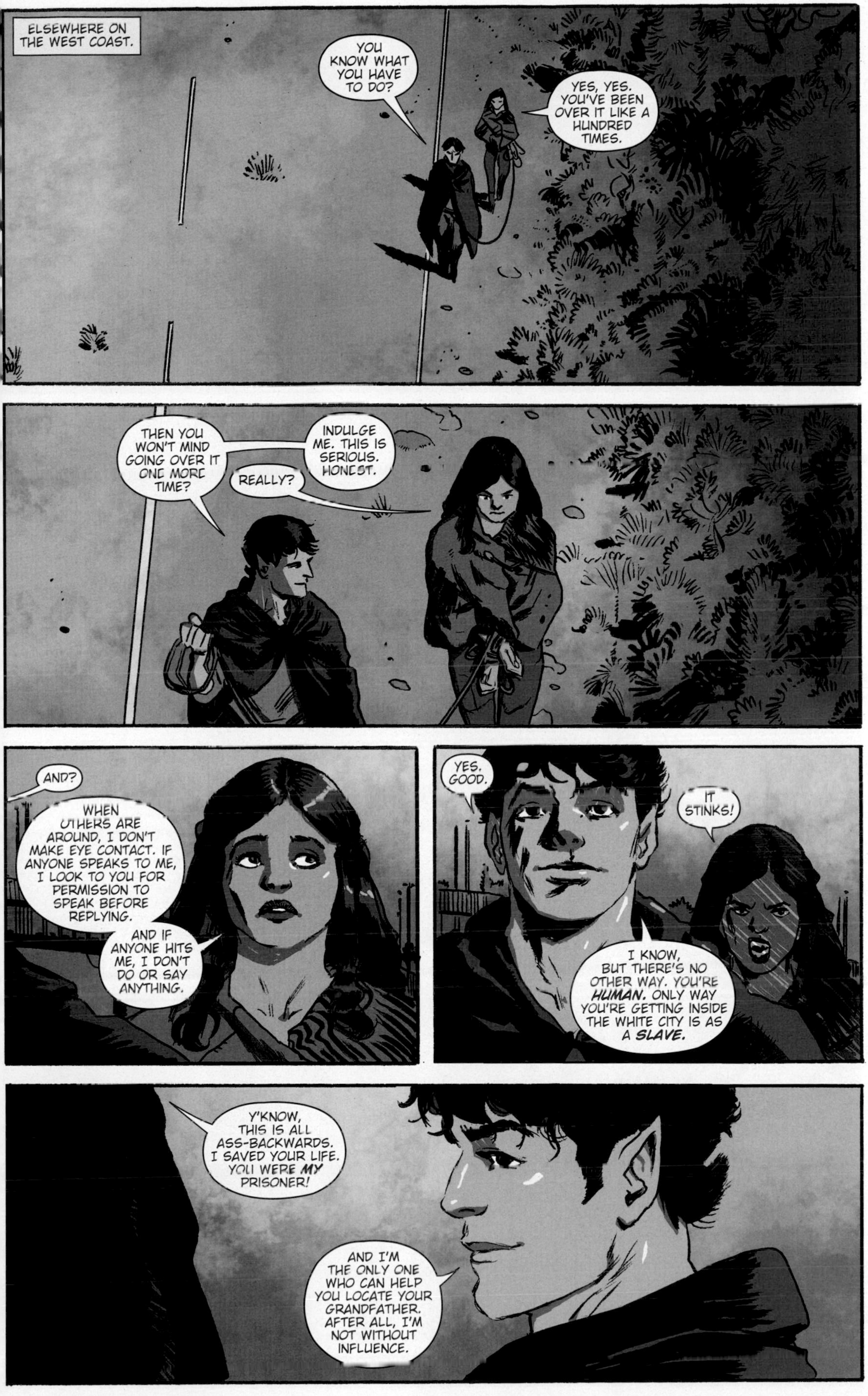
ELSEWHERE ON THE WEST COAST.
YOU KNOW WHAT YOU HAVE TO DO?
YES, YES. YOU'VE BEEN OVER IT LIKE A HUNDRED TIMES.
THEN YOU WON'T MIND GOING OVER IT ONE MORE TIME?
INDULGE ME. THIS IS SERIOUS. HONEST.
REALLY?
AND?
WHEN OTHERS ARE AROUND, I DON'T MAKE EYE CONTACT. IF ANYONE SPEAKS TO ME, I LOOK TO YOU FOR PERMISSION TO SPEAK BEFORE REPLYING.
AND IF ANYONE HITS ME, I DON'T DO OR SAY ANYTHING.
YES. GOOD.
IT STINKS!
I KNOW, BUT THERE'S NO OTHER WAY. YOU'RE HUMAN. ONLY WAY YOU'RE GETTING INSIDE THE WHITE CITY IS AS A SLAVE.
Y'KNOW, THIS IS ALL ASS-BACKWARDS. I SAVED YOUR LIFE. YOU WERE MY PRISONER!
AND I'M THE ONLY ONE WHO CAN HELP YOU LOCATE YOUR GRANDFATHER. AFTER ALL, I'M NOT WITHOUT INFLUENCE.

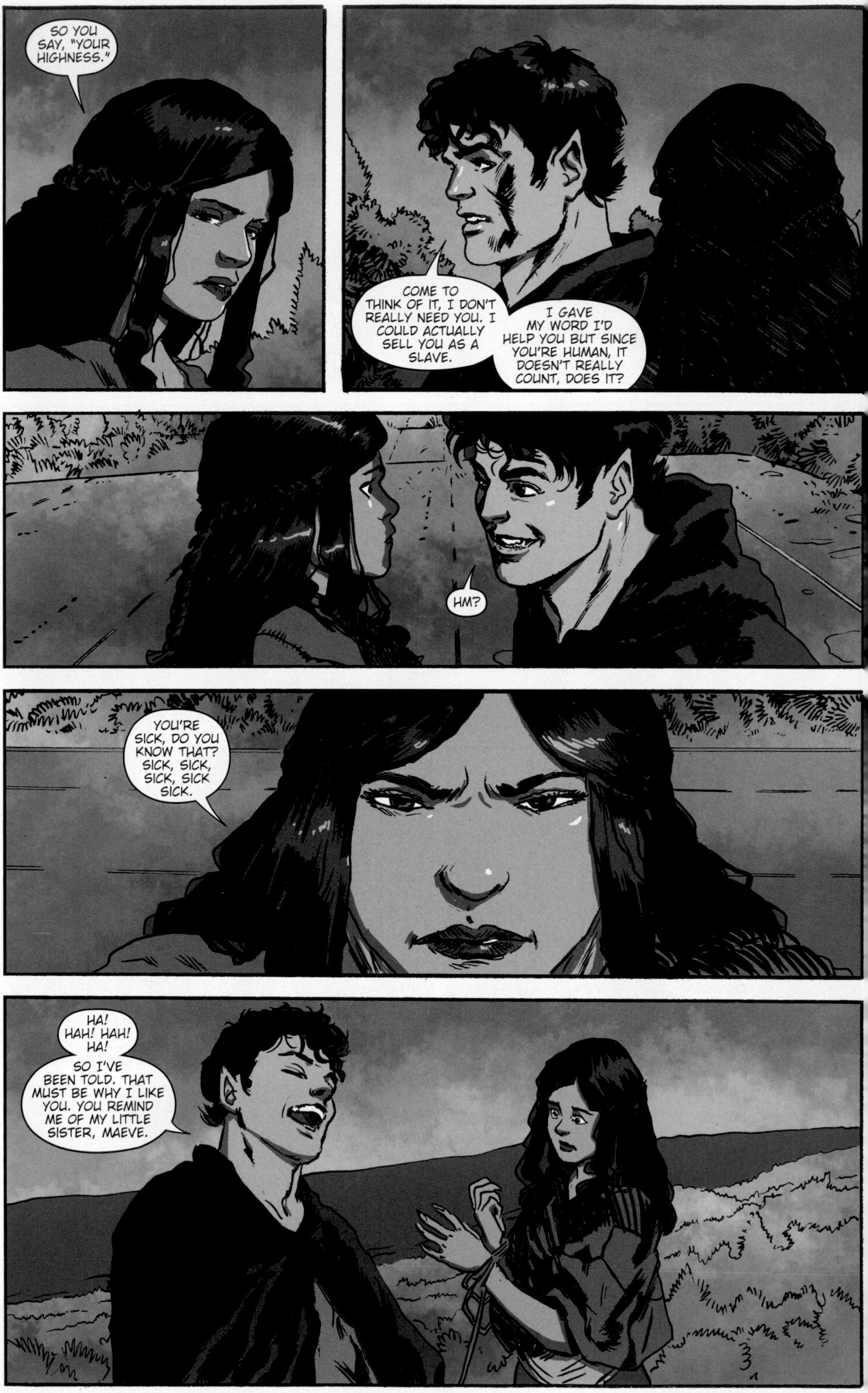
SO YOU SAY, "YOUR HIGHNESS."
COME TO THINK OF IT, I DON'T REALLY NEED YOU. I COULD ACTUALLY SELL YOU AS A SLAVE.
I GAVE MY WORD I'D HELP YOU BUT SINCE YOU'RE HUMAN, IT DOESN'T REALLY COUNT, DOES IT?
HM?
YOU'RE SICK, DO YOU KNOW THAT? SICK, SICK, SICK, SICK SICK.
HA! HAH! HAH! HA!
SO I'VE BEEN TOLD. THAT MUST BE WHY I LIKE YOU. YOU REMIND ME OF MY LITTLE SISTER, MAEVE.

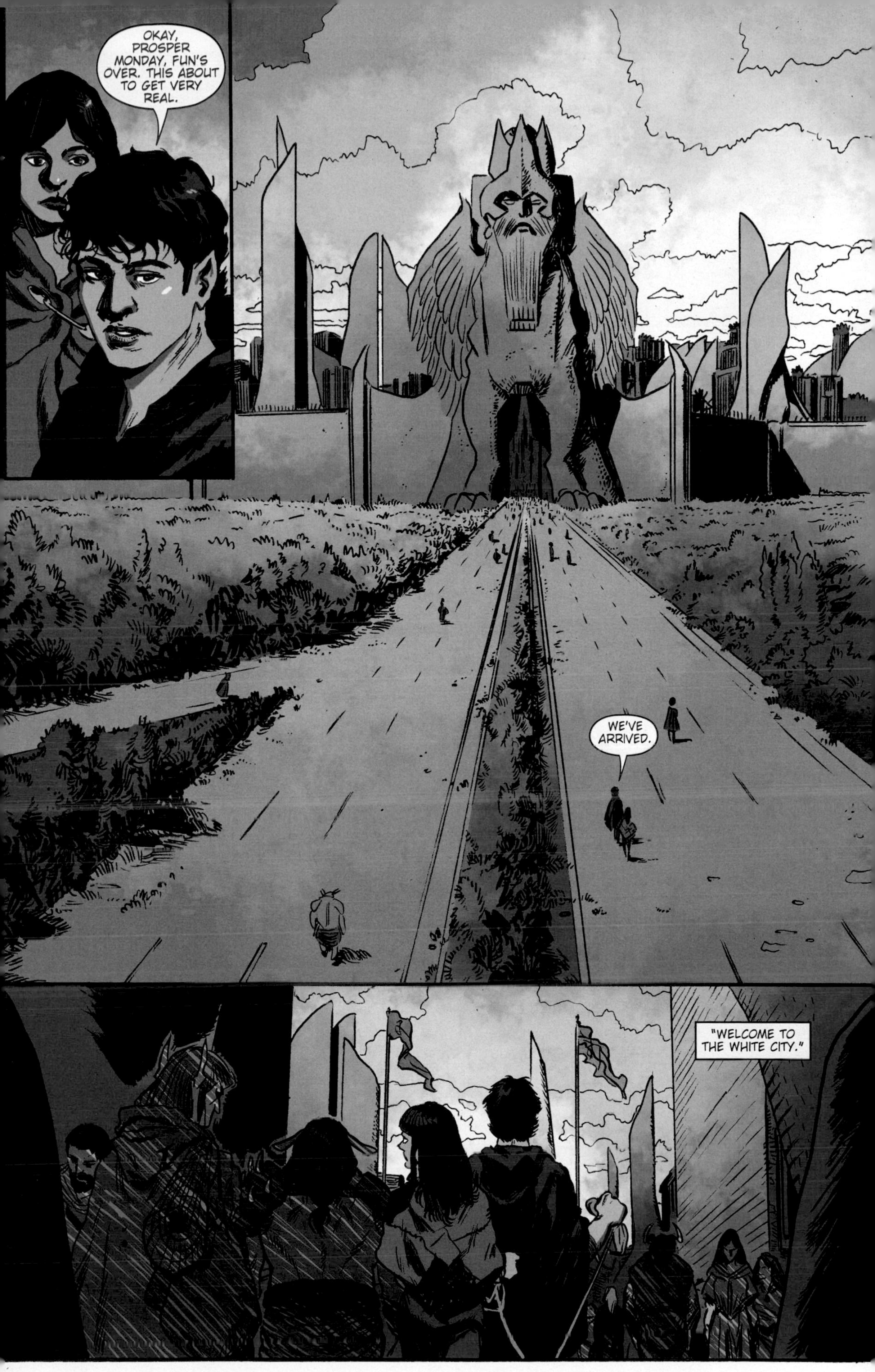
OKAY, PROSPER MONDAY, FUN'S OVER. THIS ABOUT TO GET VERY REAL.
WE'VE ARRIVED.
"WELCOME TO THE WHITE CITY."

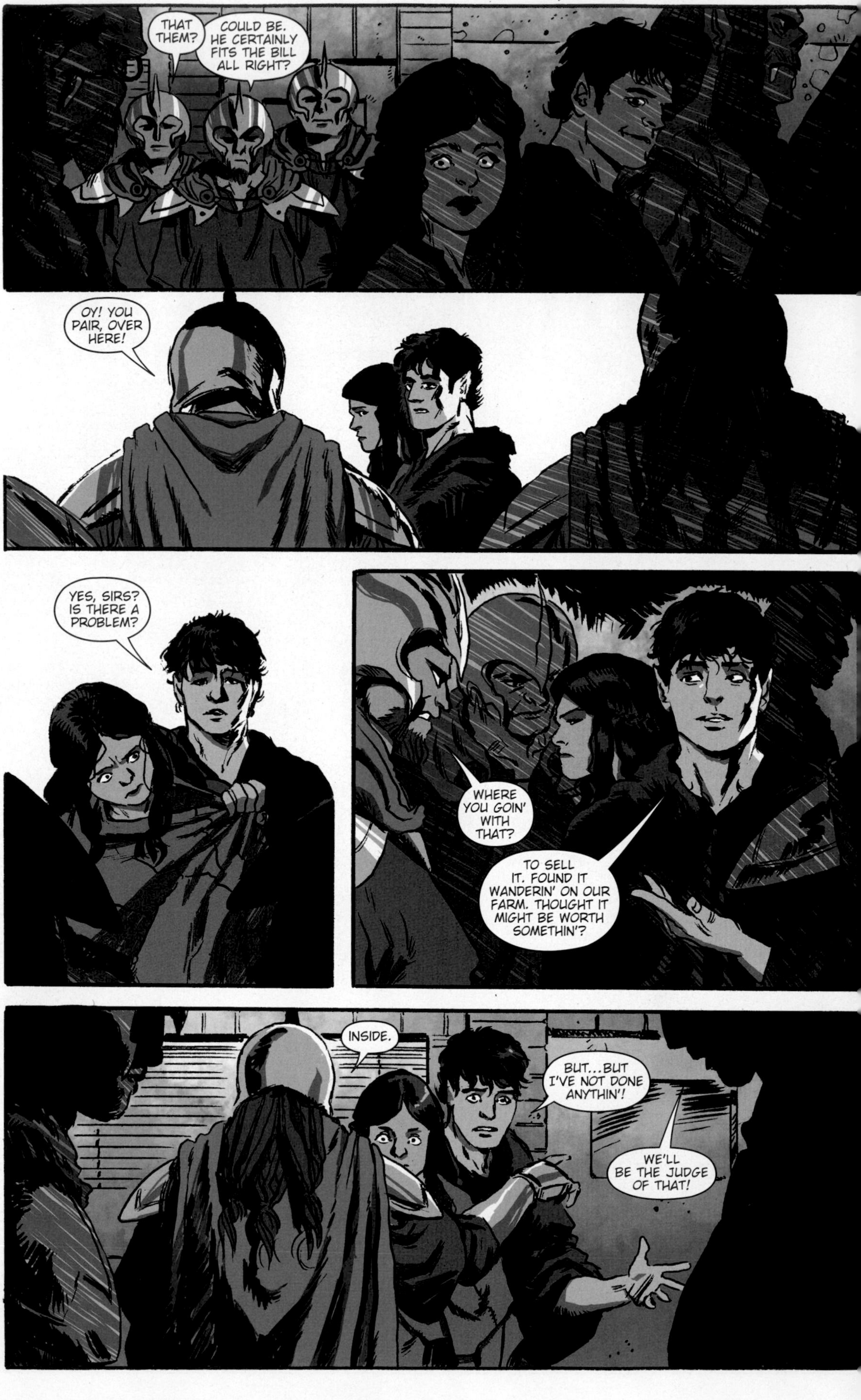
THAT THEM?
COULD BE. HE CERTAINLY FITS THE BILL ALL RIGHT?
OY! YOU PAIR, OVER HERE!
YES, SIRS? IS THERE A PROBLEM?
WHERE YOU GOIN' WITH THAT?
TO SELL IT. FOUND IT WANDERIN' ON OUR FARM. THOUGHT IT MIGHT BE WORTH SOMETHIN'?
INSIDE.
BUT...BUT I'VE NOT DONE ANYTHIN'!
WE'LL BE THE JUDGE OF THAT!

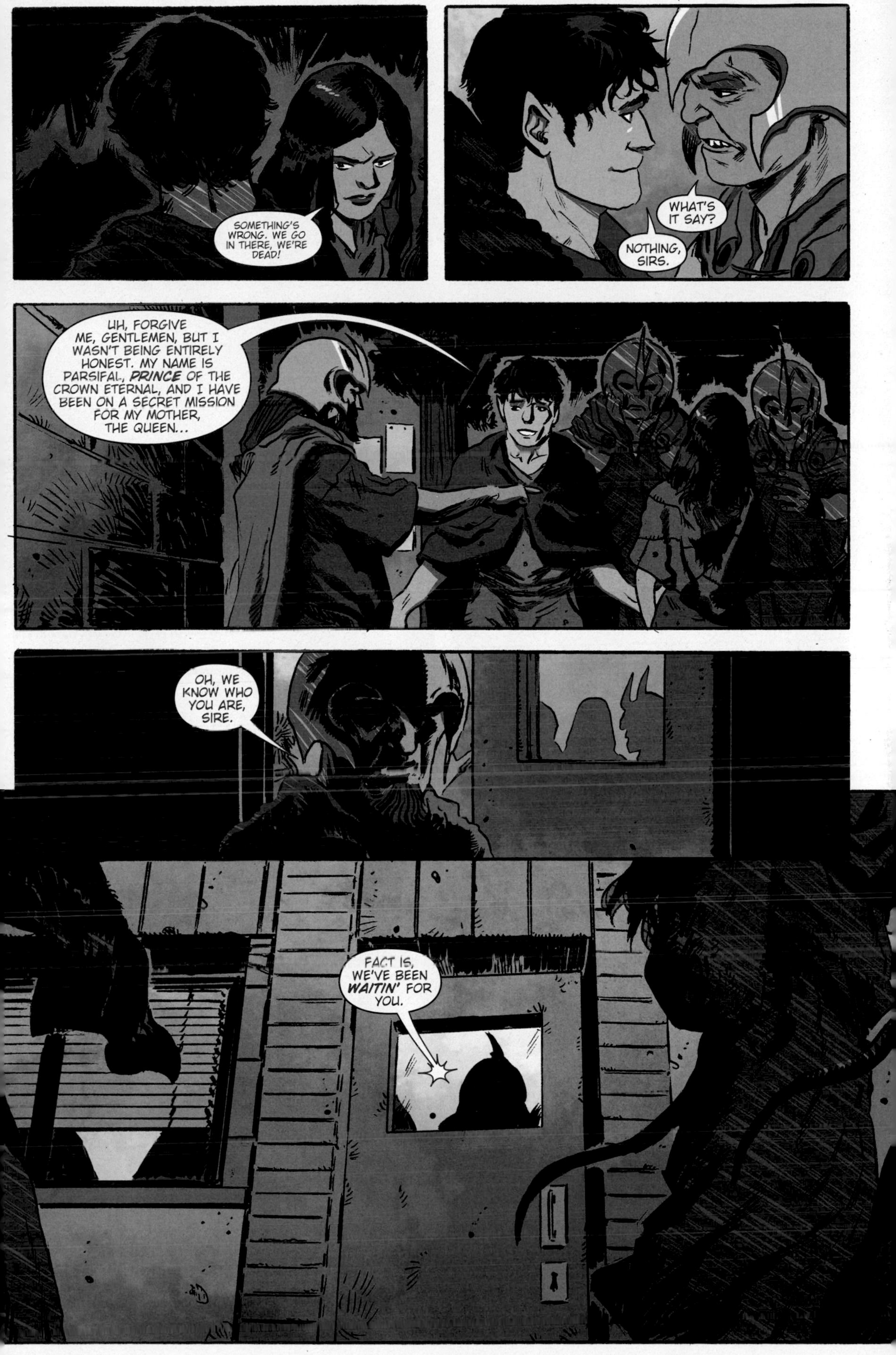
SOMETHING'S WRONG. WE GO IN THERE, WE'RE DEAD!
WHAT'S IT SAY?
NOTHING, SIRS.
UH, FORGIVE ME, GENTLEMEN, BUT I WASN'T BEING ENTIRELY HONEST. MY NAME IS PARSIFAL, PRINCE OF THE CROWN ETERNAL, AND I HAVE BEEN ON A SECRET MISSION FOR MY MOTHER, THE QUEEN...
OH, WE KNOW WHO YOU ARE, SIRE.
FACT IS, WE'VE BEEN WAITIN' FOR YOU.

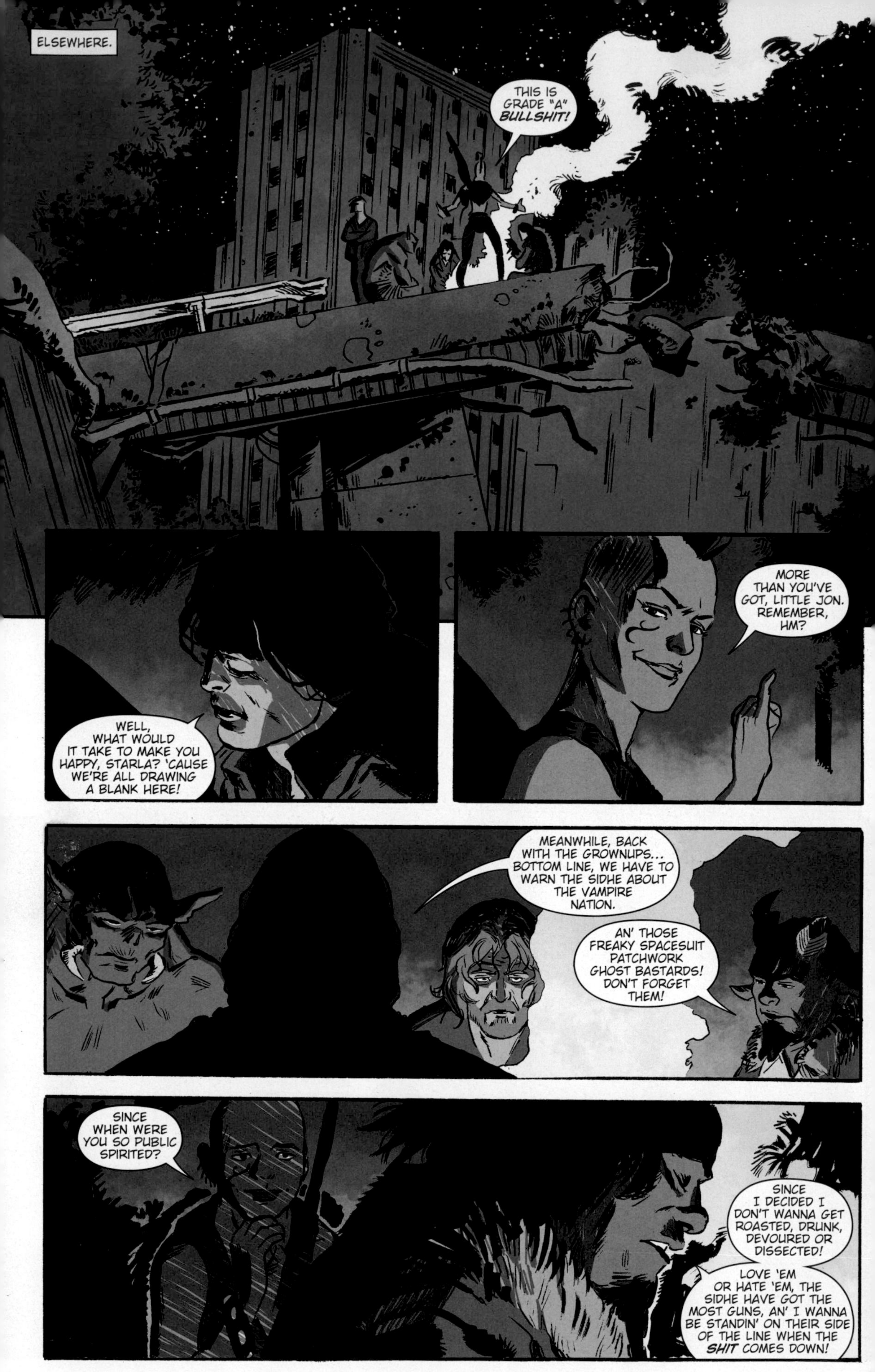
ELSEWHERE.
THIS IS GRADE "A" BULLSHIT!
WELL, WHAT WOULD IT TAKE TO MAKE YOU HAPPY, STARLA? 'CAUSE WE'RE ALL DRAWING A BLANK HERE!
MORE THAN YOU'VE GOT, LITTLE JON. REMEMBER, HM?
MEANWHILE, BACK WITH THE GROWNUPS... BOTTOM LINE, WE HAVE TO WARN THE SIDHE ABOUT THE VAMPIRE NATION.
AN' THOSE FREAKY SPACESUIT PATCHWORK GHOST BASTARDS! DON'T FORGET THEM!
SINCE WHEN WERE YOU SO PUBLIC SPIRITED?
SINCE I DECIDED I DON'T WANNA GET ROASTED, DRUNK, DEVOURED OR DISSECTED!
LOVE 'EM OR HATE 'EM, THE SIDHE HAVE GOT THE MOST GUNS, AN' I WANNA BE STANDIN' ON THEIR SIDE OF THE LINE WHEN THE SHIT COMES DOWN!

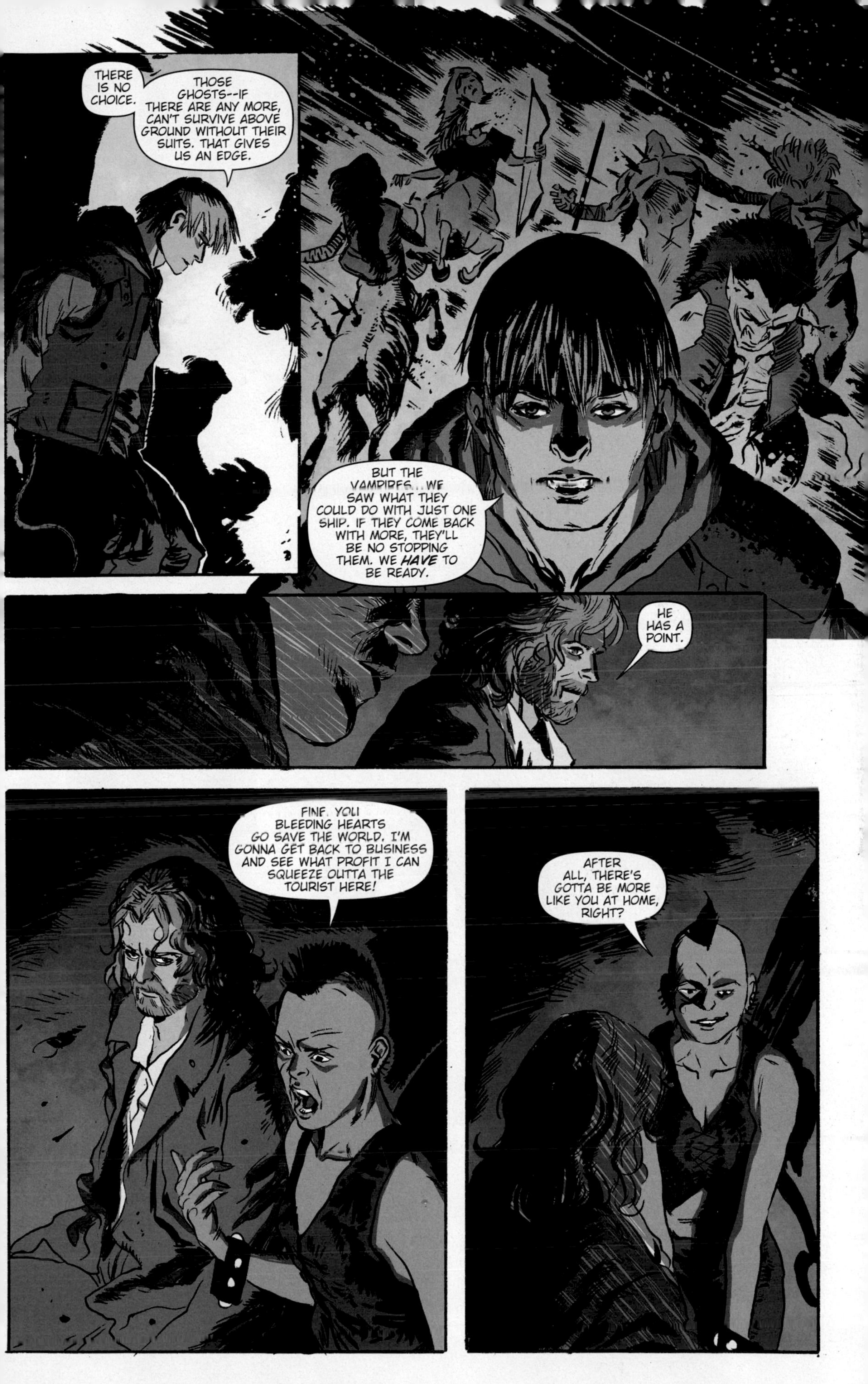
THERE IS NO CHOICE.
THOSE GHOSTS--IF THERE ARE ANY MORE, CAN'T SURVIVE ABOVE GROUND WITHOUT THEIR SUITS. THAT GIVES US AN EDGE.
BUT THE VAMPIRES... WE SAW WHAT THEY COULD DO WITH JUST ONE SHIP. IF THEY COME BACK WITH MORE, THEY'LL BE NO STOPPING THEM. WE *HAVE* TO BE READY.
HE HAS A POINT.
FINE. YOU BLEEDING HEARTS GO SAVE THE WORLD. I'M GONNA GET BACK TO BUSINESS AND SEE WHAT PROFIT I CAN SQUEEZE OUTTA THE TOURIST HERE!
AFTER ALL, THERE'S GOTTA BE MORE LIKE YOU AT HOME, RIGHT?

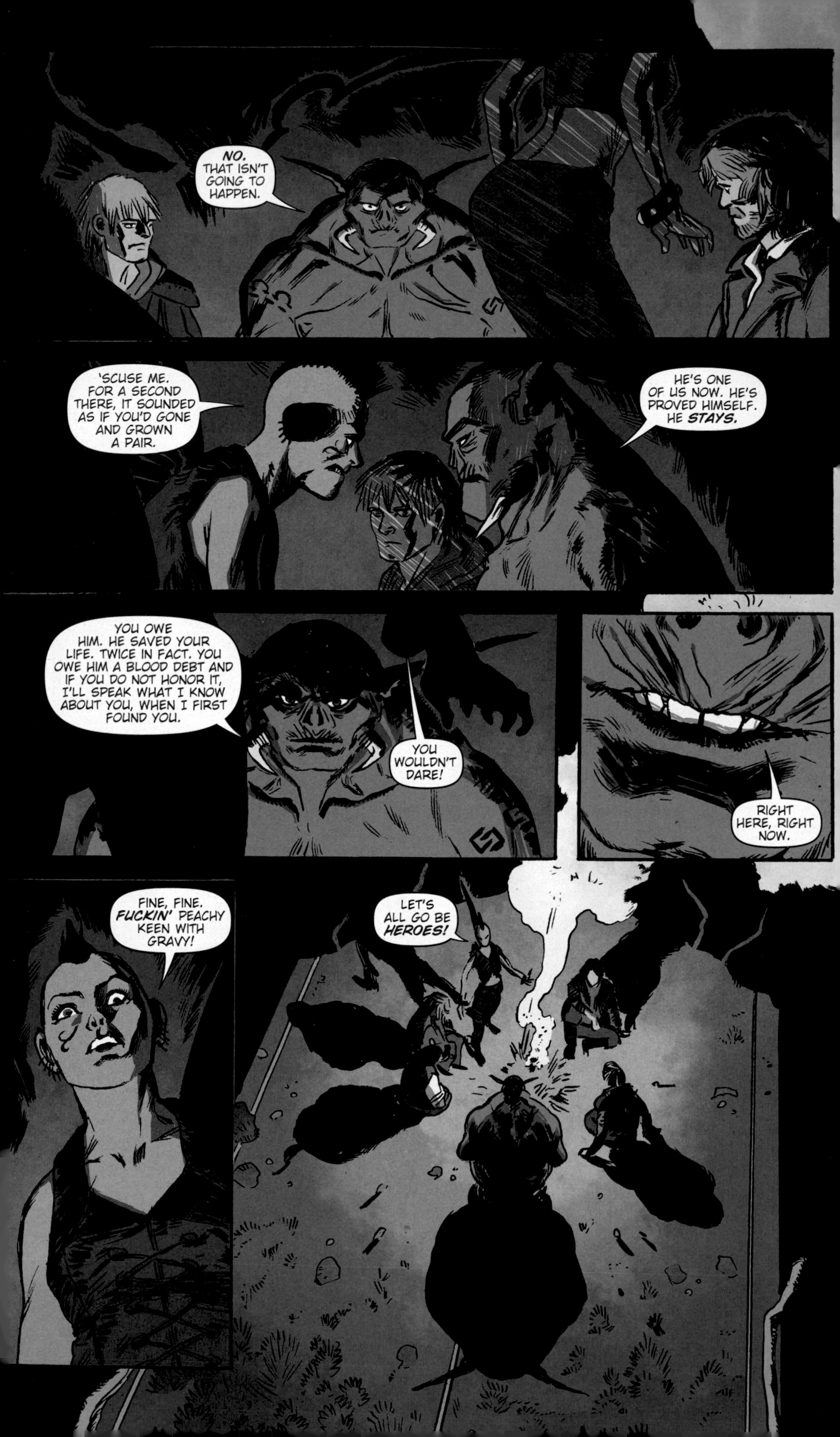
NO. THAT ISN'T GOING TO HAPPEN.
'SCUSE ME. FOR A SECOND THERE, IT SOUNDED AS IF YOU'D GONE AND GROWN A PAIR.
HE'S ONE OF US NOW. HE'S PROVED HIMSELF. HE STAYS.
YOU OWE HIM. HE SAVED YOUR LIFE. TWICE IN FACT. YOU OWE HIM A BLOOD DEBT AND IF YOU DO NOT HONOR IT, I'LL SPEAK WHAT I KNOW ABOUT YOU, WHEN I FIRST FOUND YOU.
YOU WOULDN'T DARE!
RIGHT HERE, RIGHT NOW.
FINE, FINE. FUCKIN' PEACHY KEEN WITH GRAVY!
LET'S ALL GO BE HEROES!

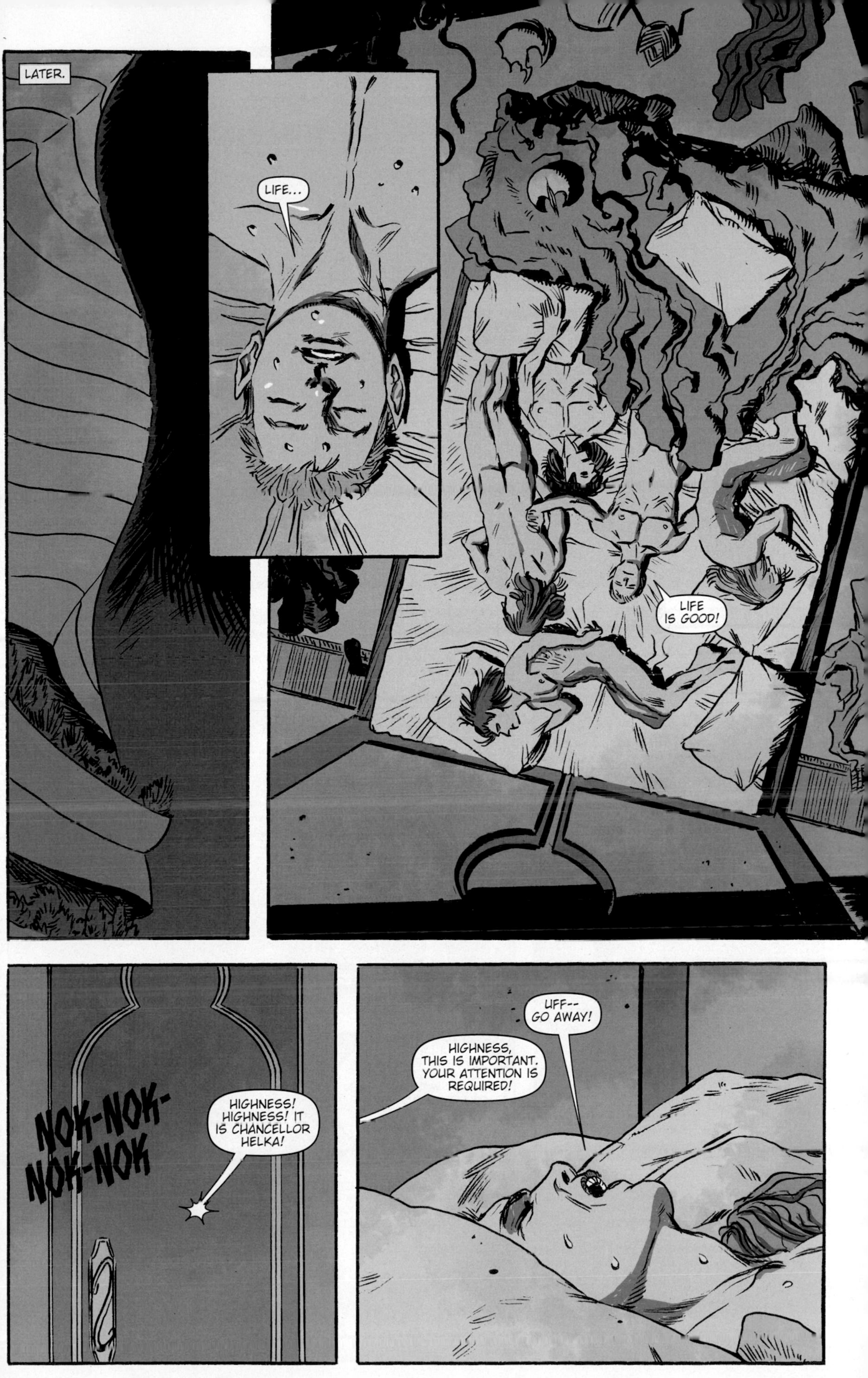
LATER.
LIFE...
LIFE IS GOOD!
NOK-NOK-NOK-NOK
HIGHNESS! HIGHNESS! IT IS CHANCELLOR HELKA!
UFF-- GO AWAY!
HIGHNESS, THIS IS IMPORTANT. YOUR ATTENTION IS REQUIRED!

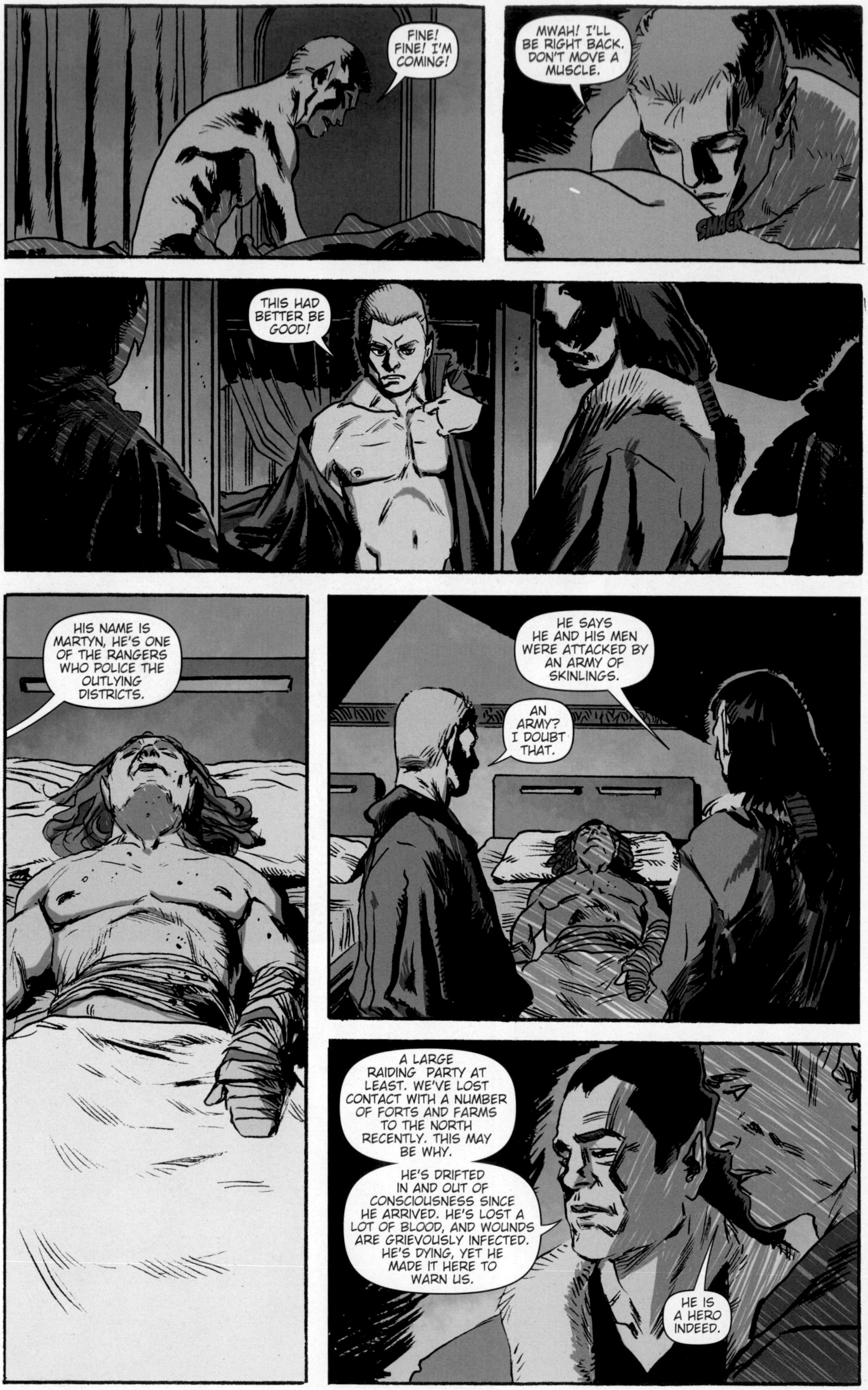
FINE! FINE! I'M COMING!
MWAH! I'LL BE RIGHT BACK. DON'T MOVE A MUSCLE.
SMACK
THIS HAD BETTER BE GOOD!
HIS NAME IS MARTYN, HE'S ONE OF THE RANGERS WHO POLICE THE OUTLYING DISTRICTS.
HE SAYS HE AND HIS MEN WERE ATTACKED BY AN ARMY OF SKINLINGS.
AN ARMY? I DOUBT THAT.
A LARGE RAIDING PARTY AT LEAST. WE'VE LOST CONTACT WITH A NUMBER OF FORTS AND FARMS TO THE NORTH RECENTLY. THIS MAY BE WHY.
HE'S DRIFTED IN AND OUT OF CONSCIOUSNESS SINCE HE ARRIVED. HE'S LOST A LOT OF BLOOD, AND WOUNDS ARE GRIEVOUSLY INFECTED. HE'S DYING, YET HE MADE IT HERE TO WARN US.
HE IS A HERO INDEED.

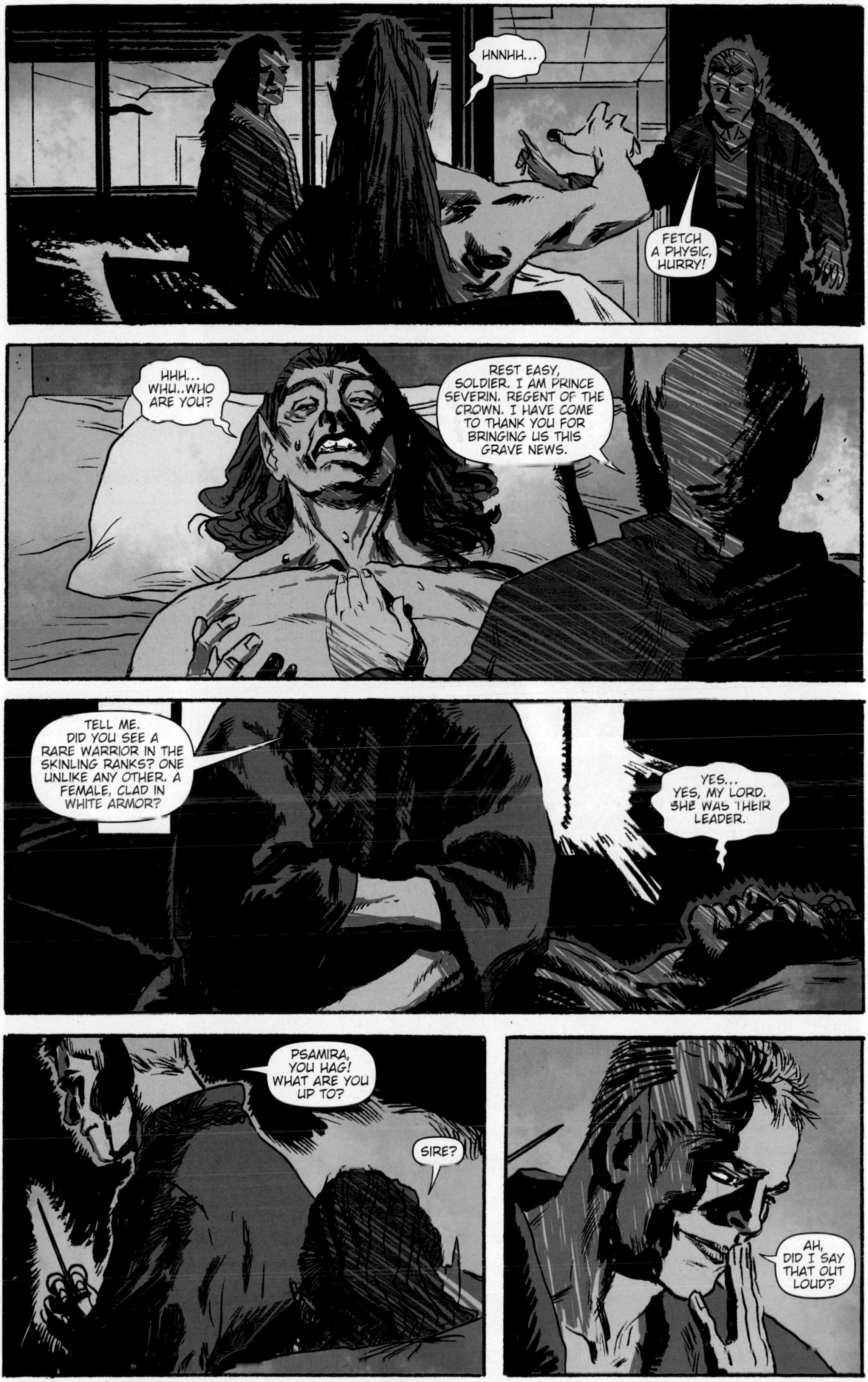
HNNHH...
FETCH A PHYSIC, HURRY!
HHH... WHU..WHO ARE YOU?
REST EASY, SOLDIER. I AM PRINCE SEVERIN. REGENT OF THE CROWN. I HAVE COME TO THANK YOU FOR BRINGING US THIS GRAVE NEWS.
TELL ME. DID YOU SEE A RARE WARRIOR IN THE SKINLING RANKS? ONE UNLIKE ANY OTHER. A FEMALE, CLAD IN WHITE ARMOR?
YES... YES, MY LORD. SHE WAS THEIR LEADER.
PSAMIRA, YOU HAG! WHAT ARE YOU UP TO?
SIRE?
AH, DID I SAY THAT OUT LOUD?

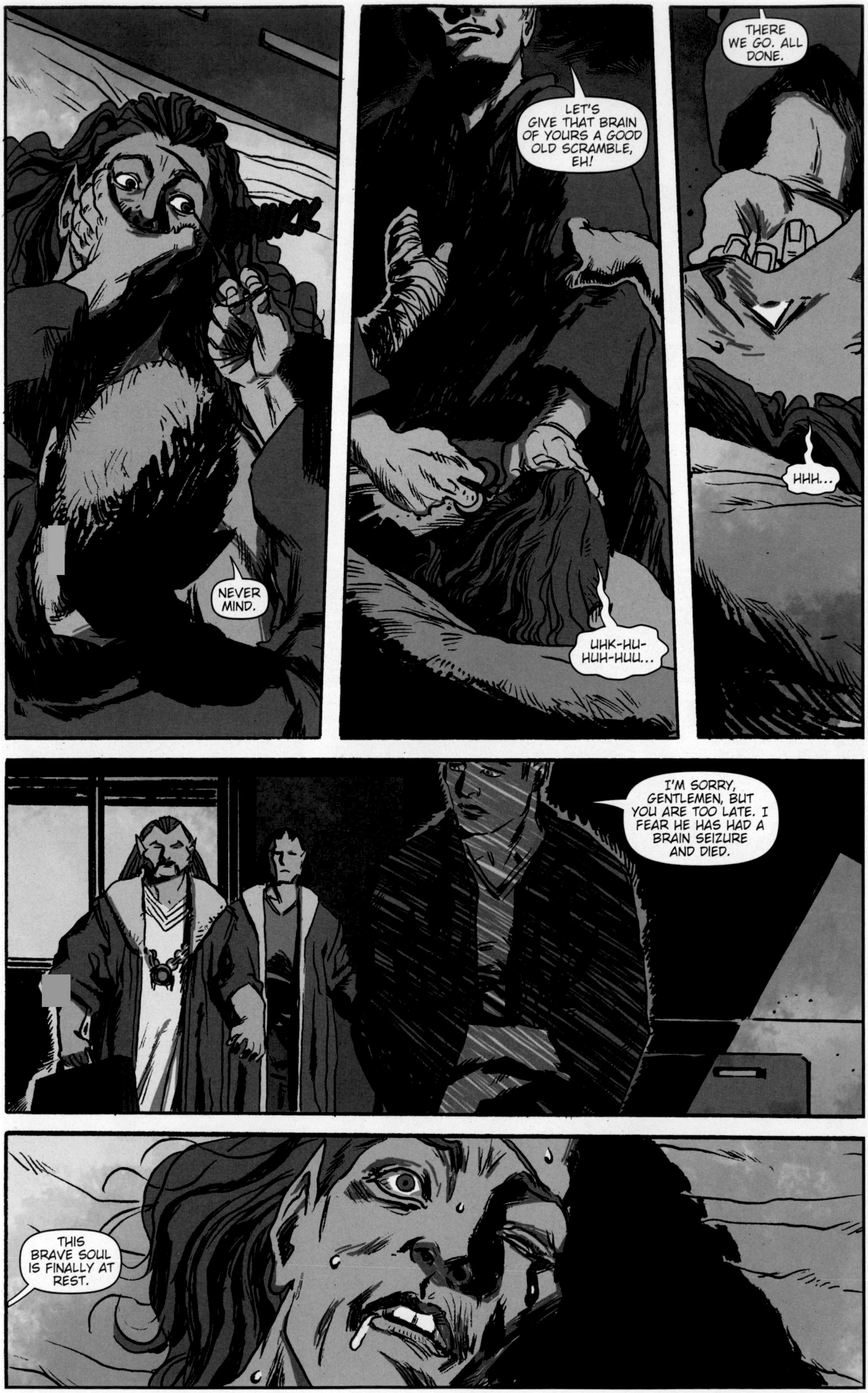
NEVER MIND.
LET'S GIVE THAT BRAIN OF YOURS A GOOD OLD SCRAMBLE, EH!
UHK-HU-HUH-HUU...
THERE WE GO. ALL DONE.
HHH...
I'M SORRY, GENTLEMEN, BUT YOU ARE TOO LATE. I FEAR HE HAS HAD A BRAIN SEIZURE AND DIED.
THIS BRAVE SOUL IS FINALLY AT REST.

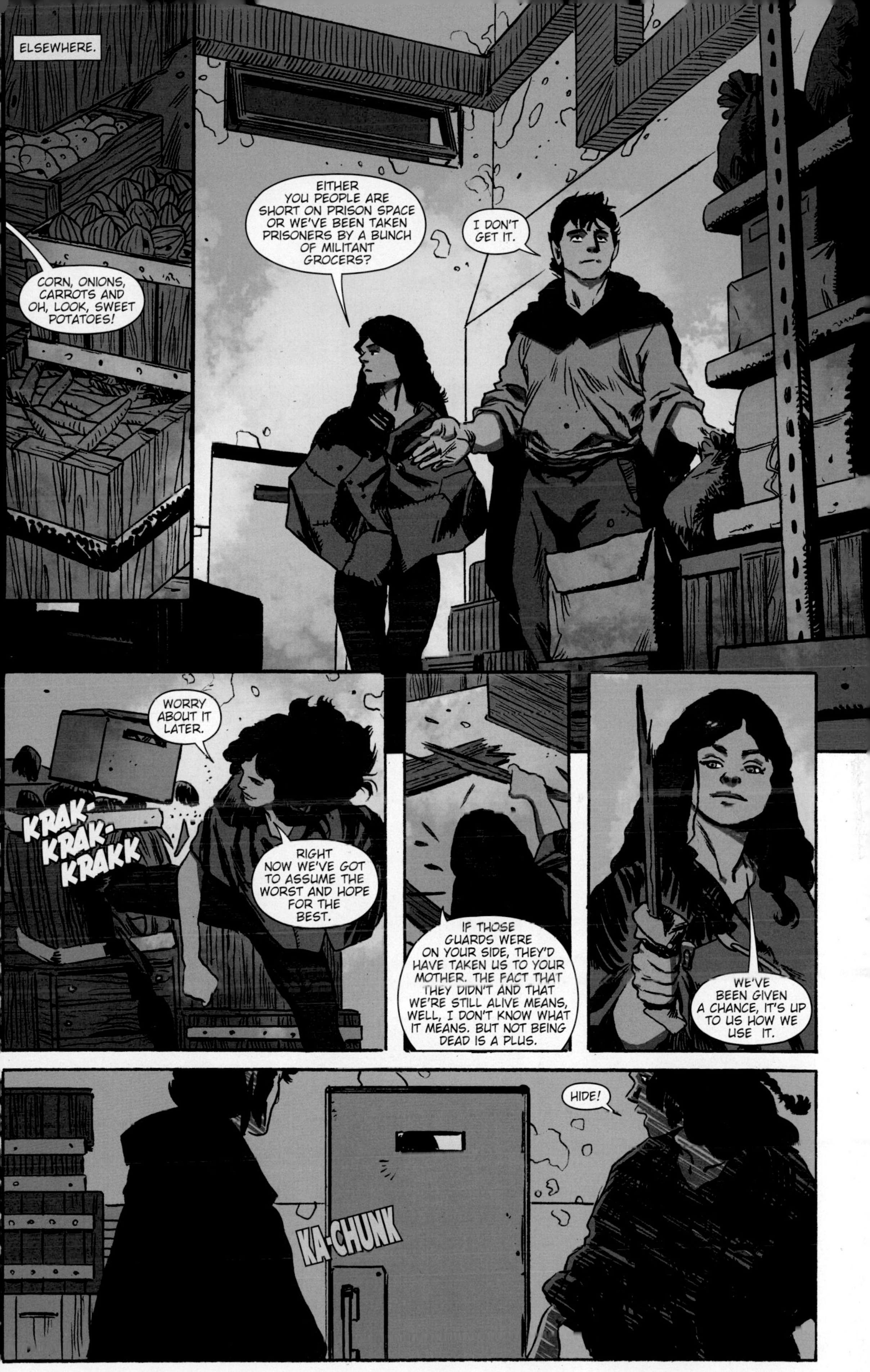
ELSEWHERE.
CORN, ONIONS, CARROTS AND OH, LOOK, SWEET POTATOES!
EITHER YOU PEOPLE ARE SHORT ON PRISON SPACE OR WE'VE BEEN TAKEN PRISONERS BY A BUNCH OF MILITANT GROCERS?
I DON'T GET IT.
WORRY ABOUT IT LATER.
KRAK-KRAK-KRAKK
RIGHT NOW WE'VE GOT TO ASSUME THE WORST AND HOPE FOR THE BEST.
IF THOSE GUARDS WERE ON YOUR SIDE, THEY'D HAVE TAKEN US TO YOUR MOTHER. THE FACT THAT THEY DIDN'T AND THAT WE'RE STILL ALIVE MEANS, WELL, I DON'T KNOW WHAT IT MEANS. BUT NOT BEING DEAD IS A PLUS.
WE'VE BEEN GIVEN A CHANCE, IT'S UP TO US HOW WE USE IT.
HIDE!
KA-CHUNK

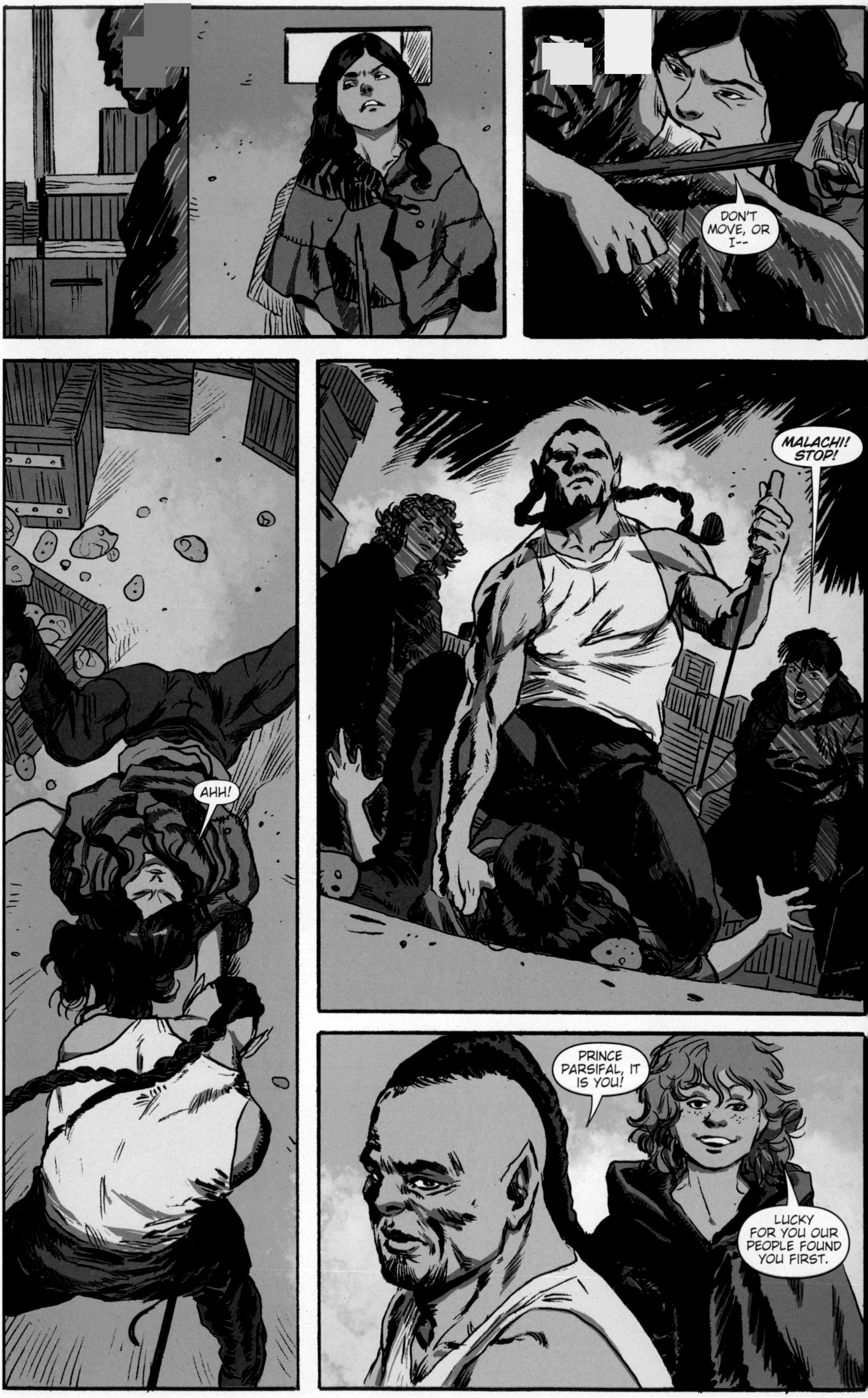
DON'T MOVE, OR I--
AHH!
MALACHI! STOP!
PRINCE PARSIFAL, IT IS YOU!
LUCKY FOR YOU OUR PEOPLE FOUND YOU FIRST.

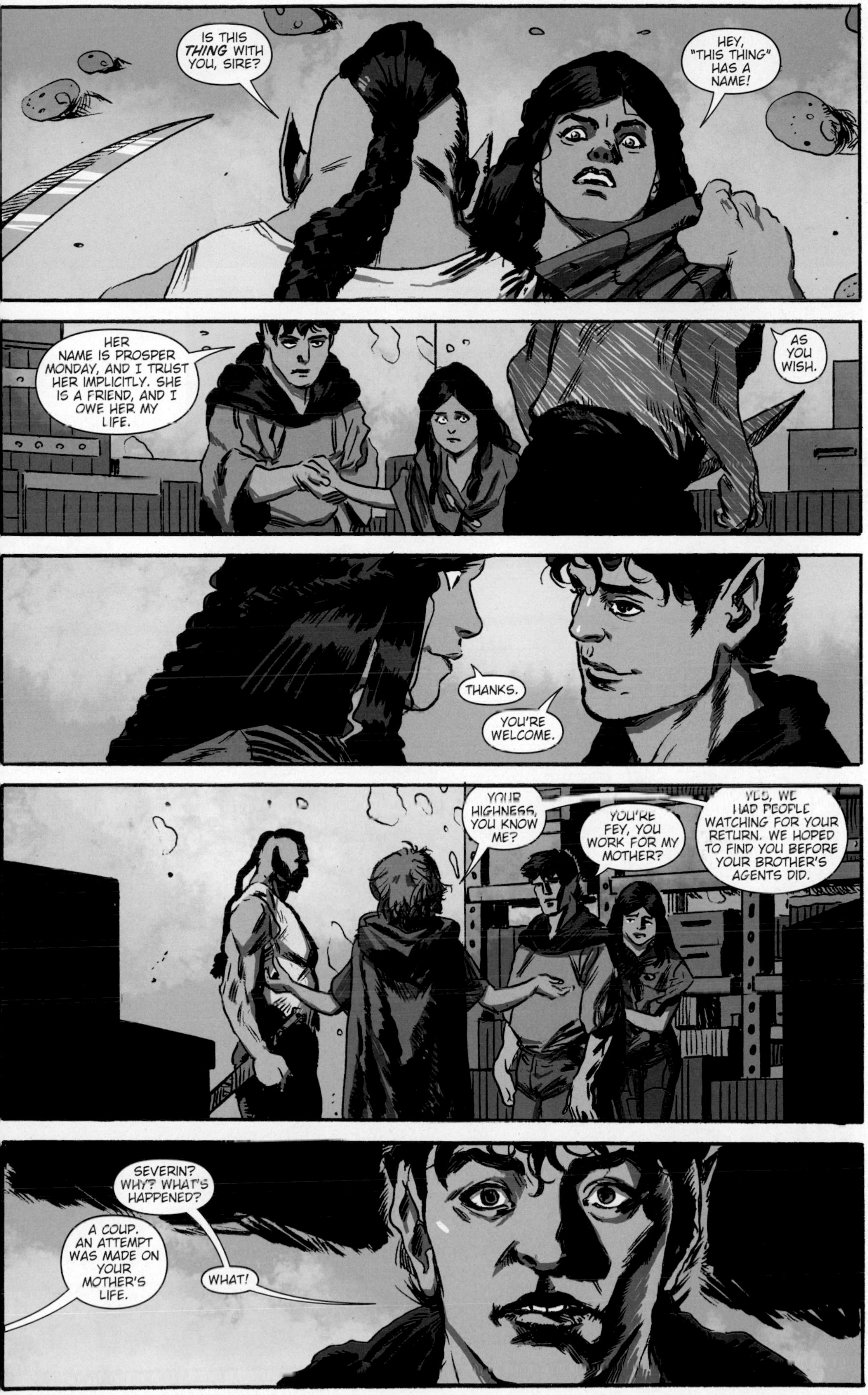
IS THIS *THING* WITH YOU, SIRE?
HEY, "THIS THING" HAS A NAME!
HER NAME IS PROSPER MONDAY, AND I TRUST HER IMPLICITLY. SHE IS A FRIEND, AND I OWE HER MY LIFE.
AS YOU WISH.
THANKS.
YOU'RE WELCOME.
YOUR HIGHNESS, YOU KNOW ME?
YOU'RE FEY, YOU WORK FOR MY MOTHER?
YES, WE HAD PEOPLE WATCHING FOR YOUR RETURN. WE HOPED TO FIND YOU BEFORE YOUR BROTHER'S AGENTS DID.
SEVERIN? WHY? WHAT'S HAPPENED?
A COUP. AN ATTEMPT WAS MADE ON YOUR MOTHER'S LIFE.
WHAT!

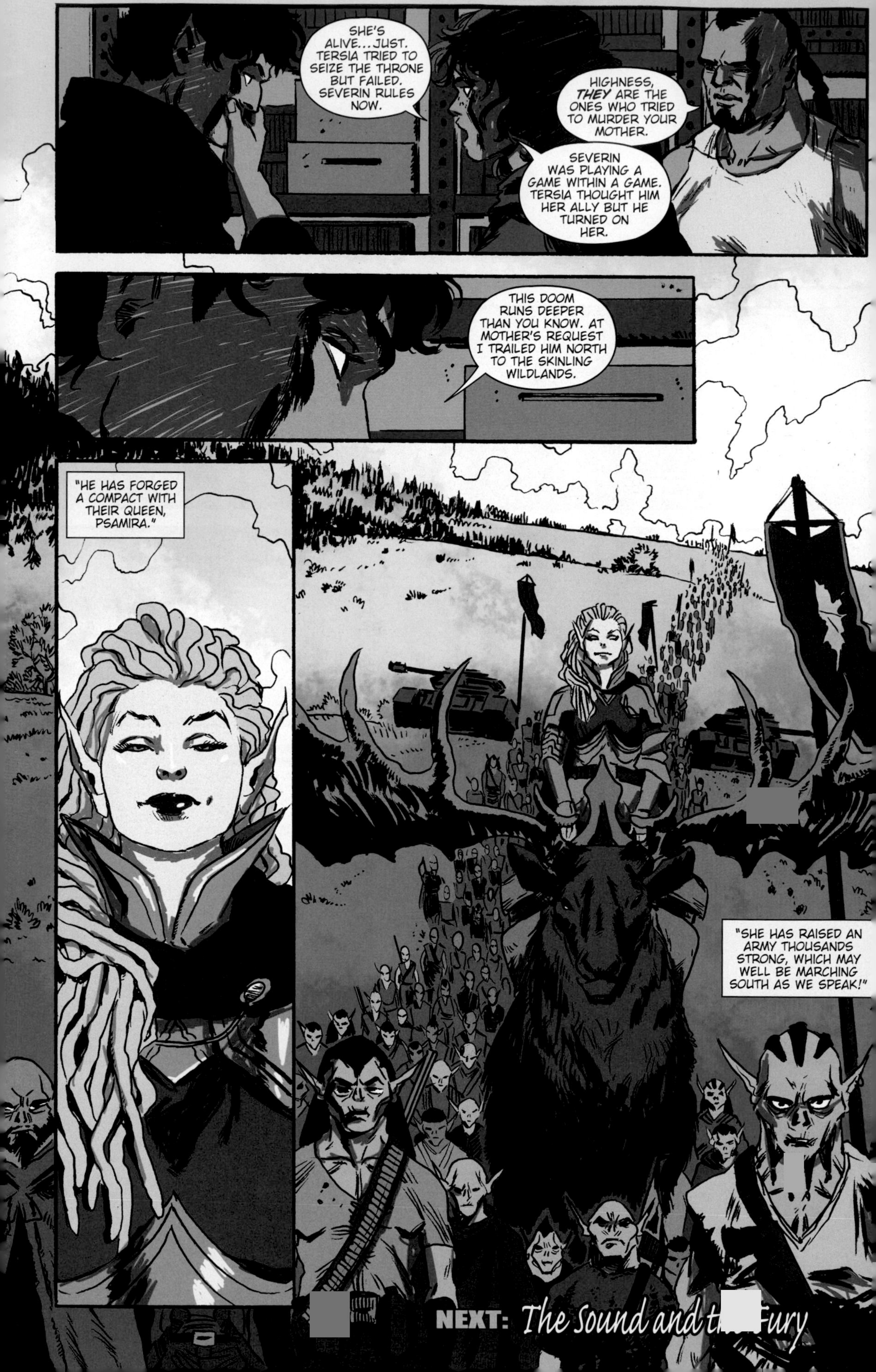
SHE'S ALIVE...JUST. TERSIA TRIED TO SEIZE THE THRONE BUT FAILED. SEVERIN RULES NOW.
HIGHNESS, THEY ARE THE ONES WHO TRIED TO MURDER YOUR MOTHER.
SEVERIN WAS PLAYING A GAME WITHIN A GAME. TERSIA THOUGHT HIM HER ALLY BUT HE TURNED ON HER.
THIS DOOM RUNS DEEPER THAN YOU KNOW. AT MOTHER'S REQUEST I TRAILED HIM NORTH TO THE SKINLING WILDLANDS.
"HE HAS FORGED A COMPACT WITH THEIR QUEEN, PSAMIRA."
"SHE HAS RAISED AN ARMY THOUSANDS STRONG, WHICH MAY WELL BE MARCHING SOUTH AS WE SPEAK!"
NEXT: The Sound and th Fury

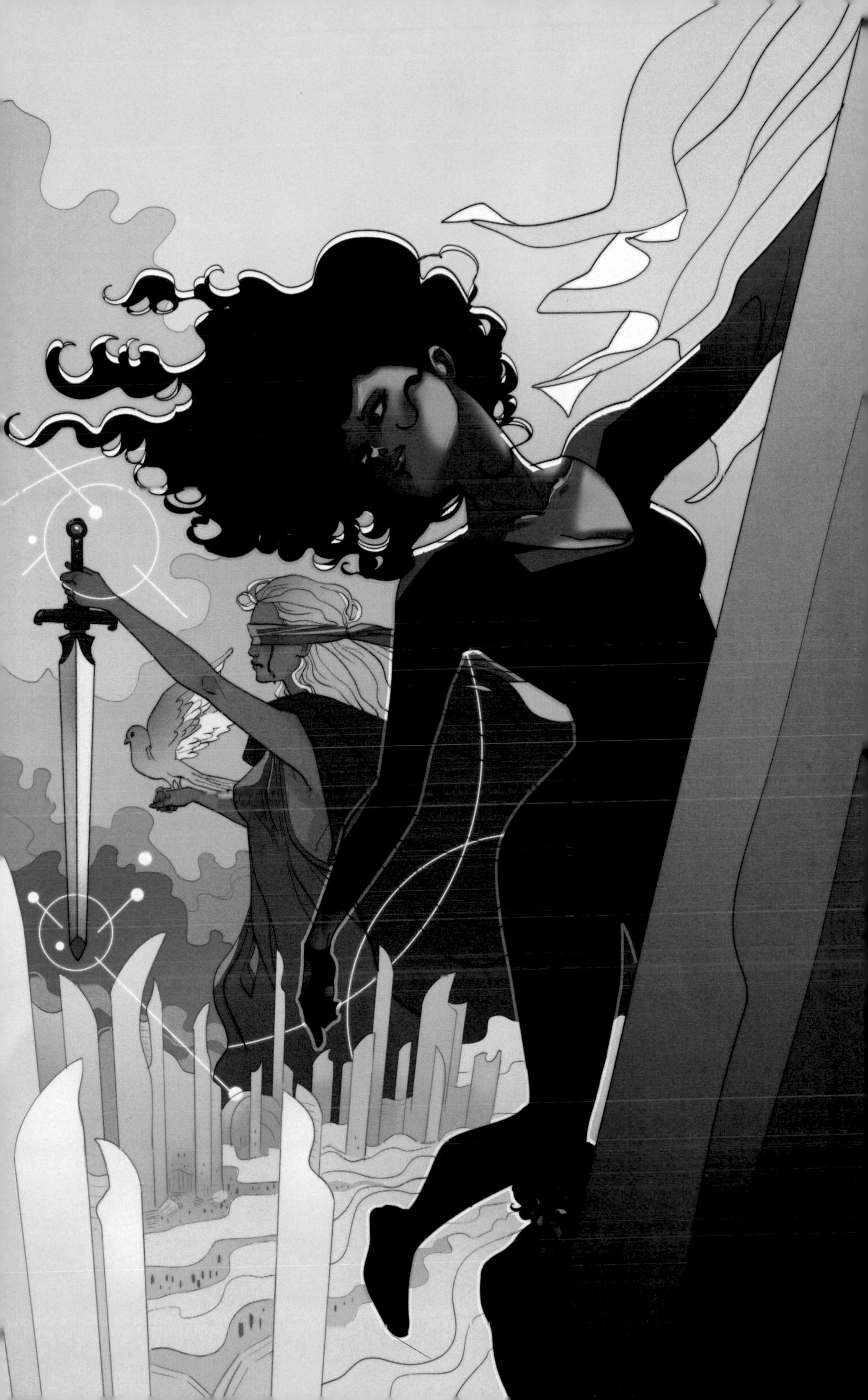

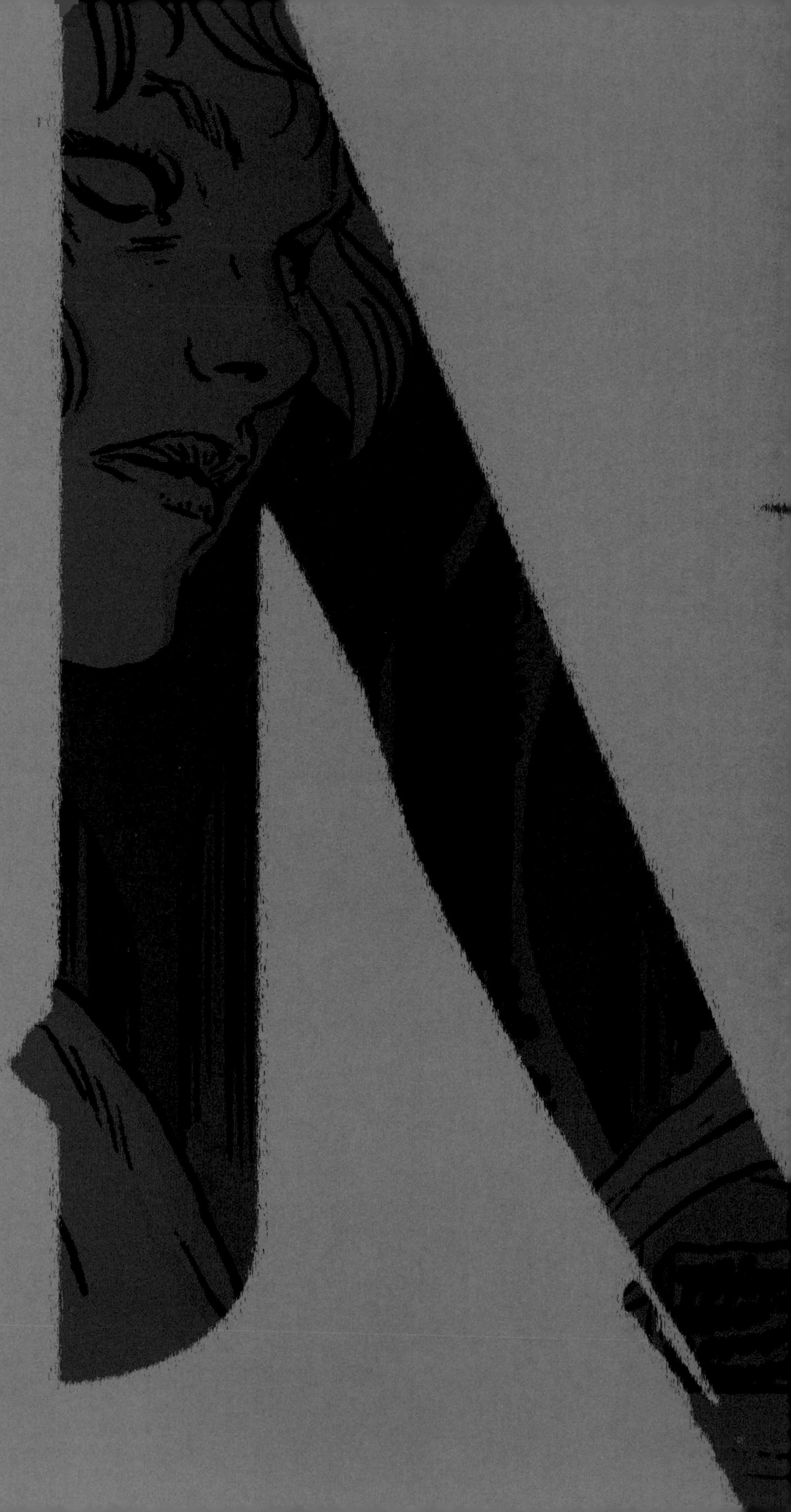

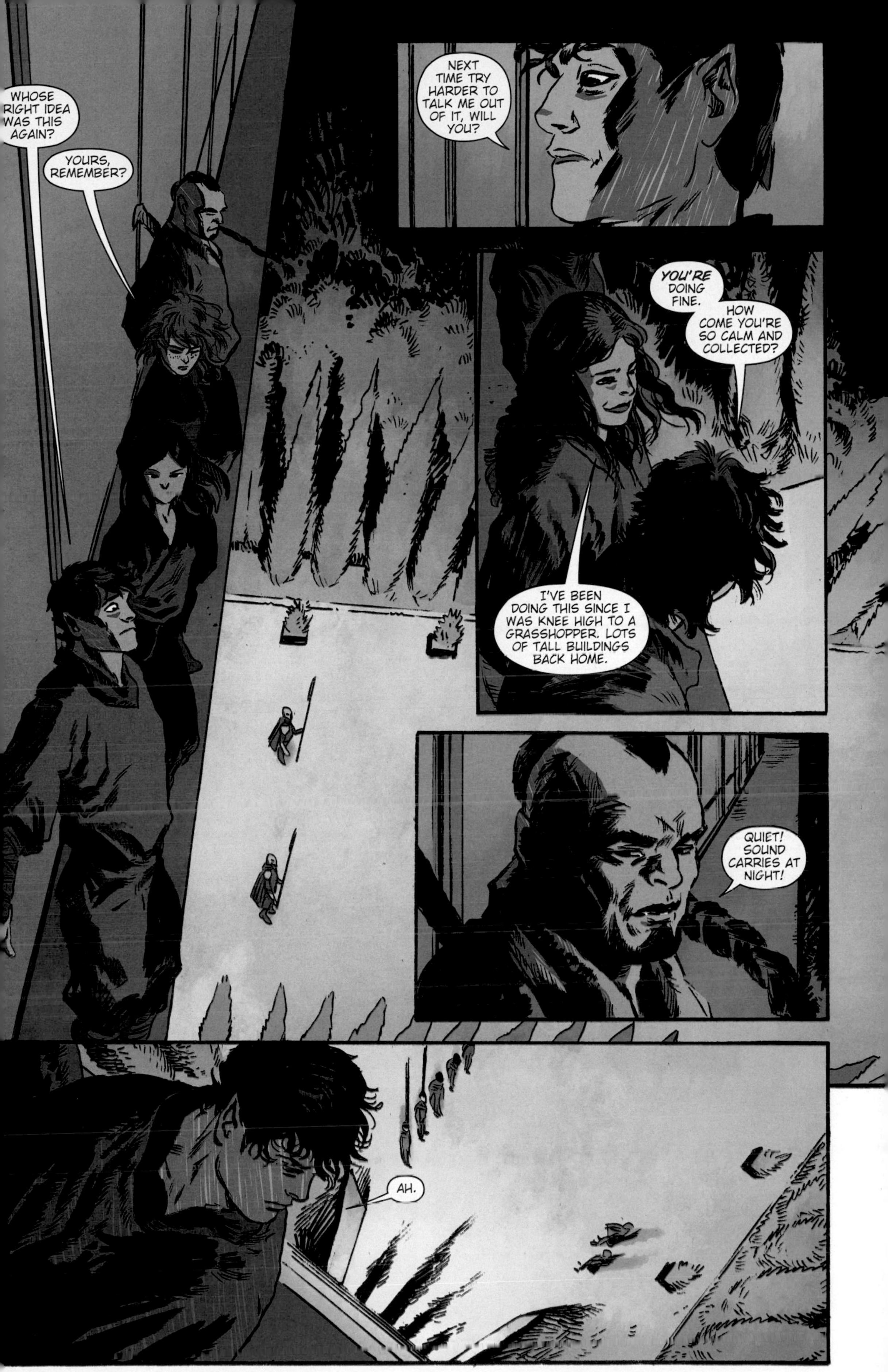
WHOSE RIGHT IDEA WAS THIS AGAIN?
YOURS, REMEMBER?
NEXT TIME TRY HARDER TO TALK ME OUT OF IT, WILL YOU?
YOU'RE DOING FINE.
HOW COME YOU'RE SO CALM AND COLLECTED?
I'VE BEEN DOING THIS SINCE I WAS KNEE HIGH TO A GRASSHOPPER. LOTS OF TALL BUILDINGS BACK HOME.
QUIET! SOUND CARRIES AT NIGHT!
AH.

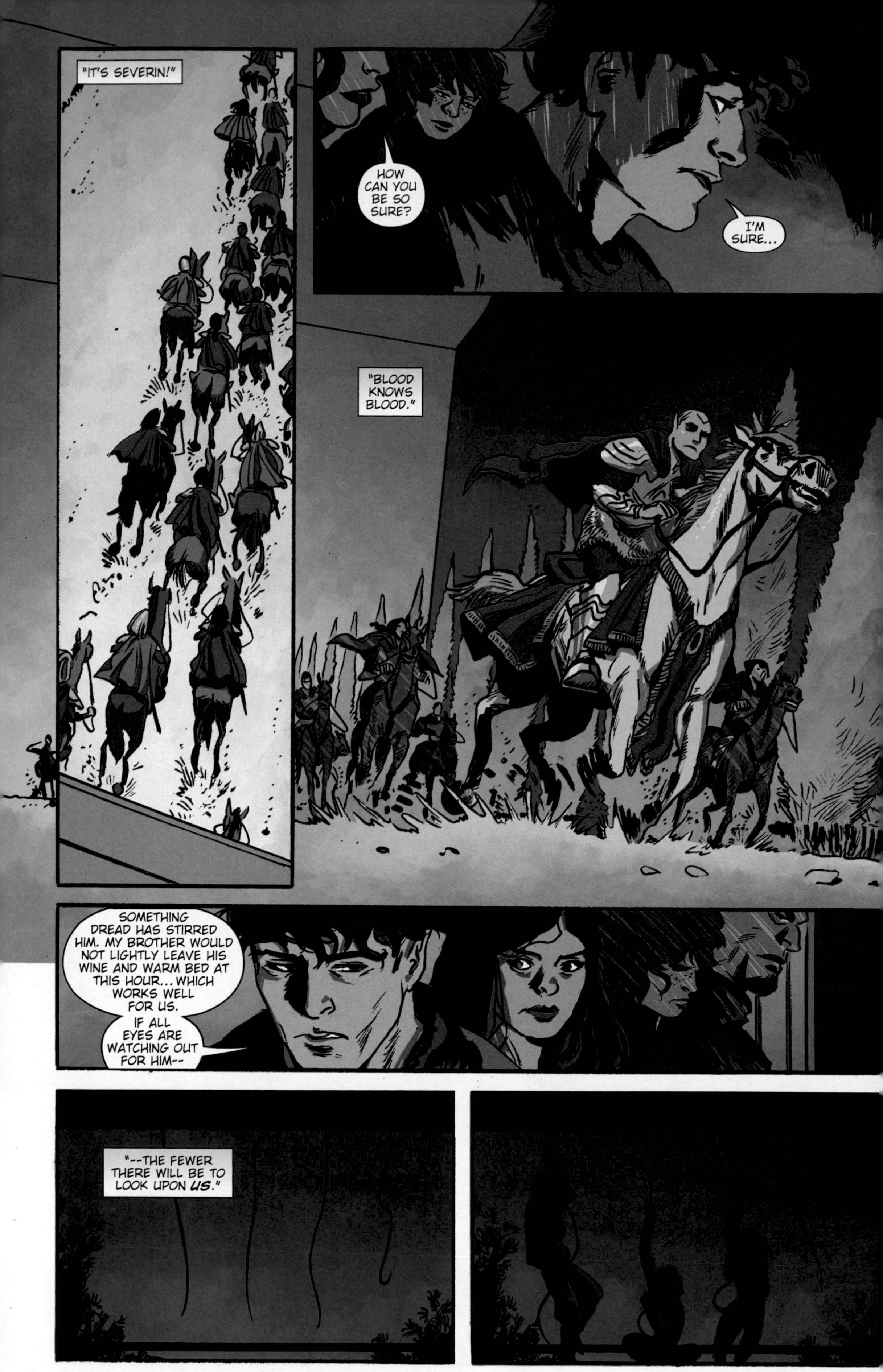
"IT'S SEVERIN!"
HOW CAN YOU BE SO SURE?
I'M SURE...
"BLOOD KNOWS BLOOD."
SOMETHING DREAD HAS STIRRED HIM. MY BROTHER WOULD NOT LIGHTLY LEAVE HIS WINE AND WARM BED AT THIS HOUR... WHICH WORKS WELL FOR US.
IF ALL EYES ARE WATCHING OUT FOR HIM--
"--THE FEWER THERE WILL BE TO LOOK UPON *US*."

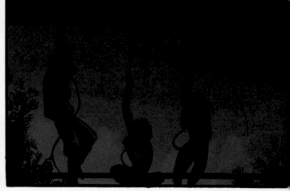

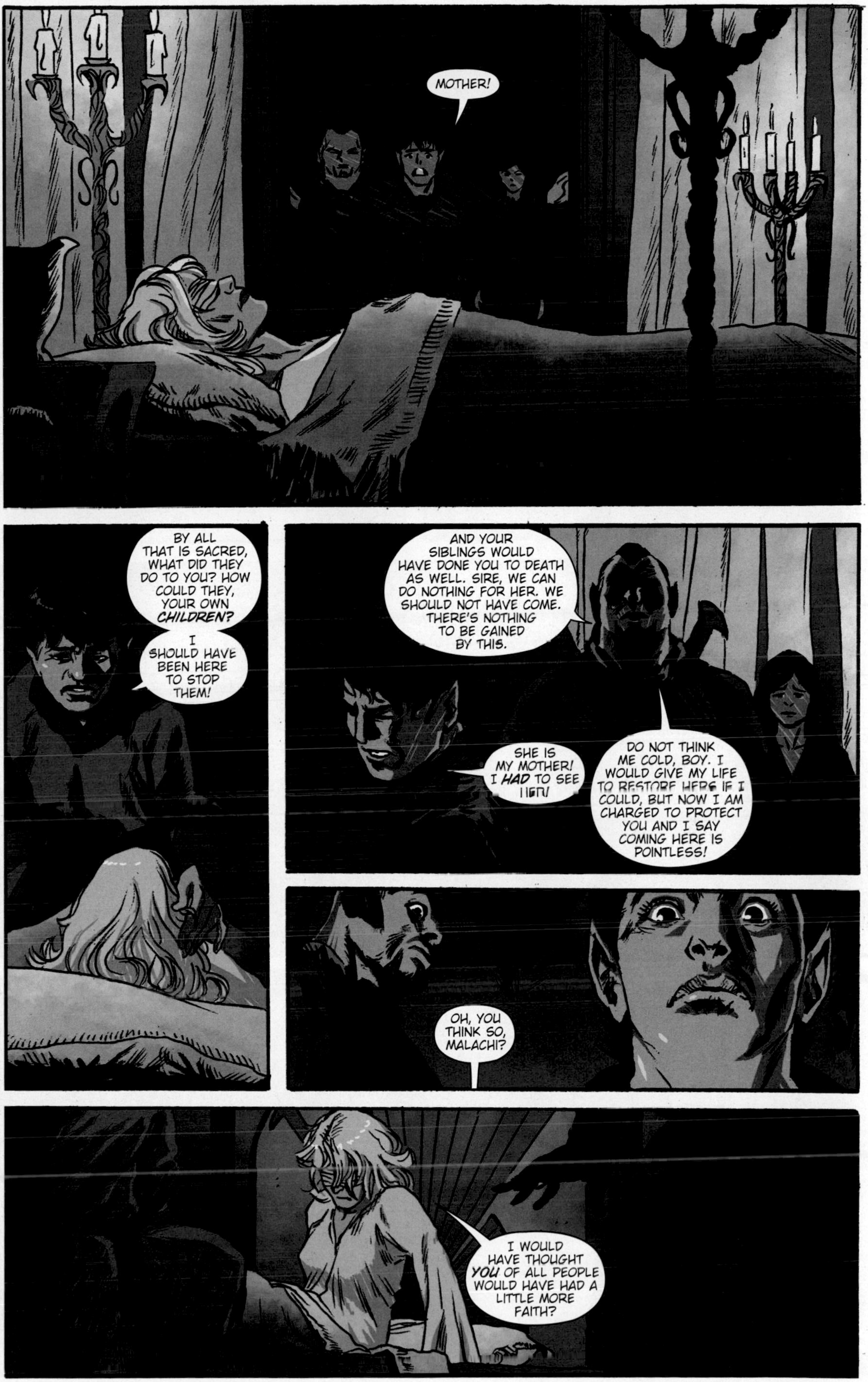
MOTHER!
BY ALL THAT IS SACRED, WHAT DID THEY DO TO YOU? HOW COULD THEY, YOUR OWN *CHILDREN*?
I SHOULD HAVE BEEN HERE TO STOP THEM!
AND YOUR SIBLINGS WOULD HAVE DONE YOU TO DEATH AS WELL. SIRE, WE CAN DO NOTHING FOR HER. WE SHOULD NOT HAVE COME. THERE'S NOTHING TO BE GAINED BY THIS.
SHE IS MY MOTHER! I *HAD* TO SEE HER!
DO NOT THINK ME COLD, BOY. I WOULD GIVE MY LIFE TO RESTORE HERS IF I COULD, BUT NOW I AM CHARGED TO PROTECT YOU AND I SAY COMING HERE IS POINTLESS!
OH, YOU THINK SO, MALACHI?
I WOULD HAVE THOUGHT *YOU* OF ALL PEOPLE WOULD HAVE HAD A LITTLE MORE FAITH?

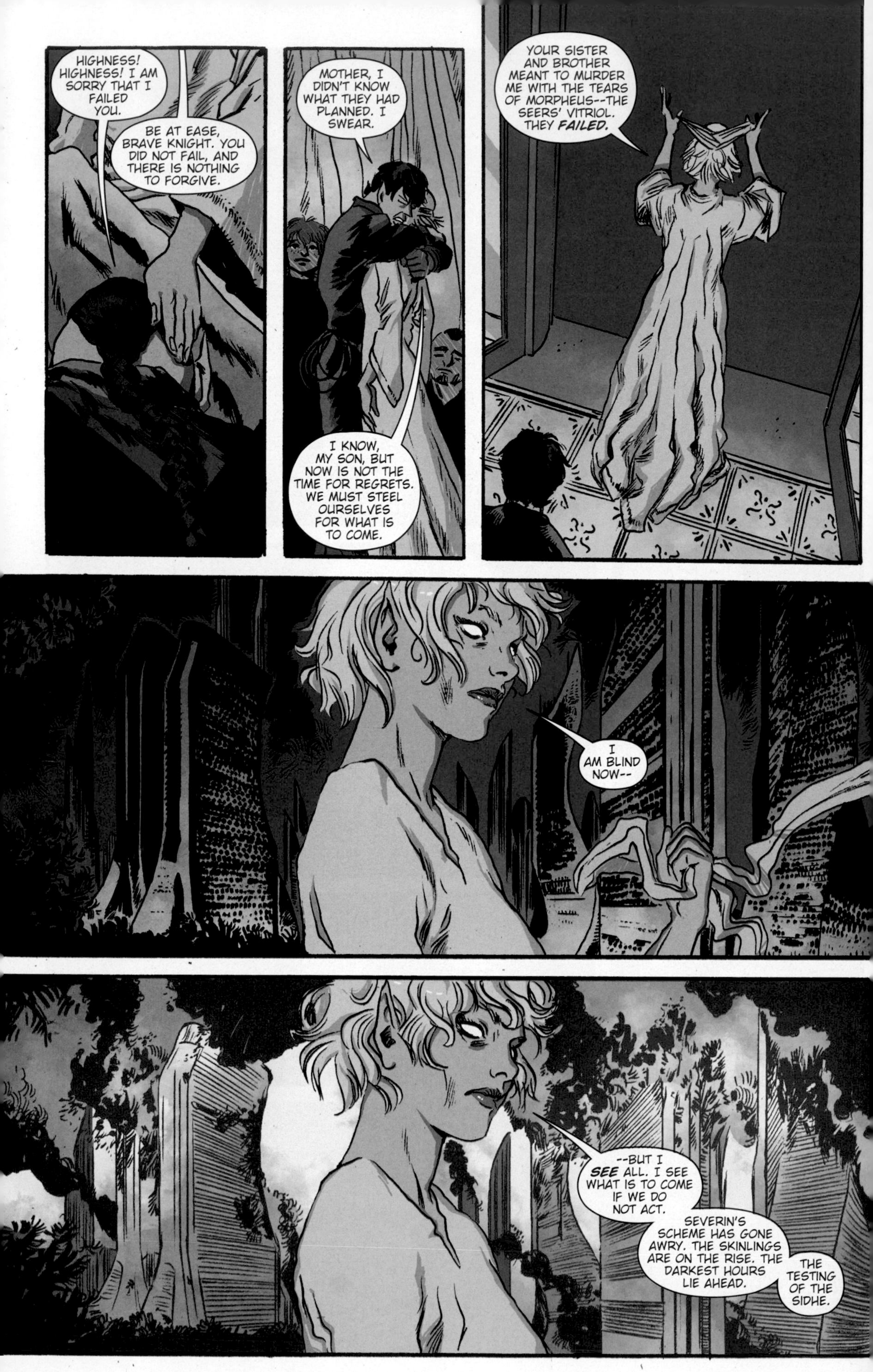
HIGHNESS! HIGHNESS! I AM SORRY THAT I FAILED YOU.
BE AT EASE, BRAVE KNIGHT. YOU DID NOT FAIL, AND THERE IS NOTHING TO FORGIVE.
MOTHER, I DIDN'T KNOW WHAT THEY HAD PLANNED. I SWEAR.
I KNOW, MY SON, BUT NOW IS NOT THE TIME FOR REGRETS. WE MUST STEEL OURSELVES FOR WHAT IS TO COME.
YOUR SISTER AND BROTHER MEANT TO MURDER ME WITH THE TEARS OF MORPHEUS--THE SEERS' VITRIOL. THEY *FAILED.*
I AM BLIND NOW--
--BUT I *SEE* ALL. I SEE WHAT IS TO COME IF WE DO NOT ACT.
SEVERIN'S SCHEME HAS GONE AWRY. THE SKINLINGS ARE ON THE RISE. THE DARKEST HOURS LIE AHEAD.
THE TESTING OF THE SIDHE.

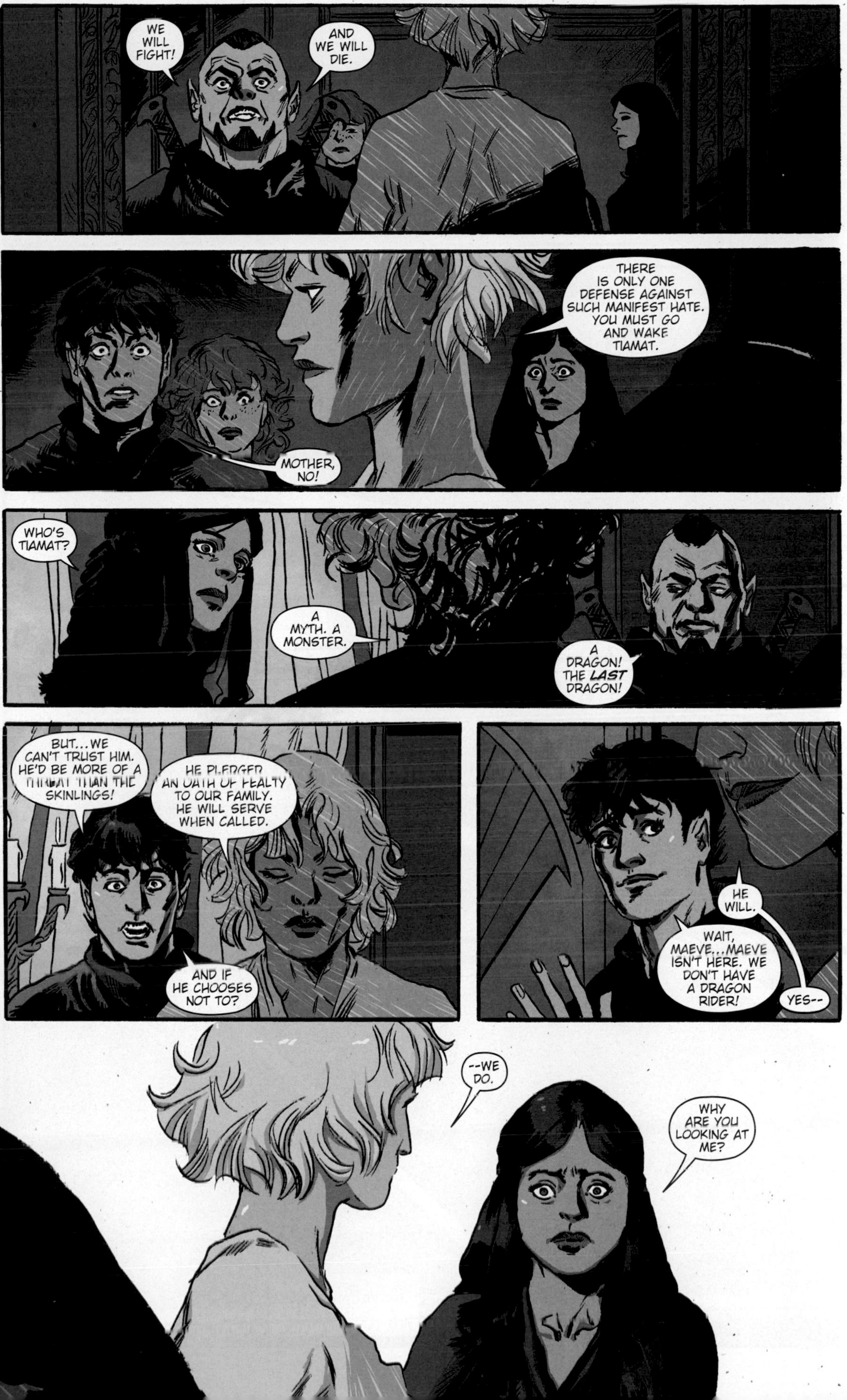
WE WILL FIGHT!
AND WE WILL DIE.
THERE IS ONLY ONE DEFENSE AGAINST SUCH MANIFEST HATE. YOU MUST GO AND WAKE TIAMAT.
MOTHER, NO!
WHO'S TIAMAT?
A MYTH. A MONSTER.
A DRAGON! THE LAST DRAGON!
BUT...WE CAN'T TRUST HIM. HE'D BE MORE OF A THREAT THAN THE SKINLINGS!
HE PLEDGED AN OATH OF FEALTY TO OUR FAMILY. HE WILL SERVE WHEN CALLED.
AND IF HE CHOOSES NOT TO?
HE WILL.
WAIT, MAEVE...MAEVE ISN'T HERE. WE DON'T HAVE A DRAGON RIDER!
YES--
--WE DO.
WHY ARE YOU LOOKING AT ME?

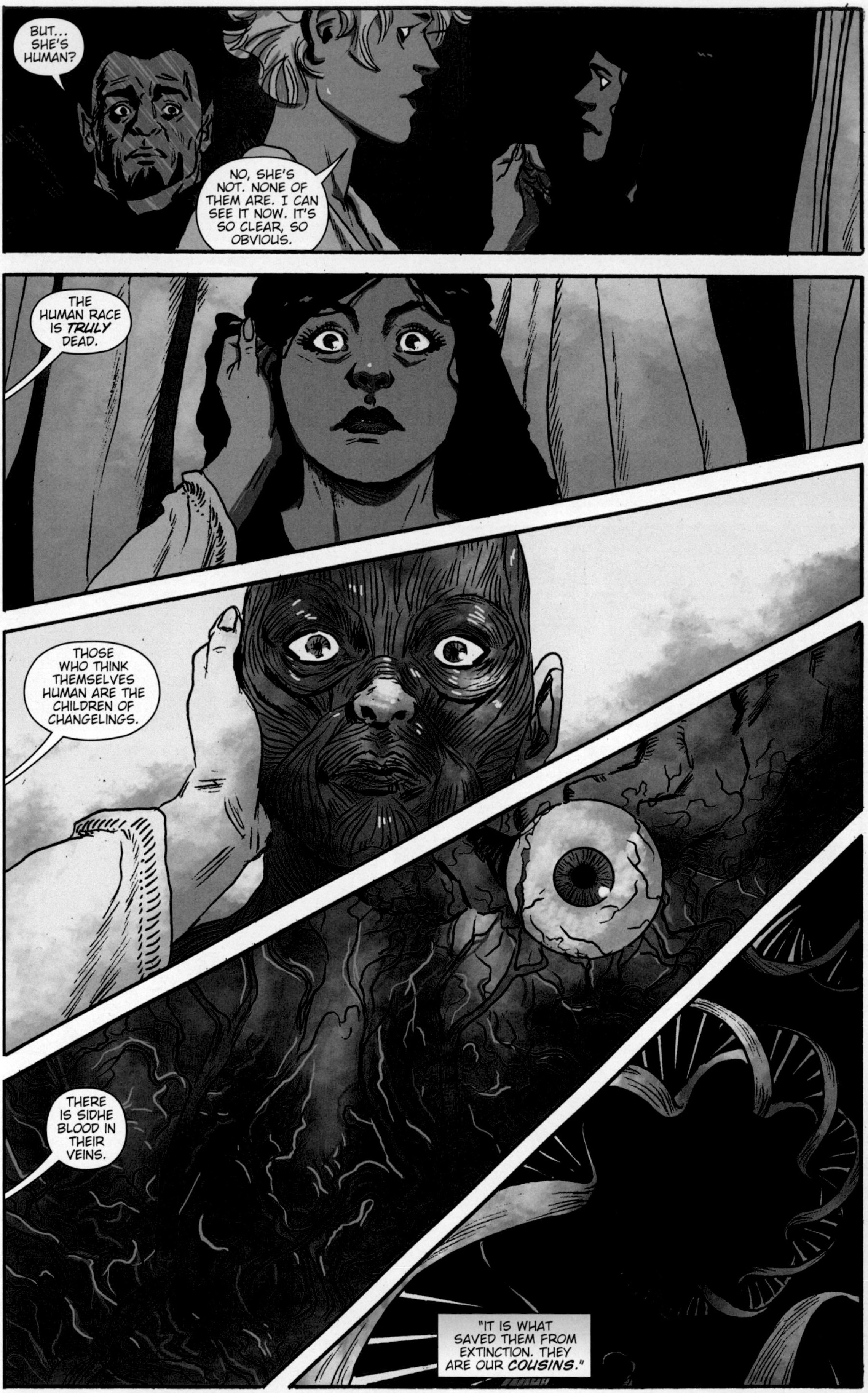
BUT... SHE'S HUMAN?
NO, SHE'S NOT. NONE OF THEM ARE. I CAN SEE IT NOW. IT'S SO CLEAR, SO OBVIOUS.
THE HUMAN RACE IS *TRULY* DEAD.
THOSE WHO THINK THEMSELVES HUMAN ARE THE CHILDREN OF CHANGELINGS.
THERE IS SIDHE BLOOD IN THEIR VEINS.
"IT IS WHAT SAVED THEM FROM EXTINCTION. THEY ARE OUR *COUSINS*."

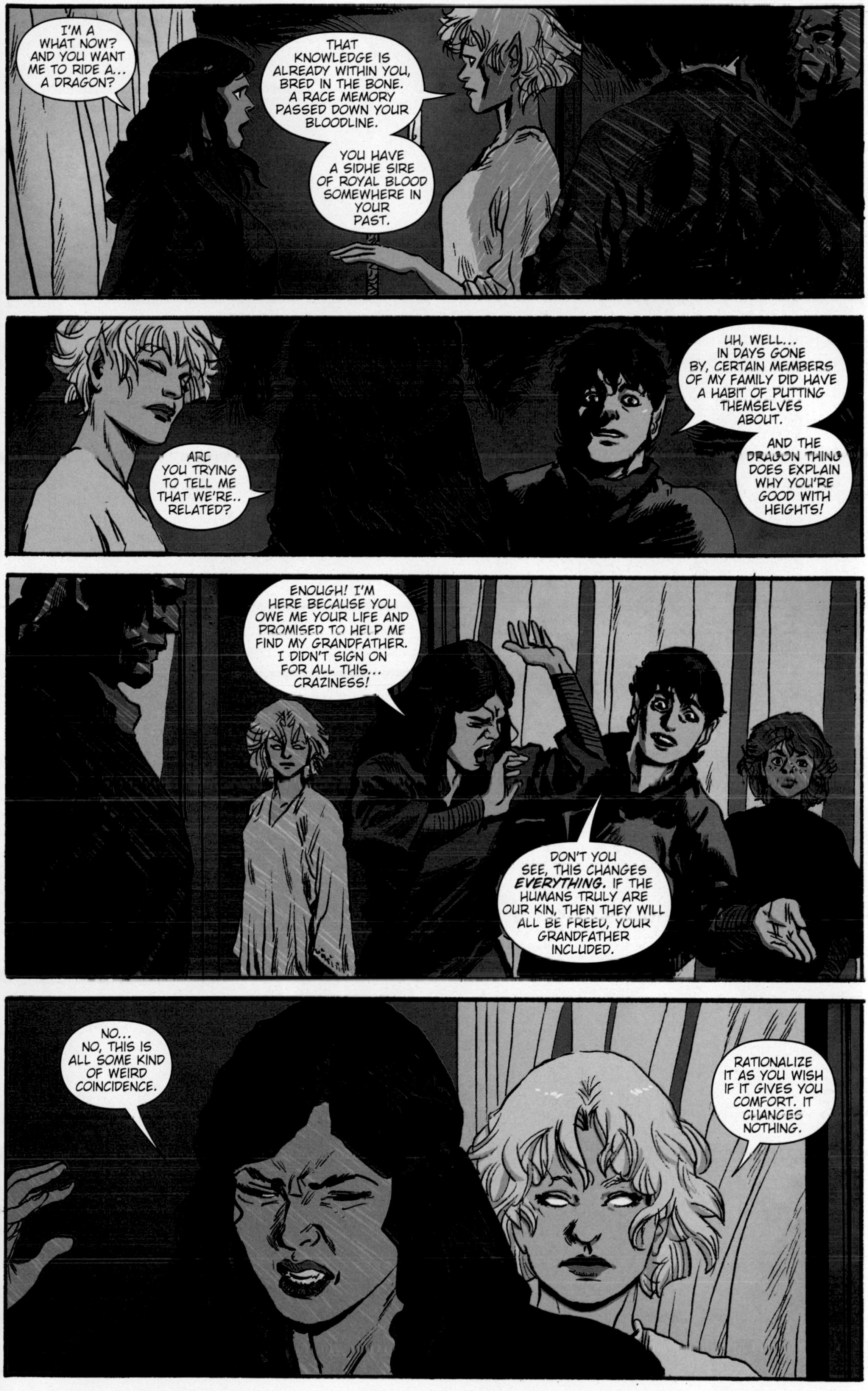
I'M A WHAT NOW? AND YOU WANT ME TO RIDE A... A DRAGON?
THAT KNOWLEDGE IS ALREADY WITHIN YOU, BRED IN THE BONE. A RACE MEMORY PASSED DOWN YOUR BLOODLINE.
YOU HAVE A SIDHE SIRE OF ROYAL BLOOD SOMEWHERE IN YOUR PAST.
ARE YOU TRYING TO TELL ME THAT WE'RE.. RELATED?
UH, WELL... IN DAYS GONE BY, CERTAIN MEMBERS OF MY FAMILY DID HAVE A HABIT OF PUTTING THEMSELVES ABOUT.
AND THE DRAGON THING DOES EXPLAIN WHY YOU'RE GOOD WITH HEIGHTS!
ENOUGH! I'M HERE BECAUSE YOU OWE ME YOUR LIFE AND PROMISED TO HELP ME FIND MY GRANDFATHER. I DIDN'T SIGN ON FOR ALL THIS... CRAZINESS!
DON'T YOU SEE, THIS CHANGES EVERYTHING. IF THE HUMANS TRULY ARE OUR KIN, THEN THEY WILL ALL BE FREED, YOUR GRANDFATHER INCLUDED.
NO... NO, THIS IS ALL SOME KIND OF WEIRD COINCIDENCE.
RATIONALIZE IT AS YOU WISH IF IT GIVES YOU COMFORT. IT CHANGES NOTHING.

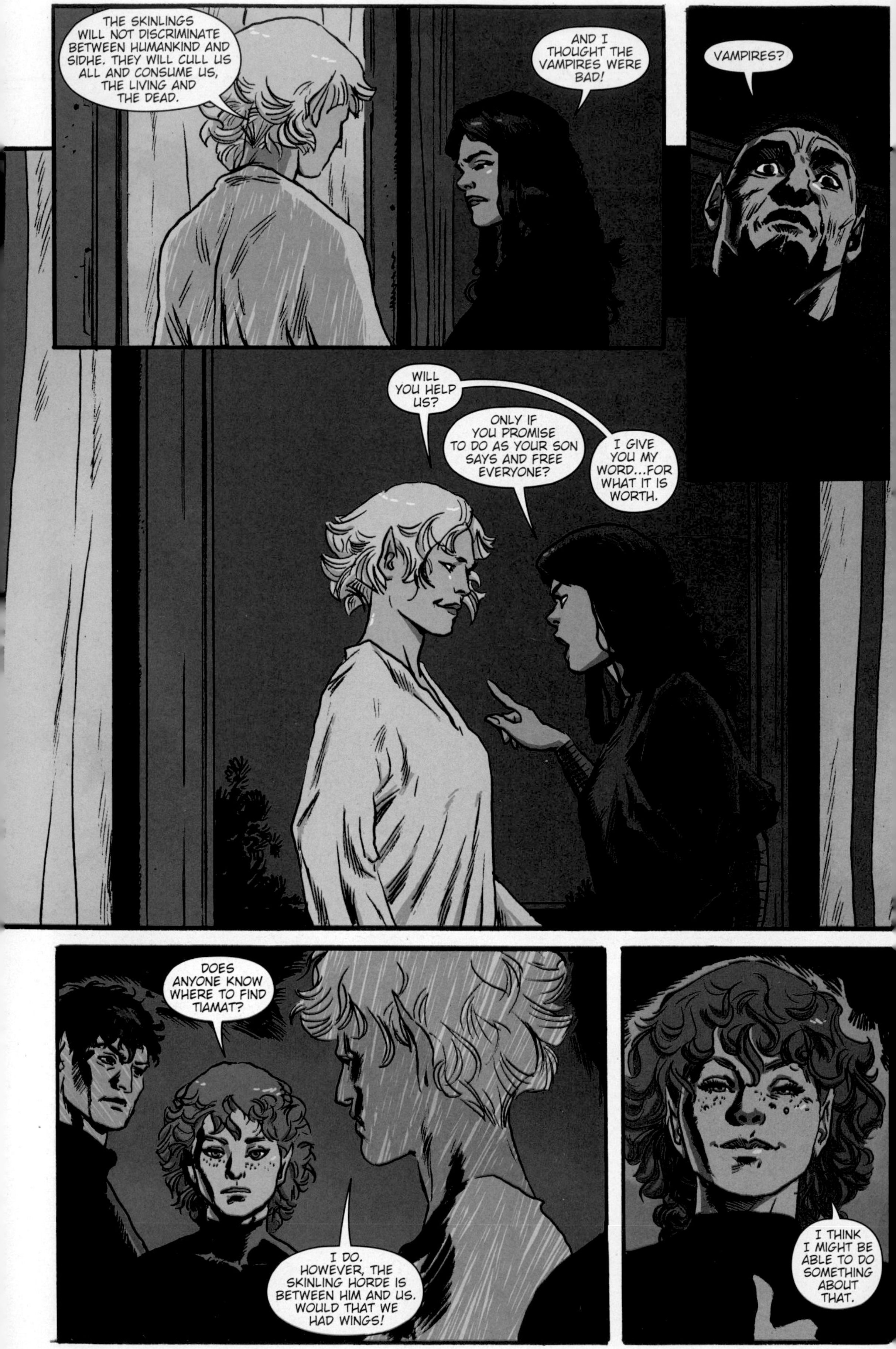
THE SKINLINGS WILL NOT DISCRIMINATE BETWEEN HUMANKIND AND SIDHE. THEY WILL CULL US ALL AND CONSUME US, THE LIVING AND THE DEAD.
AND I THOUGHT THE VAMPIRES WERE BAD!
VAMPIRES?
WILL YOU HELP US?
ONLY IF YOU PROMISE TO DO AS YOUR SON SAYS AND FREE EVERYONE?
I GIVE YOU MY WORD...FOR WHAT IT IS WORTH.
DOES ANYONE KNOW WHERE TO FIND TIAMAT?
I DO. HOWEVER, THE SKINLING HORDE IS BETWEEN HIM AND US. WOULD THAT WE HAD WINGS!
I THINK I MIGHT BE ABLE TO DO SOMETHING ABOUT THAT.

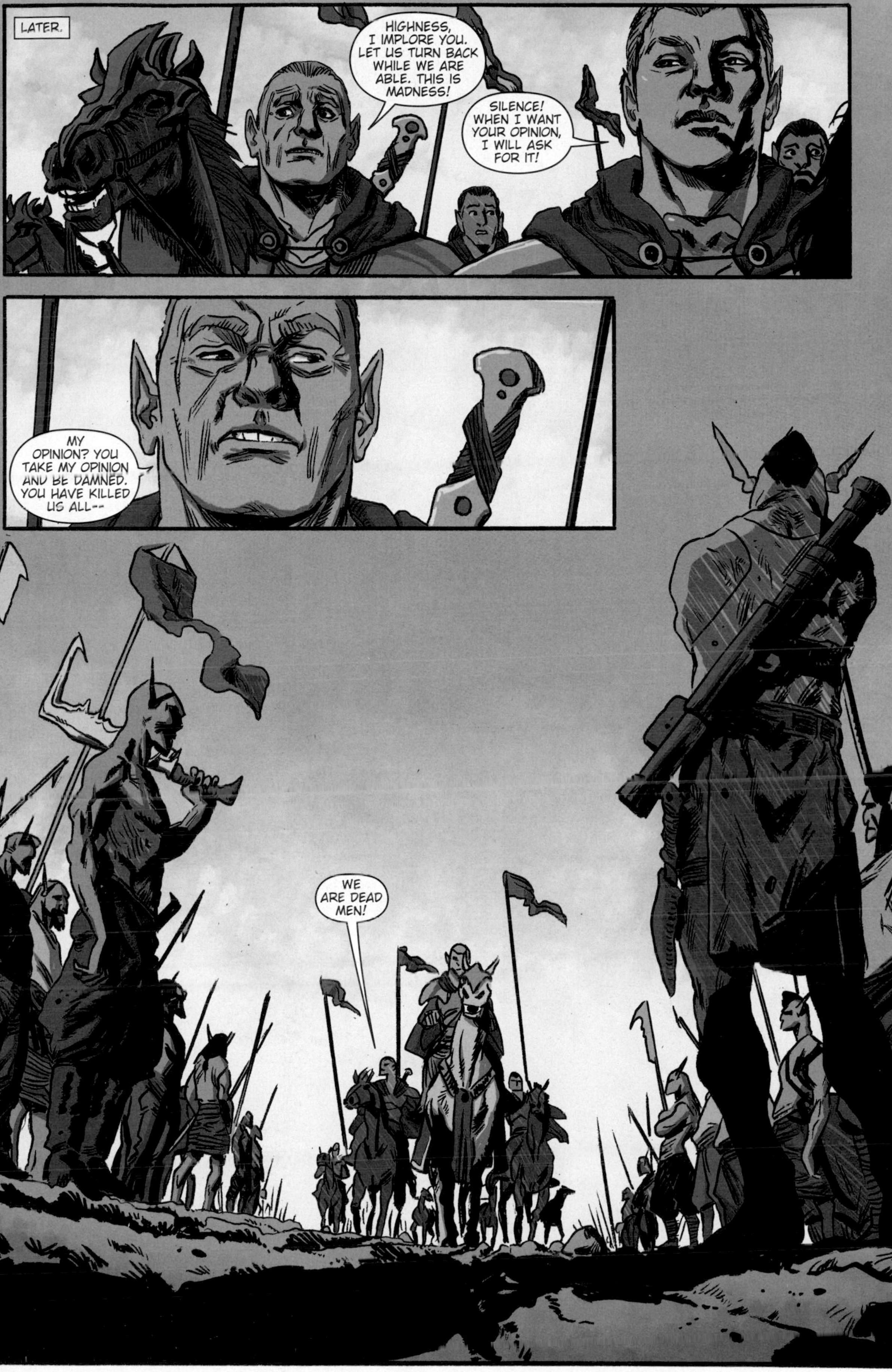
LATER.
HIGHNESS, I IMPLORE YOU. LET US TURN BACK WHILE WE ARE ABLE. THIS IS MADNESS!
SILENCE! WHEN I WANT YOUR OPINION, I WILL ASK FOR IT!
MY OPINION? YOU TAKE MY OPINION AND BE DAMNED. YOU HAVE KILLED US ALL--
WE ARE DEAD MEN!

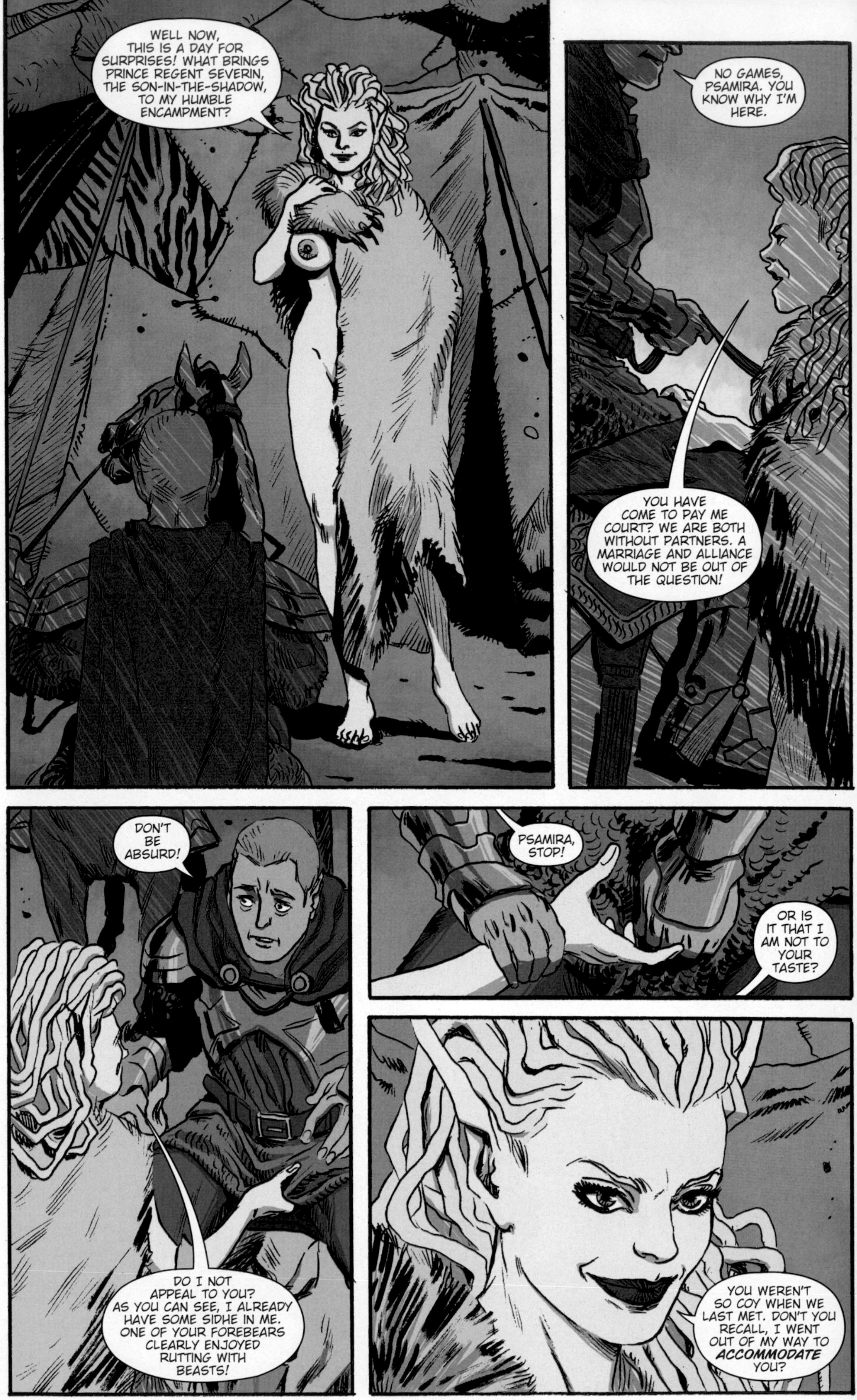
WELL NOW, THIS IS A DAY FOR SURPRISES! WHAT BRINGS PRINCE REGENT SEVERIN, THE SON-IN-THE-SHADOW, TO MY HUMBLE ENCAMPMENT?
NO GAMES, PSAMIRA. YOU KNOW WHY I'M HERE.
YOU HAVE COME TO PAY ME COURT? WE ARE BOTH WITHOUT PARTNERS. A MARRIAGE AND ALLIANCE WOULD NOT BE OUT OF THE QUESTION!
DON'T BE ABSURD!
DO I NOT APPEAL TO YOU? AS YOU CAN SEE, I ALREADY HAVE SOME SIDHE IN ME. ONE OF YOUR FOREBEARS CLEARLY ENJOYED RUTTING WITH BEASTS!
PSAMIRA, STOP!
OR IS IT THAT I AM NOT TO YOUR TASTE?
YOU WEREN'T SO COY WHEN WE LAST MET. DON'T YOU RECALL, I WENT OUT OF MY WAY TO ACCOMMODATE YOU?

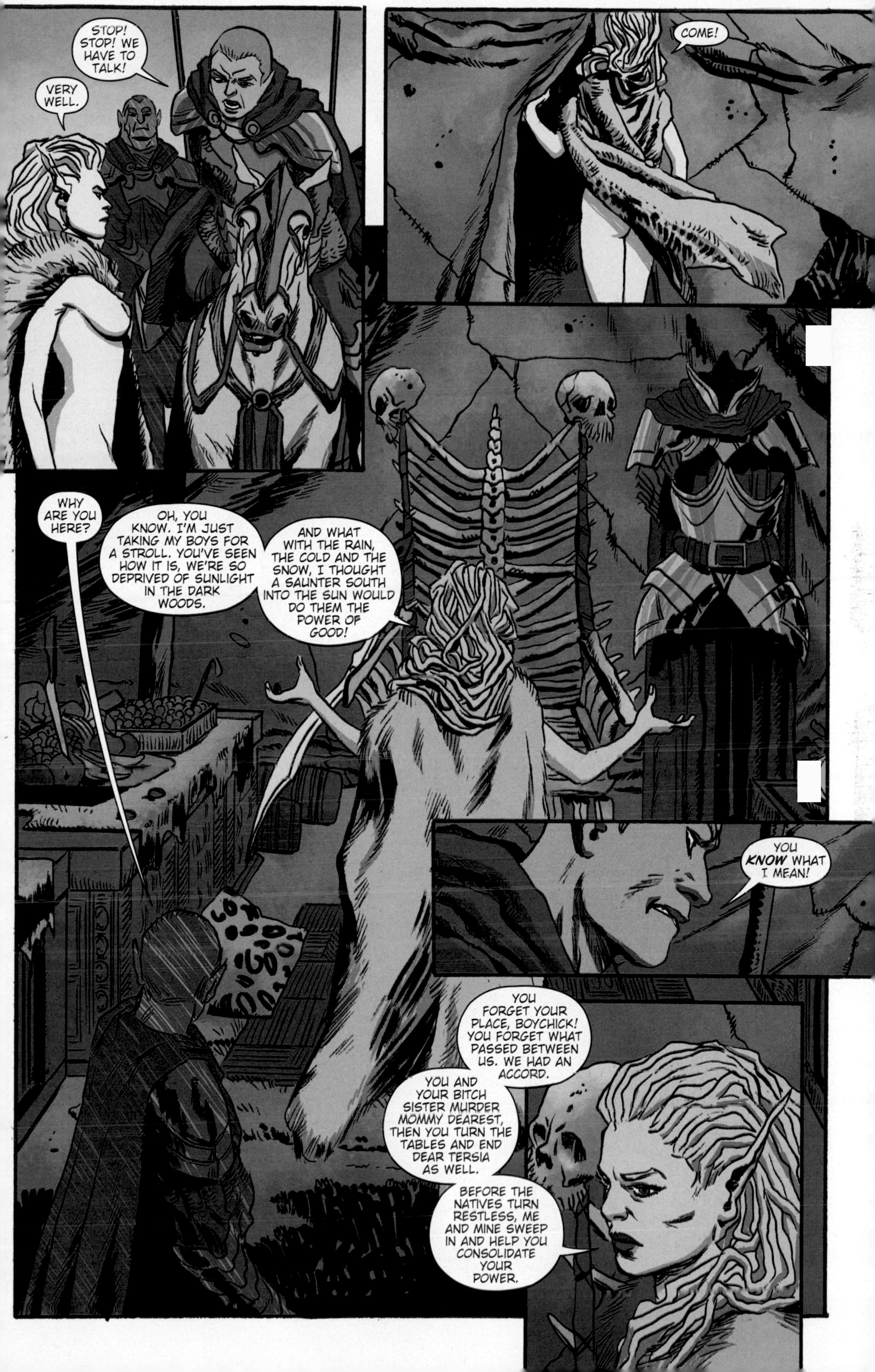

STOP! STOP! WE HAVE TO TALK!
VERY WELL.
COME!
WHY ARE YOU HERE?
OH, YOU KNOW. I'M JUST TAKING MY BOYS FOR A STROLL. YOU'VE SEEN HOW IT IS, WE'RE SO DEPRIVED OF SUNLIGHT IN THE DARK WOODS.
AND WHAT WITH THE RAIN, THE COLD AND THE SNOW, I THOUGHT A SAUNTER SOUTH INTO THE SUN WOULD DO THEM THE POWER OF GOOD!
YOU **KNOW** WHAT I MEAN!
YOU FORGET YOUR PLACE, BOYCHICK! YOU FORGET WHAT PASSED BETWEEN US. WE HAD AN ACCORD.
YOU AND YOUR BITCH SISTER MURDER MOMMY DEAREST, THEN YOU TURN THE TABLES AND END DEAR TERSIA AS WELL.
BEFORE THE NATIVES TURN RESTLESS, ME AND MINE SWEEP IN AND HELP YOU CONSOLIDATE YOUR POWER.

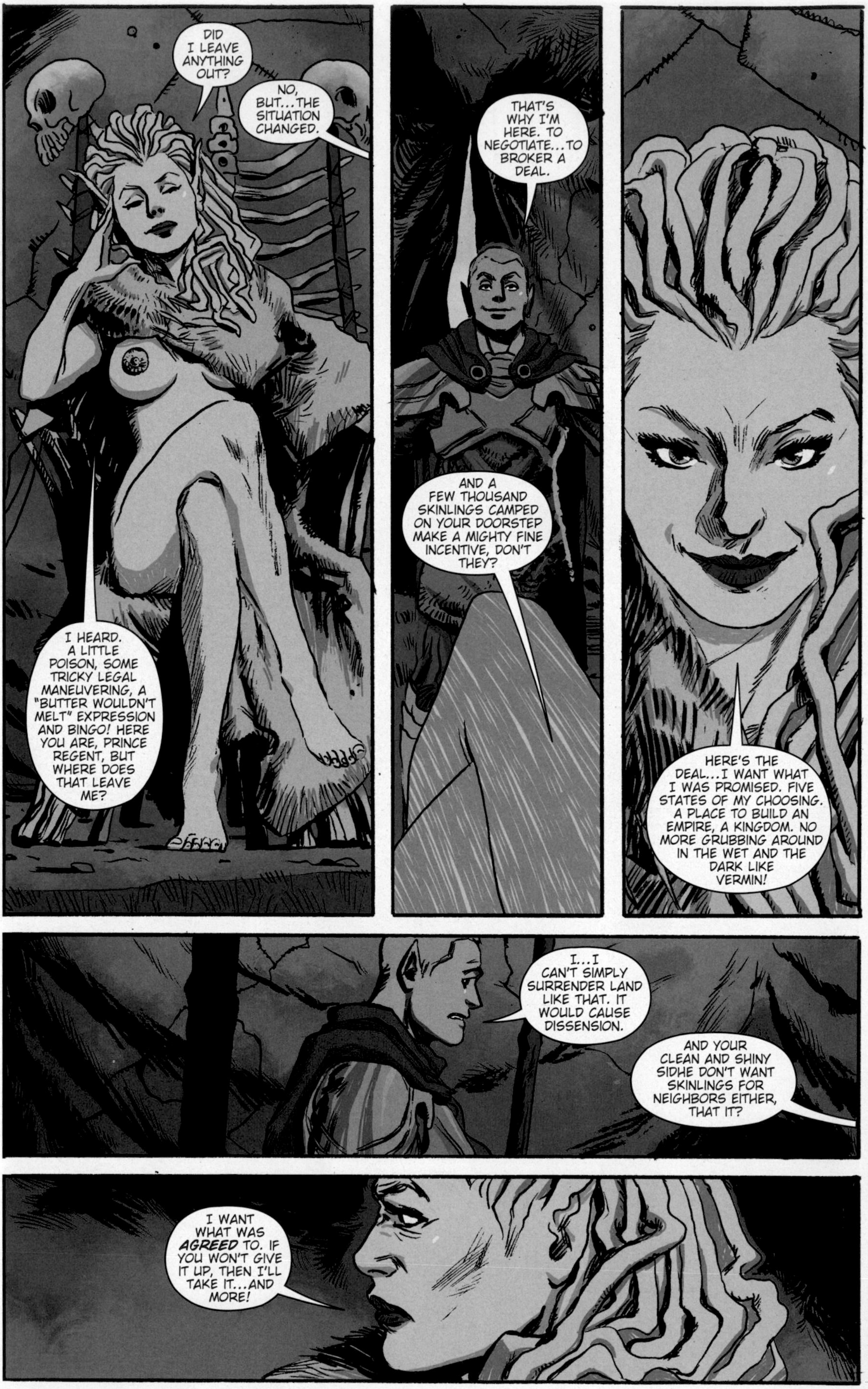
DID I LEAVE ANYTHING OUT?
NO, BUT...THE SITUATION CHANGED.
I HEARD. A LITTLE POISON, SOME TRICKY LEGAL MANEUVERING, A "BUTTER WOULDN'T MELT" EXPRESSION AND BINGO! HERE YOU ARE, PRINCE REGENT, BUT WHERE DOES THAT LEAVE ME?
THAT'S WHY I'M HERE. TO NEGOTIATE...TO BROKER A DEAL.
AND A FEW THOUSAND SKINLINGS CAMPED ON YOUR DOORSTEP MAKE A MIGHTY FINE INCENTIVE, DON'T THEY?
HERE'S THE DEAL...I WANT WHAT I WAS PROMISED. FIVE STATES OF MY CHOOSING. A PLACE TO BUILD AN EMPIRE, A KINGDOM. NO MORE GRUBBING AROUND IN THE WET AND THE DARK LIKE VERMIN!
I...I CAN'T SIMPLY SURRENDER LAND LIKE THAT. IT WOULD CAUSE DISSENSION.
AND YOUR CLEAN AND SHINY SIDHE DON'T WANT SKINLINGS FOR NEIGHBORS EITHER, THAT IT?
I WANT WHAT WAS *AGREED* TO. IF YOU WON'T GIVE IT UP, THEN I'LL TAKE IT...AND MORE!

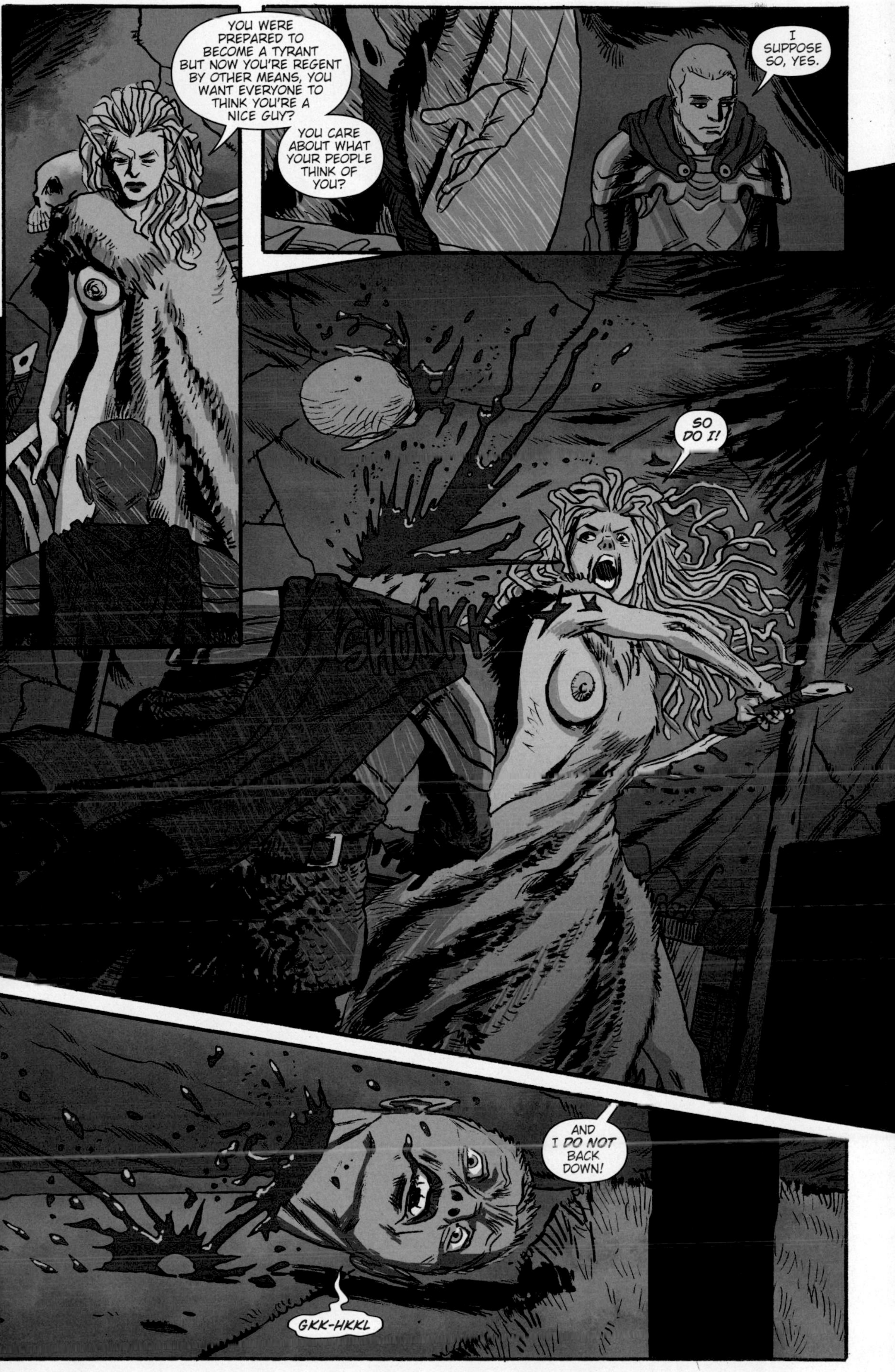
YOU WERE PREPARED TO BECOME A TYRANT BUT NOW YOU'RE REGENT BY OTHER MEANS, YOU WANT EVERYONE TO THINK YOU'RE A NICE GUY?
YOU CARE ABOUT WHAT YOUR PEOPLE THINK OF YOU?
I SUPPOSE SO, YES.
SO DO I!
SHUNKK
AND I DO NOT BACK DOWN!
GKK-HKKL

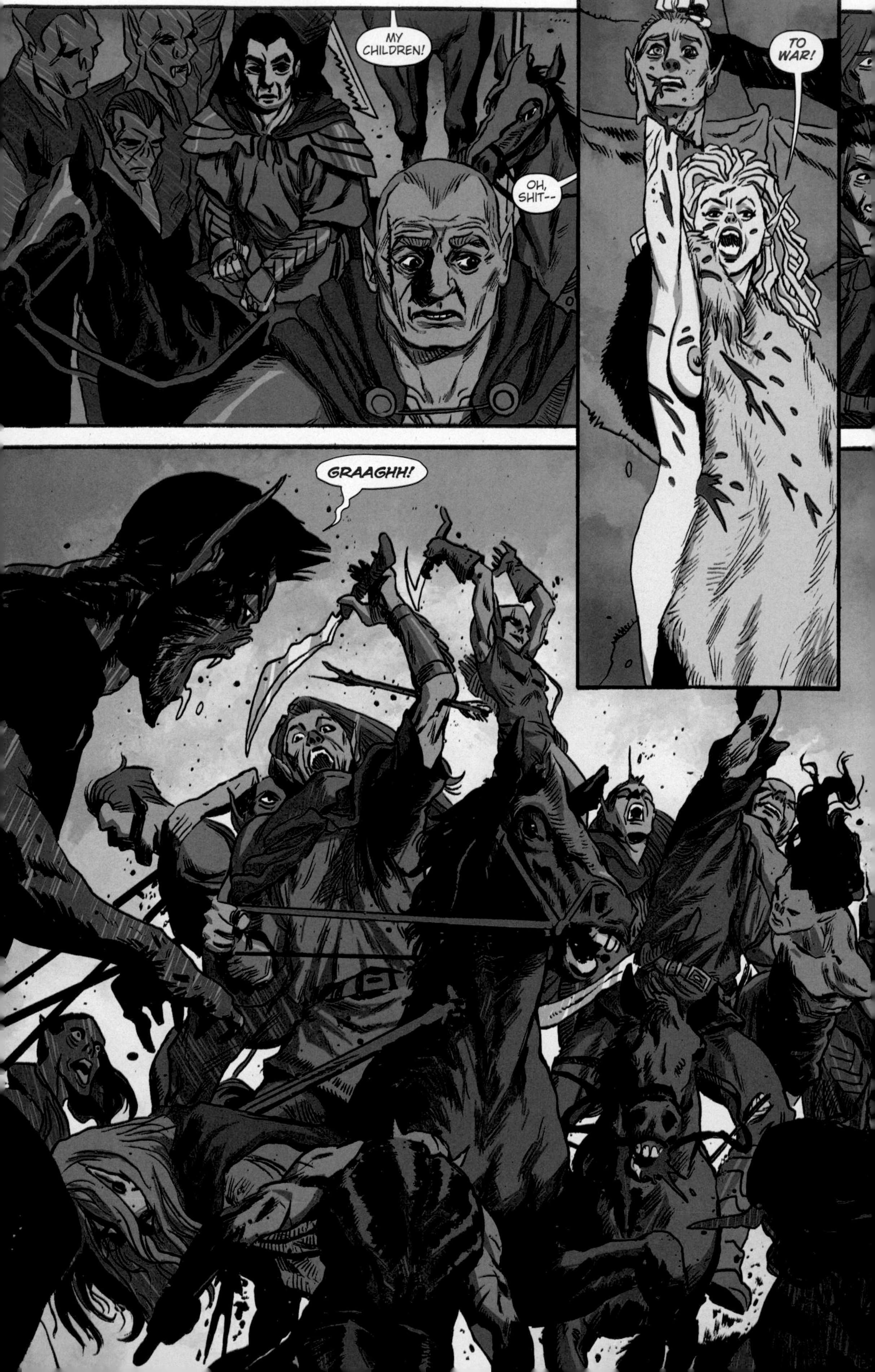
MY CHILDREN!
OH, SHIT--
TO WAR!
GRAAGHH!

HOLY MARY MOTHER OF GOD!

OKAY, THAT'S IT WE'RE DONE HERE. WE CAN'T GO ANY FURTHER, IT'S TOO RISKY.

WE HAVE TO TRY! WE CAN'T JUST QUIT!

LISTEN, DOC. THERE ARE THOUSANDS OF THOSE SKINLING BASTARDS BETWEEN US AND THE WHITE CITY AND I JUST WATCHED 'EM TEAR APART A SIDHE COLUMN LIKE THEY WAS STRING CHEESE.

I AM NOT GOIN' DOWN THERE.

LET ME SEE.

YOU WANTED T'WARN 'EM ABOUT VAMPIRES. BROTHER, IT'S TOO LATE. THEY GOT A DOG AT THEIR THROAT ALREADY.

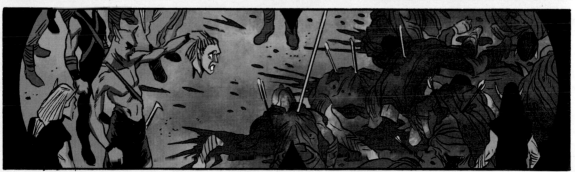

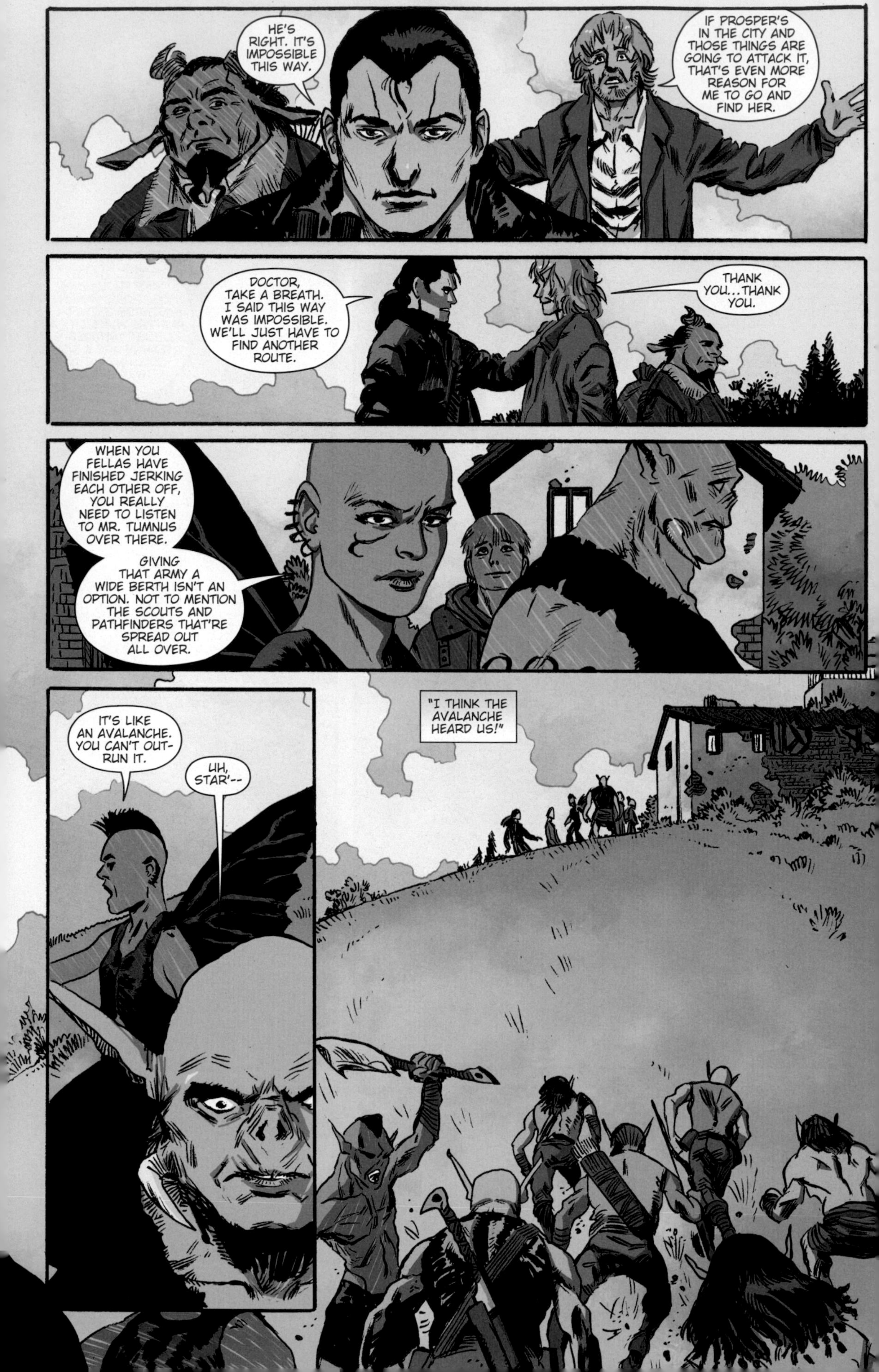
HE'S RIGHT. IT'S IMPOSSIBLE THIS WAY.
IF PROSPER'S IN THE CITY AND THOSE THINGS ARE GOING TO ATTACK IT, THAT'S EVEN MORE REASON FOR ME TO GO AND FIND HER.
DOCTOR, TAKE A BREATH. I SAID THIS WAY WAS IMPOSSIBLE. WE'LL JUST HAVE TO FIND ANOTHER ROUTE.
THANK YOU...THANK YOU.
WHEN YOU FELLAS HAVE FINISHED JERKING EACH OTHER OFF, YOU REALLY NEED TO LISTEN TO MR. TUMNUS OVER THERE.
GIVING THAT ARMY A WIDE BERTH ISN'T AN OPTION. NOT TO MENTION THE SCOUTS AND PATHFINDERS THAT'RE SPREAD OUT ALL OVER.
IT'S LIKE AN AVALANCHE. YOU CAN'T OUT-RUN IT.
UH, STAR'--
"I THINK THE AVALANCHE HEARD US!"

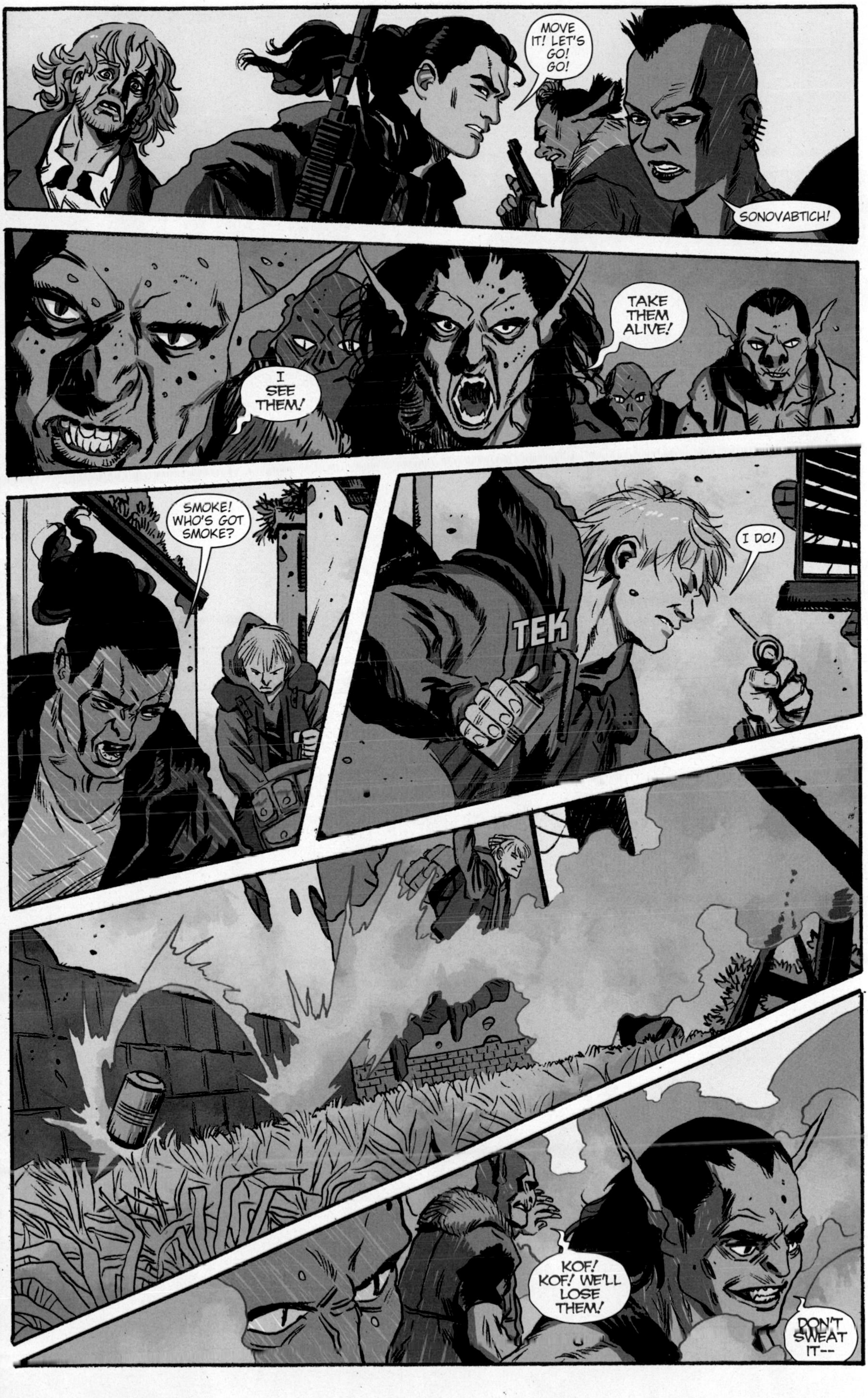
MOVE IT! LET'S GO! GO!
SONOVABTICH!
TAKE THEM ALIVE!
I SEE THEM!
SMOKE! WHO'S GOT SMOKE?
I DO!
TEK
KOF! KOF! WE'LL LOSE THEM!
DON'T SWEAT IT--

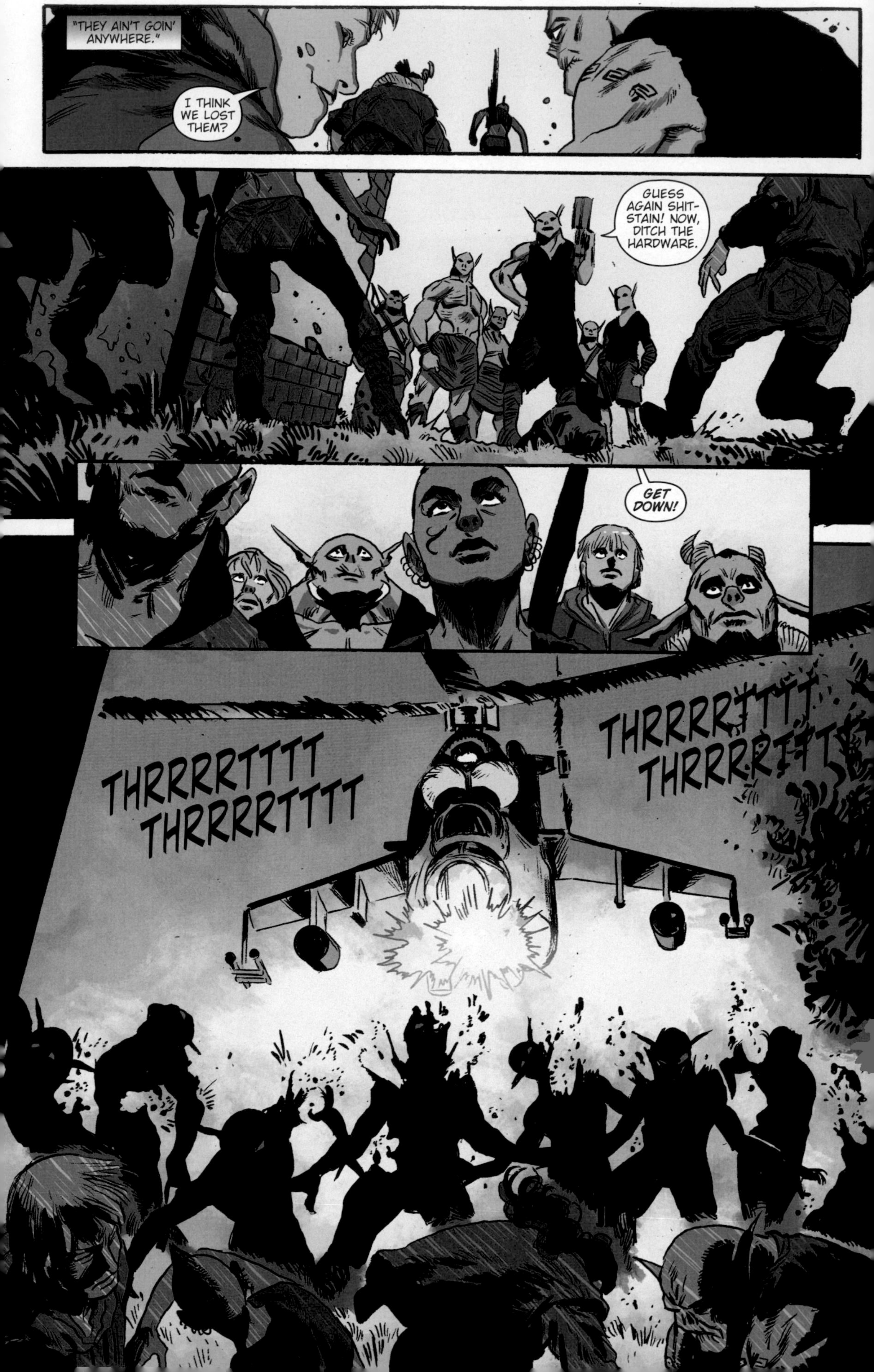
"THEY AIN'T GOIN' ANYWHERE."
I THINK WE LOST THEM?
GUESS AGAIN SHIT-STAIN! NOW, DITCH THE HARDWARE.
GET DOWN!
THRRRRTTTT THRRRRTTTT
THRRRRTTTT THRRRRTTTT

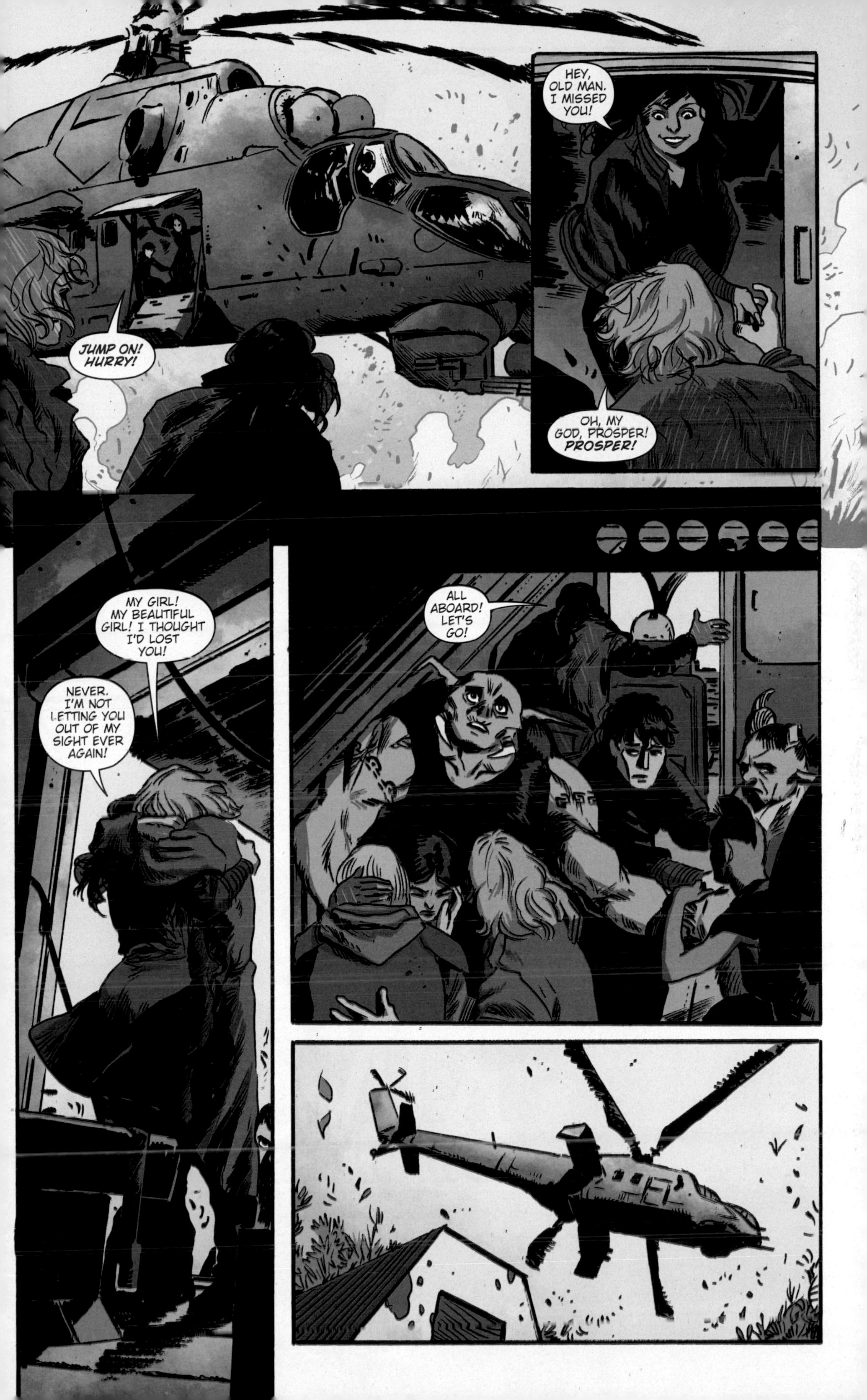
JUMP ON! HURRY!
HEY, OLD MAN. I MISSED YOU!
OH, MY GOD, PROSPER! PROSPER!
MY GIRL! MY BEAUTIFUL GIRL! I THOUGHT I'D LOST YOU!
NEVER. I'M NOT LETTING YOU OUT OF MY SIGHT EVER AGAIN!
ALL ABOARD! LET'S GO!

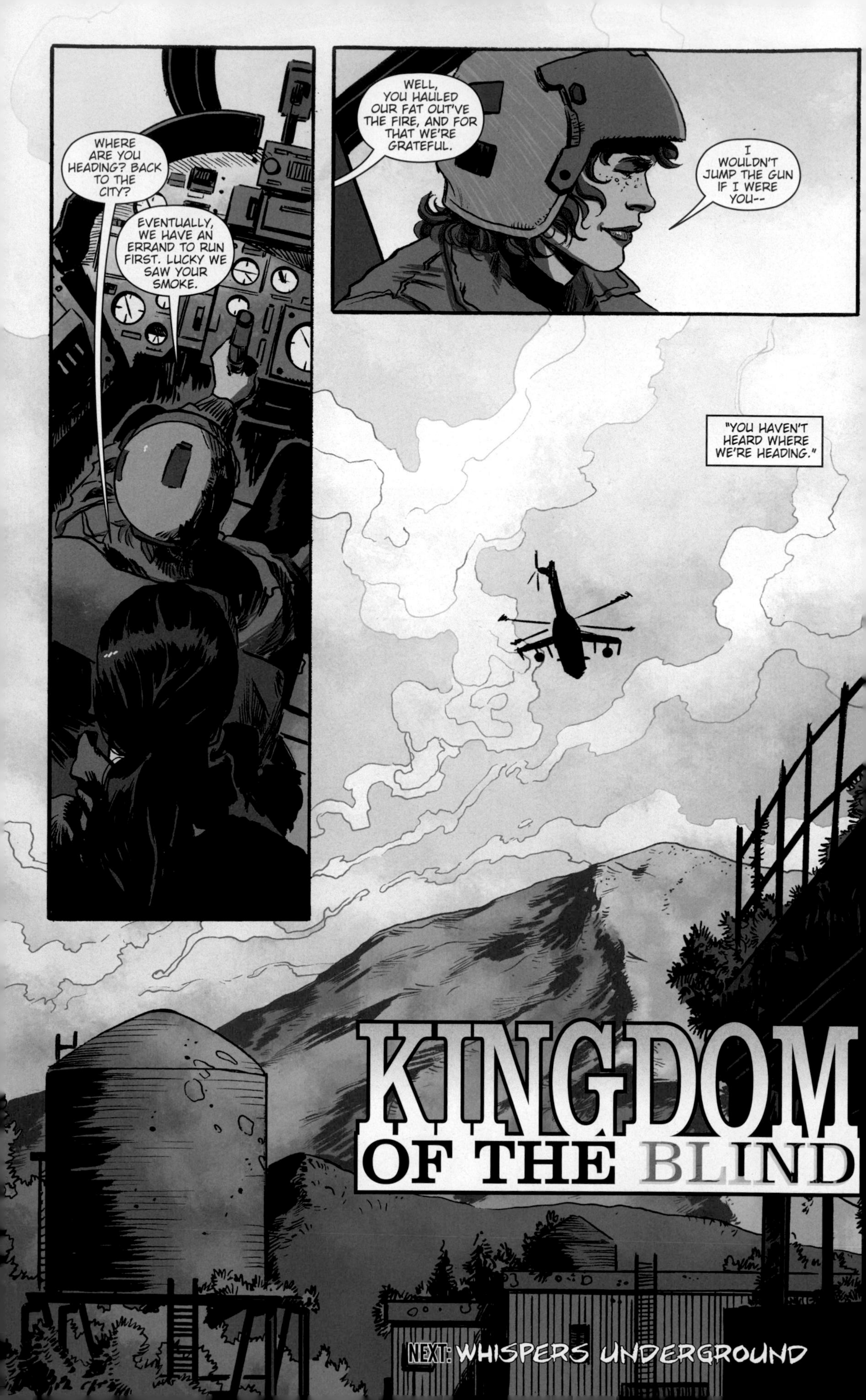

WHERE ARE YOU HEADING? BACK TO THE CITY?
EVENTUALLY, WE HAVE AN ERRAND TO RUN FIRST. LUCKY WE SAW YOUR SMOKE.
WELL, YOU HAULED OUR FAT OUT'VE THE FIRE, AND FOR THAT WE'RE GRATEFUL.
I WOULDN'T JUMP THE GUN IF I WERE YOU--
"YOU HAVEN'T HEARD WHERE WE'RE HEADING."
KINGDOM OF THE BLIND
NEXT: WHISPERS UNDERGROUND

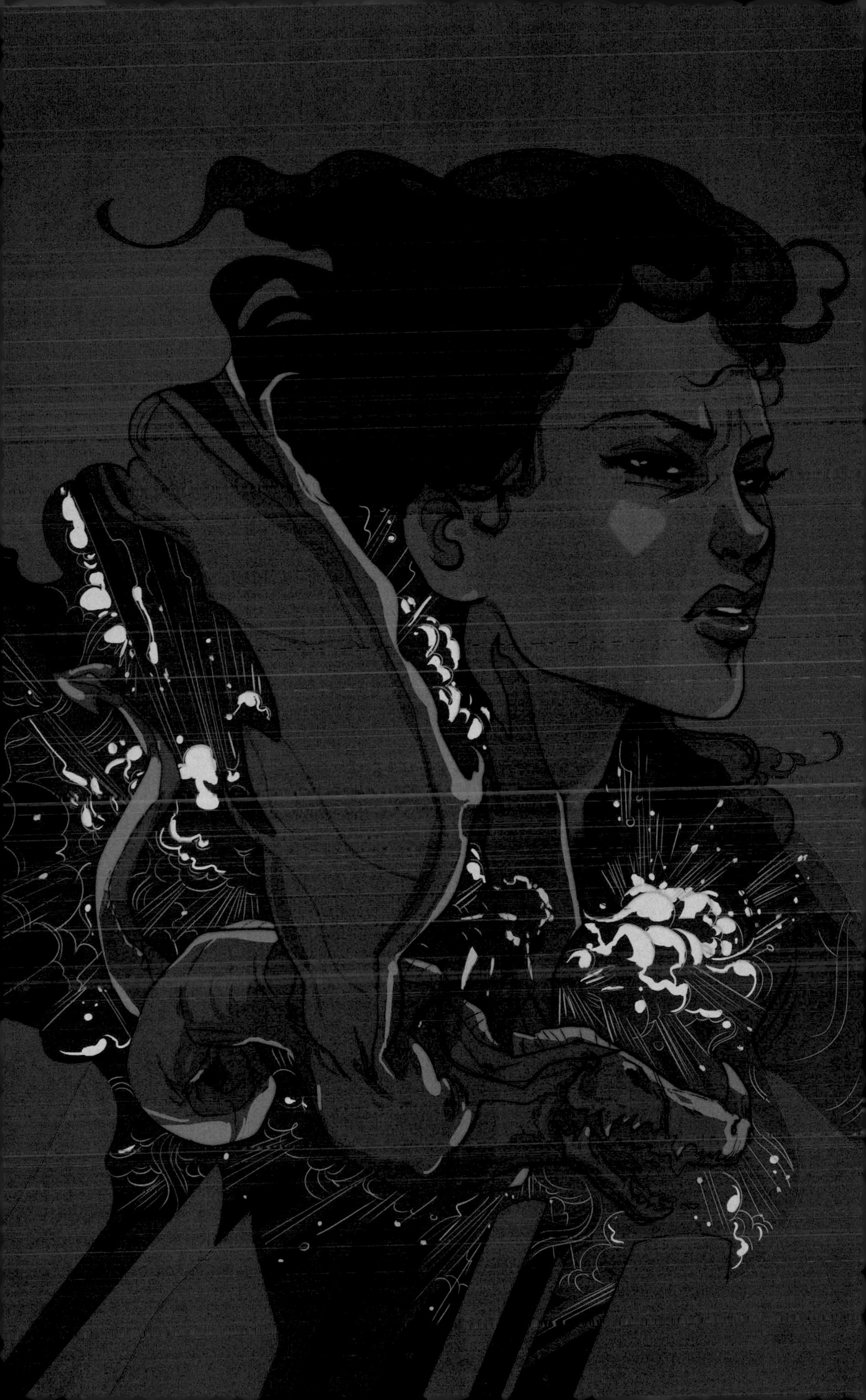

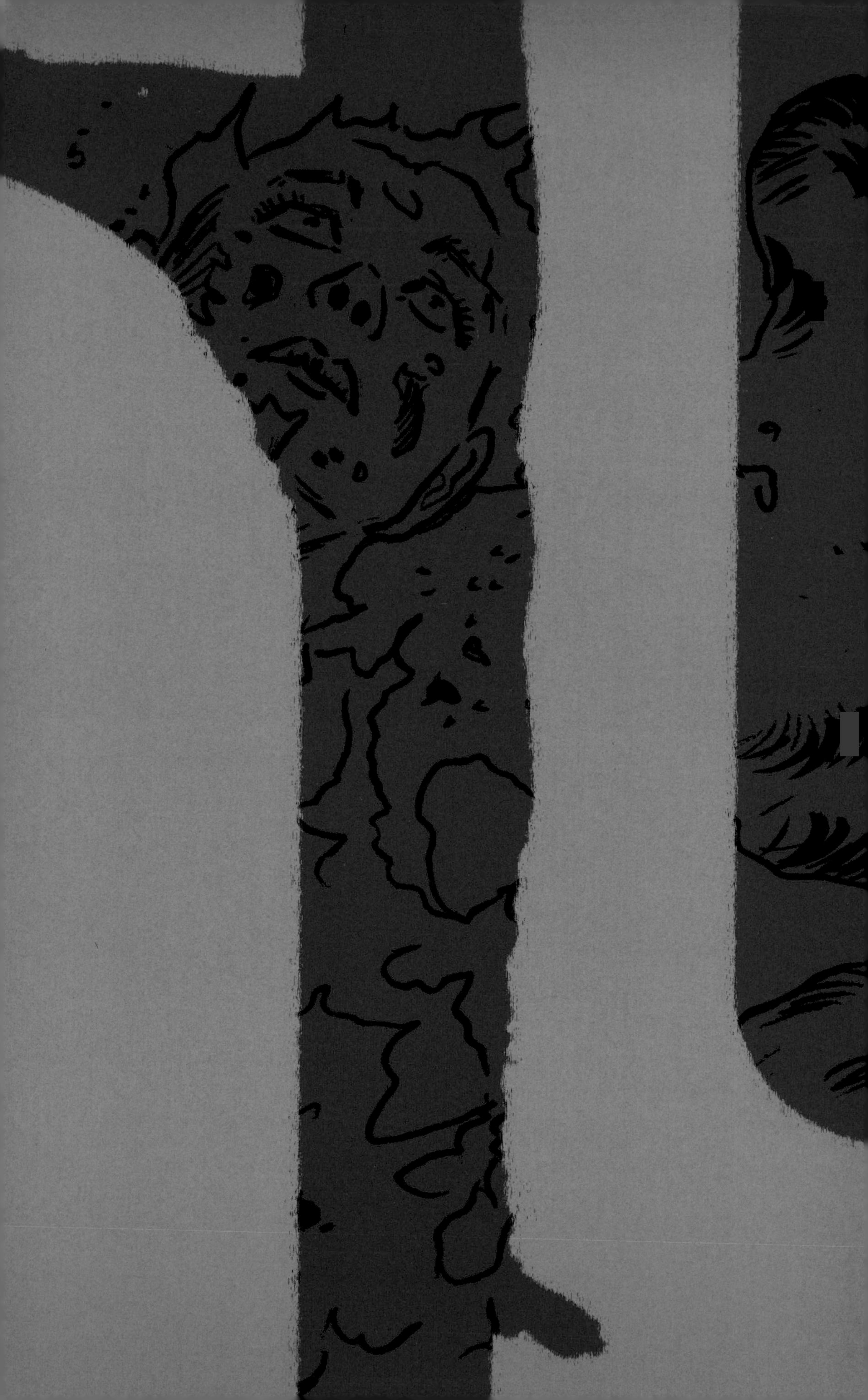

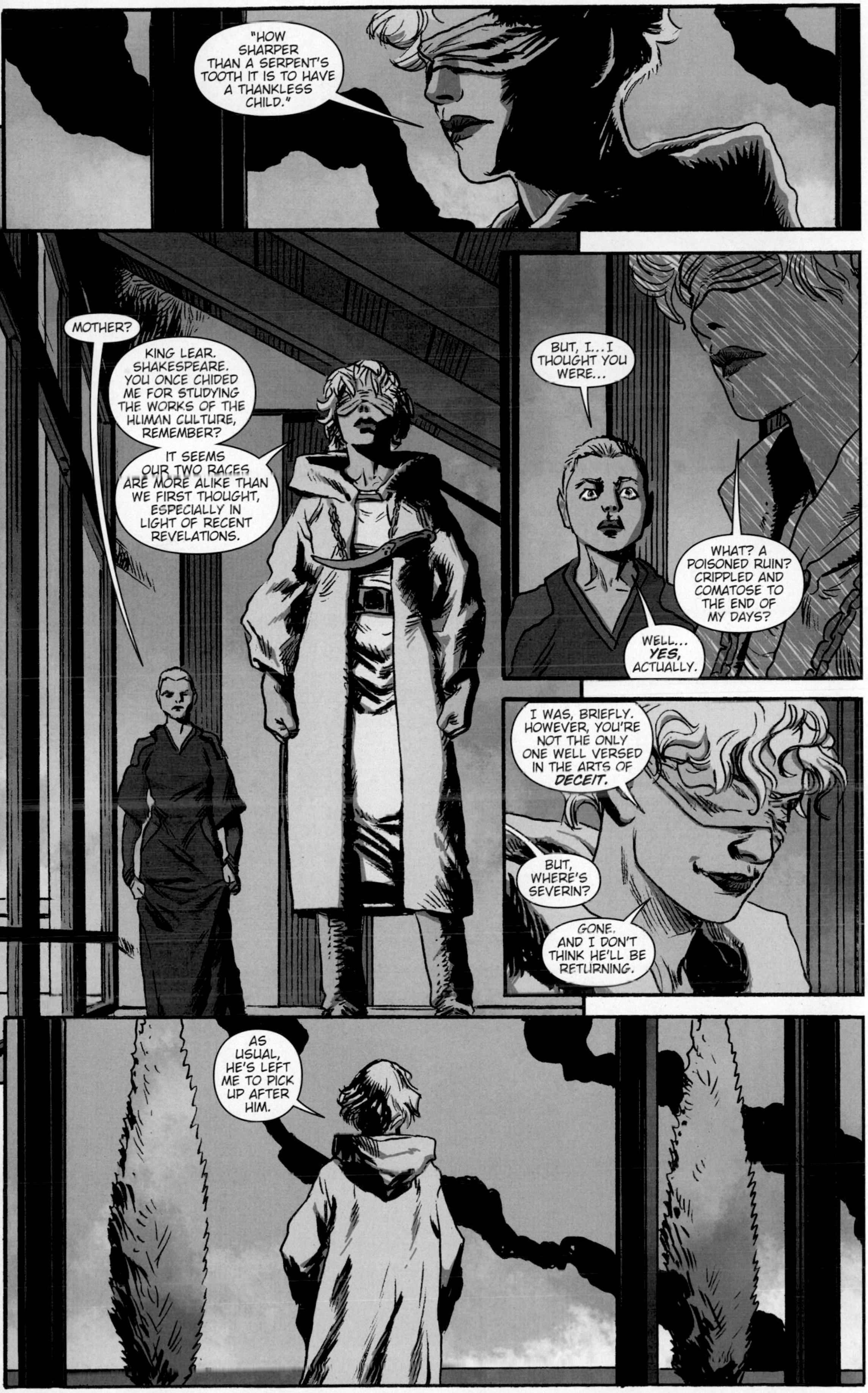
"HOW SHARPER THAN A SERPENT'S TOOTH IT IS TO HAVE A THANKLESS CHILD."
MOTHER?
KING LEAR. SHAKESPEARE. YOU ONCE CHIDED ME FOR STUDYING THE WORKS OF THE HUMAN CULTURE, REMEMBER?
IT SEEMS OUR TWO RACES ARE MORE ALIKE THAN WE FIRST THOUGHT, ESPECIALLY IN LIGHT OF RECENT REVELATIONS.
BUT, I...I THOUGHT YOU WERE...
WHAT? A POISONED RUIN? CRIPPLED AND COMATOSE TO THE END OF MY DAYS?
WELL... YES, ACTUALLY.
I WAS, BRIEFLY. HOWEVER, YOU'RE NOT THE ONLY ONE WELL VERSED IN THE ARTS OF DECEIT.
BUT, WHERE'S SEVERIN?
GONE. AND I DON'T THINK HE'LL BE RETURNING.
AS USUAL, HE'S LEFT ME TO PICK UP AFTER HIM.

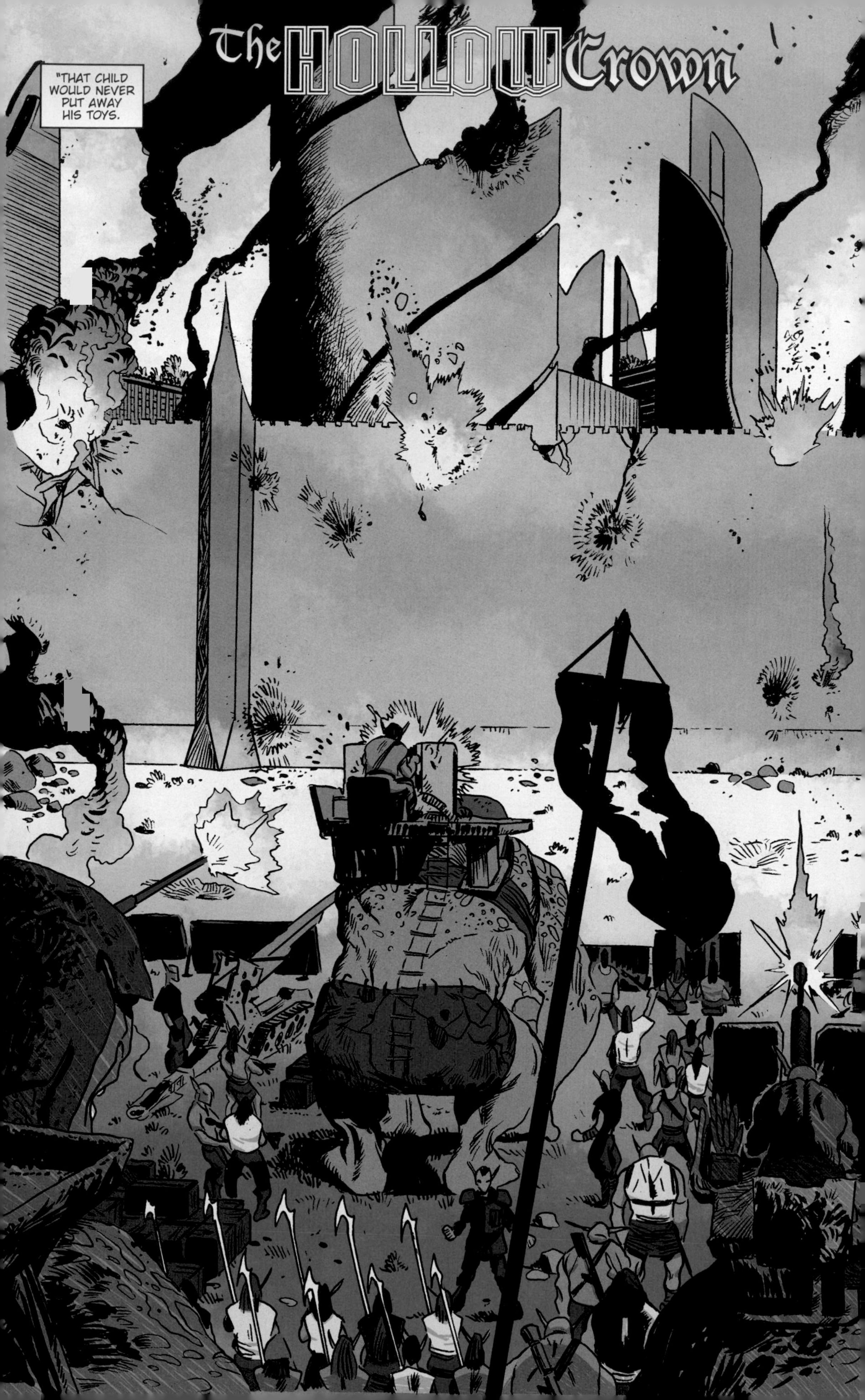
The HOLLOW Crown
"THAT CHILD WOULD NEVER PUT AWAY HIS TOYS.

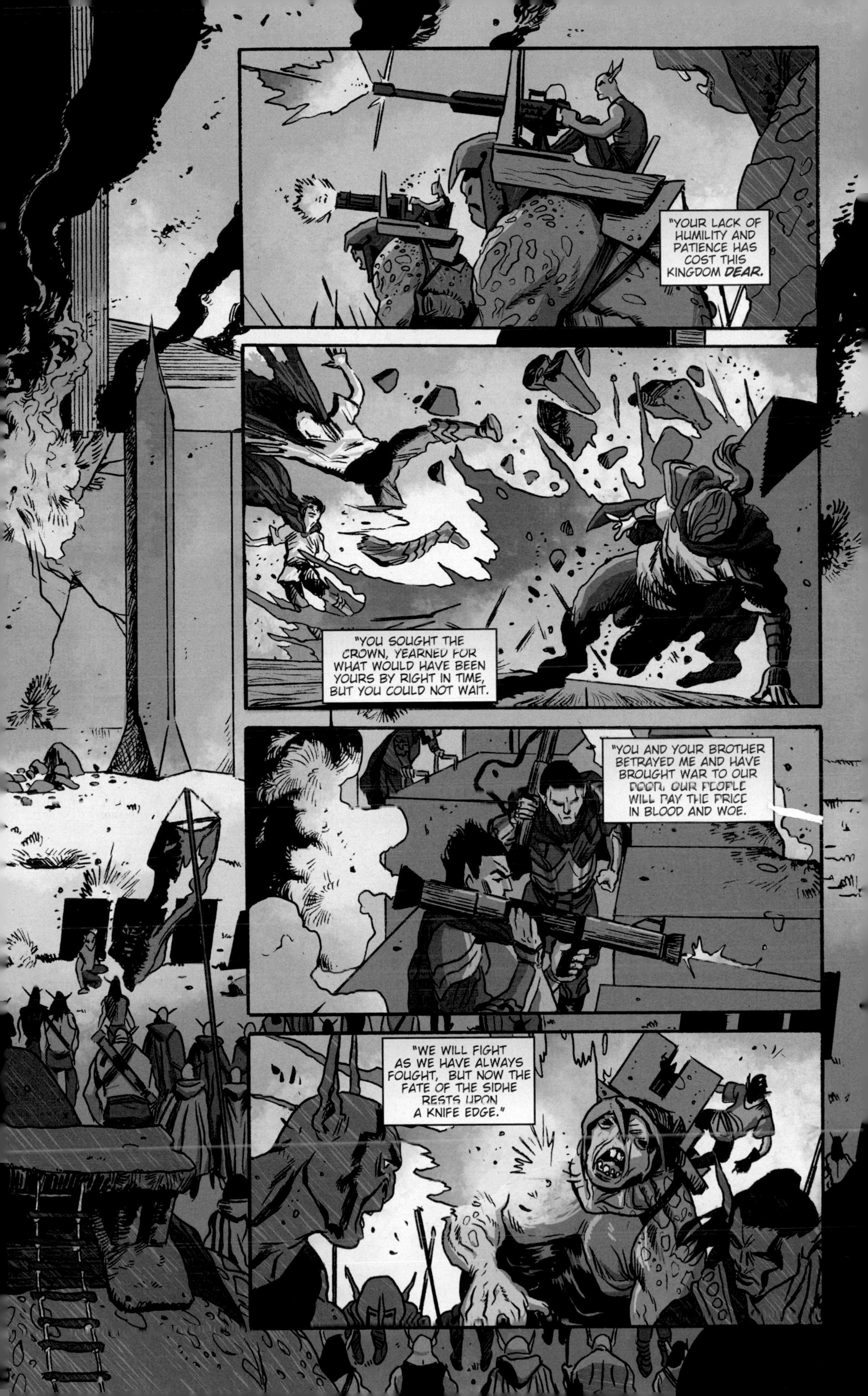
"YOUR LACK OF HUMILITY AND PATIENCE HAS COST THIS KINGDOM *DEAR.*
"YOU SOUGHT THE CROWN, YEARNED FOR WHAT WOULD HAVE BEEN YOURS BY RIGHT IN TIME, BUT YOU COULD NOT WAIT.
"YOU AND YOUR BROTHER BETRAYED ME AND HAVE BROUGHT WAR TO OUR DOOR. OUR PEOPLE WILL PAY THE PRICE IN BLOOD AND WOE.
"WE WILL FIGHT AS WE HAVE ALWAYS FOUGHT, BUT NOW THE FATE OF THE SIDHE RESTS UPON A KNIFE EDGE."

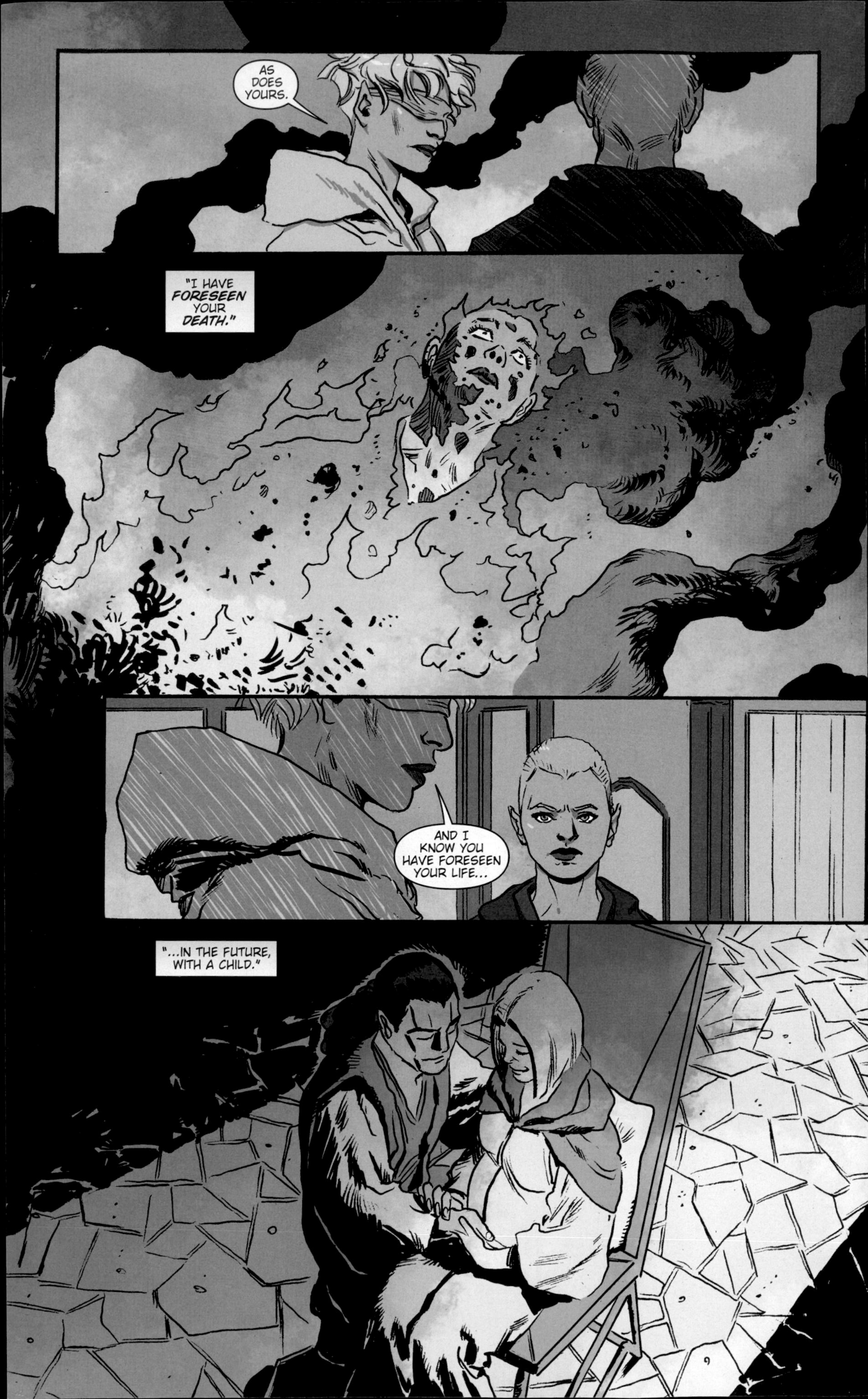
AS DOES YOURS.
"I HAVE *FORESEEN* YOUR *DEATH*."
AND I KNOW YOU HAVE FORESEEN YOUR LIFE...
"...IN THE FUTURE, WITH A CHILD."

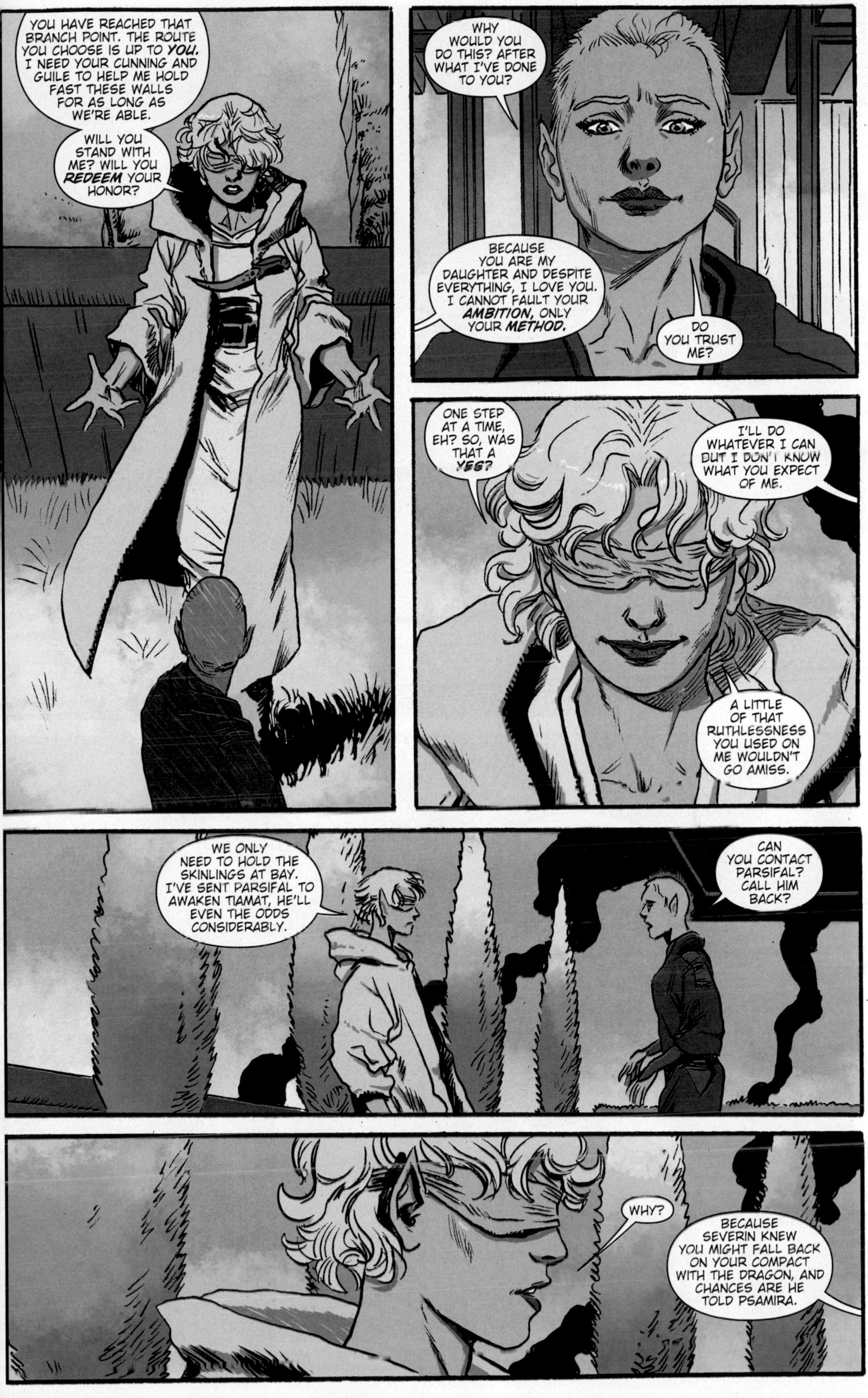
YOU HAVE REACHED THAT BRANCH POINT. THE ROUTE YOU CHOOSE IS UP TO YOU. I NEED YOUR CUNNING AND GUILE TO HELP ME HOLD FAST THESE WALLS FOR AS LONG AS WE'RE ABLE.
WILL YOU STAND WITH ME? WILL YOU REDEEM YOUR HONOR?
WHY WOULD YOU DO THIS? AFTER WHAT I'VE DONE TO YOU?
BECAUSE YOU ARE MY DAUGHTER AND DESPITE EVERYTHING, I LOVE YOU. I CANNOT FAULT YOUR AMBITION, ONLY YOUR METHOD.
DO YOU TRUST ME?
I'LL DO WHATEVER I CAN BUT I DON'T KNOW WHAT YOU EXPECT OF ME.
ONE STEP AT A TIME, EH? SO, WAS THAT A YES?
A LITTLE OF THAT RUTHLESSNESS YOU USED ON ME WOULDN'T GO AMISS.
WE ONLY NEED TO HOLD THE SKINLINGS AT BAY. I'VE SENT PARSIFAL TO AWAKEN TIAMAT, HE'LL EVEN THE ODDS CONSIDERABLY.
CAN YOU CONTACT PARSIFAL? CALL HIM BACK?
WHY?
BECAUSE SEVERIN KNEW YOU MIGHT FALL BACK ON YOUR COMPACT WITH THE DRAGON, AND CHANCES ARE HE TOLD PSAMIRA.

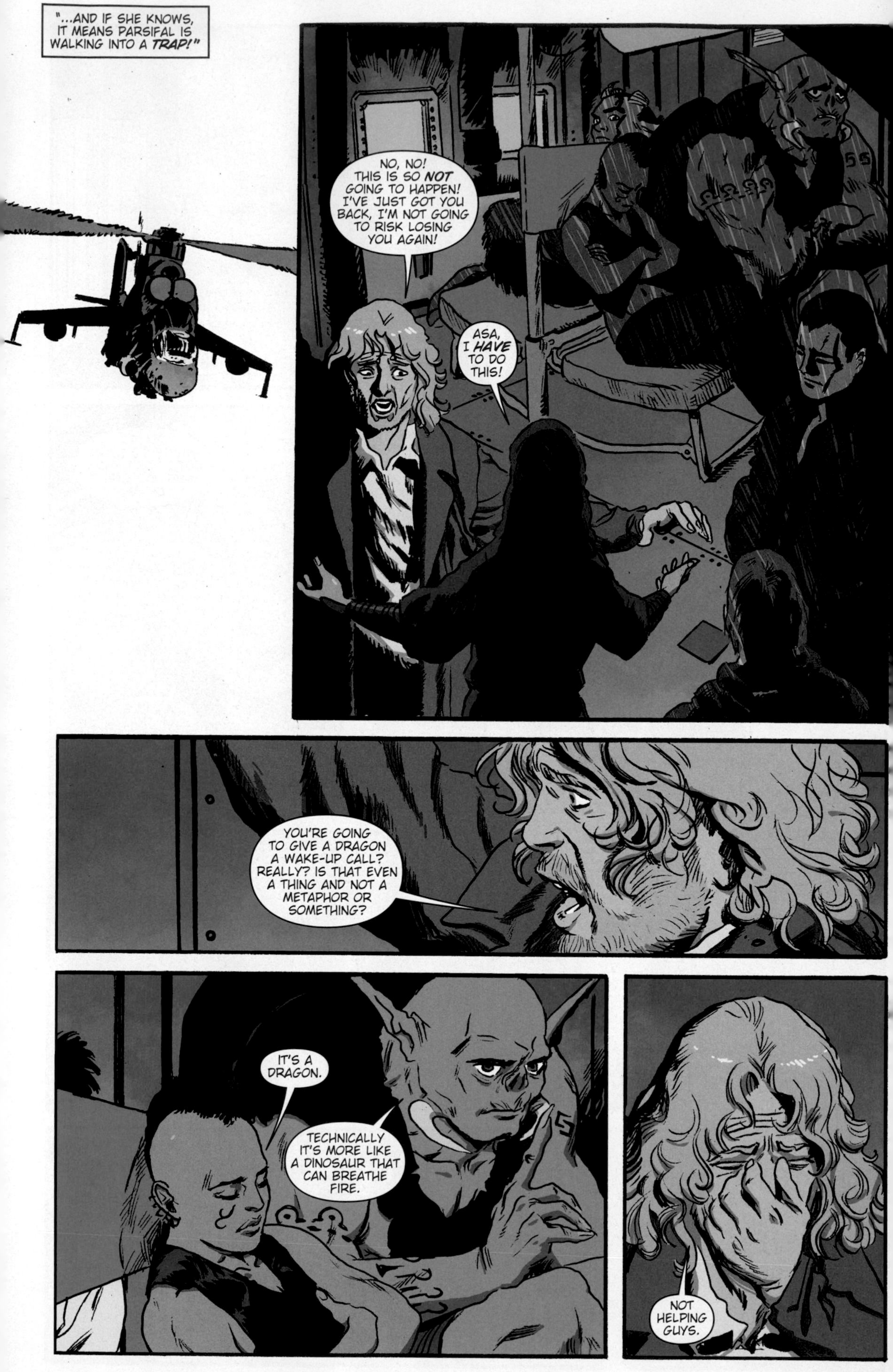
"...AND IF SHE KNOWS, IT MEANS PARSIFAL IS WALKING INTO A *TRAP!*"
NO, NO! THIS IS SO *NOT* GOING TO HAPPEN! I'VE JUST GOT YOU BACK, I'M NOT GOING TO RISK LOSING YOU AGAIN!
ASA, I *HAVE* TO DO THIS!
YOU'RE GOING TO GIVE A DRAGON A WAKE-UP CALL? REALLY? IS THAT EVEN A THING AND NOT A METAPHOR OR SOMETHING?
IT'S A DRAGON.
TECHNICALLY IT'S MORE LIKE A DINOSAUR THAT CAN BREATHE FIRE.
NOT HELPING GUYS.

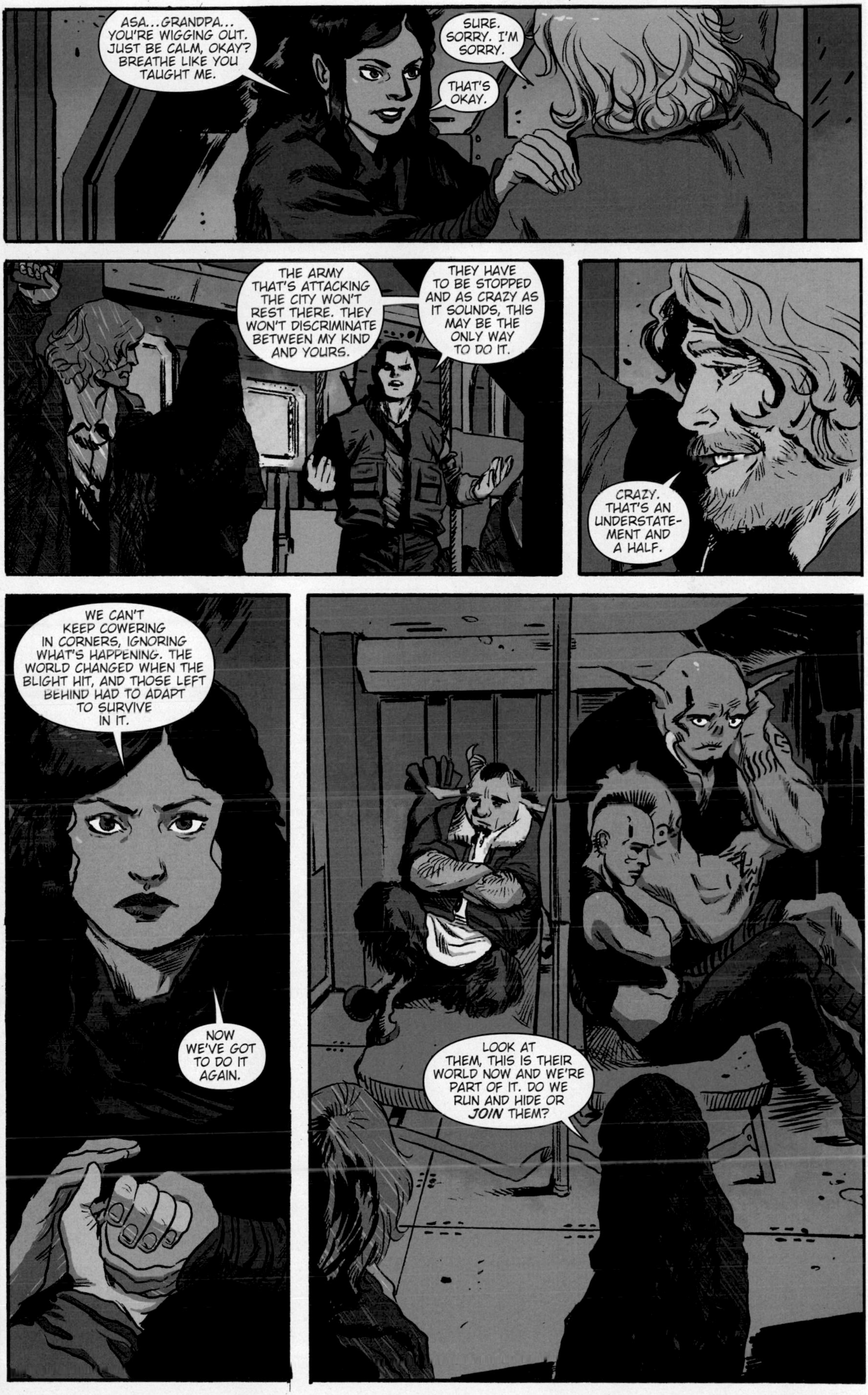
ASA...GRANDPA... YOU'RE WIGGING OUT. JUST BE CALM, OKAY? BREATHE LIKE YOU TAUGHT ME.
SURE. SORRY. I'M SORRY.
THAT'S OKAY.
THE ARMY THAT'S ATTACKING THE CITY WON'T REST THERE. THEY WON'T DISCRIMINATE BETWEEN MY KIND AND YOURS.
THEY HAVE TO BE STOPPED AND AS CRAZY AS IT SOUNDS, THIS MAY BE THE ONLY WAY TO DO IT.
CRAZY. THAT'S AN UNDERSTATE-MENT AND A HALF.
WE CAN'T KEEP COWERING IN CORNERS, IGNORING WHAT'S HAPPENING. THE WORLD CHANGED WHEN THE BLIGHT HIT, AND THOSE LEFT BEHIND HAD TO ADAPT TO SURVIVE IN IT.
NOW WE'VE GOT TO DO IT AGAIN.
LOOK AT THEM, THIS IS THEIR WORLD NOW AND WE'RE PART OF IT. DO WE RUN AND HIDE OR JOIN THEM?

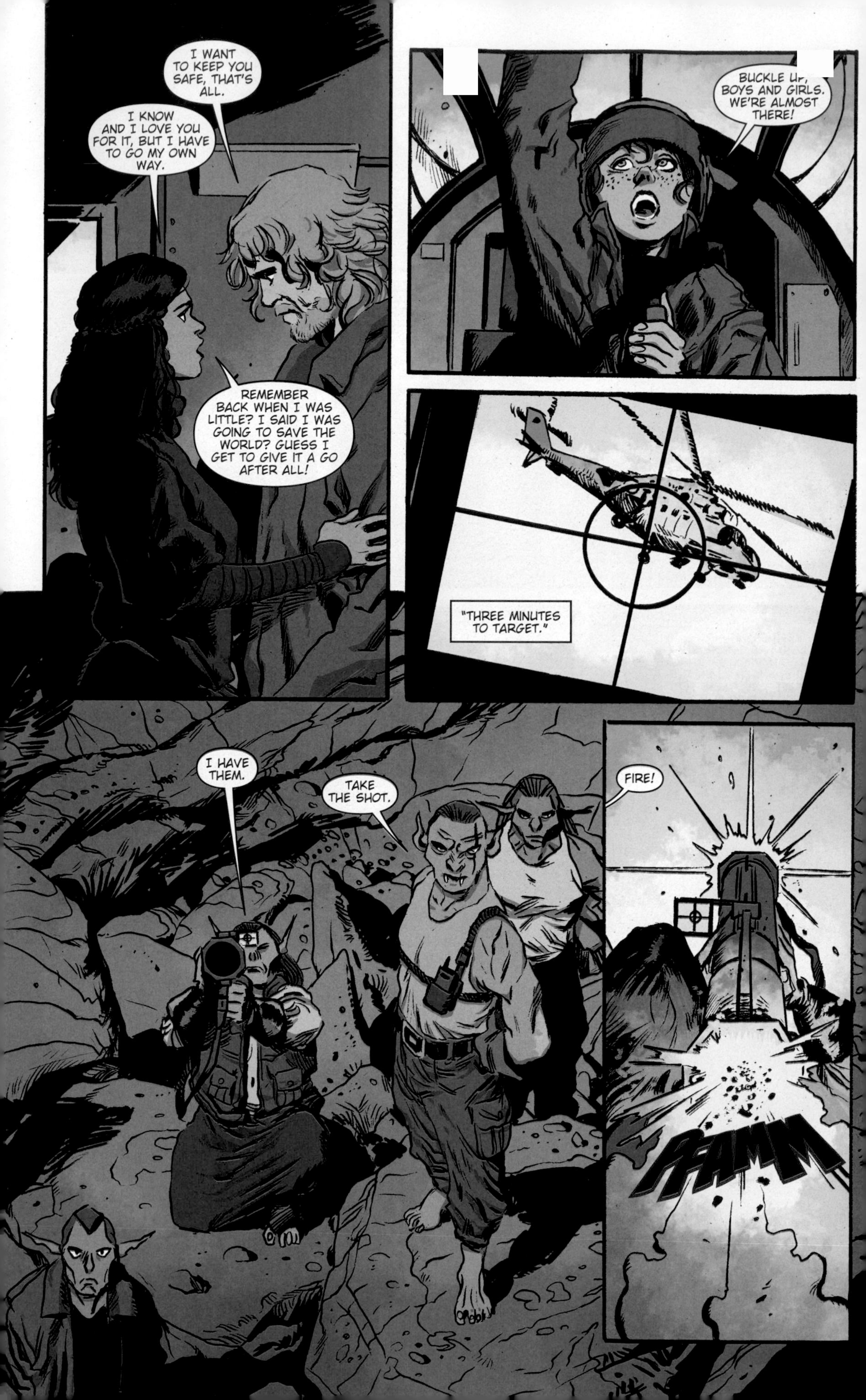
I WANT TO KEEP YOU SAFE, THAT'S ALL.
I KNOW AND I LOVE YOU FOR IT, BUT I HAVE TO GO MY OWN WAY.
REMEMBER BACK WHEN I WAS LITTLE? I SAID I WAS GOING TO SAVE THE WORLD? GUESS I GET TO GIVE IT A GO AFTER ALL!
BUCKLE UP, BOYS AND GIRLS. WE'RE ALMOST THERE!
"THREE MINUTES TO TARGET."
I HAVE THEM.
TAKE THE SHOT.
FIRE!
FFAMM

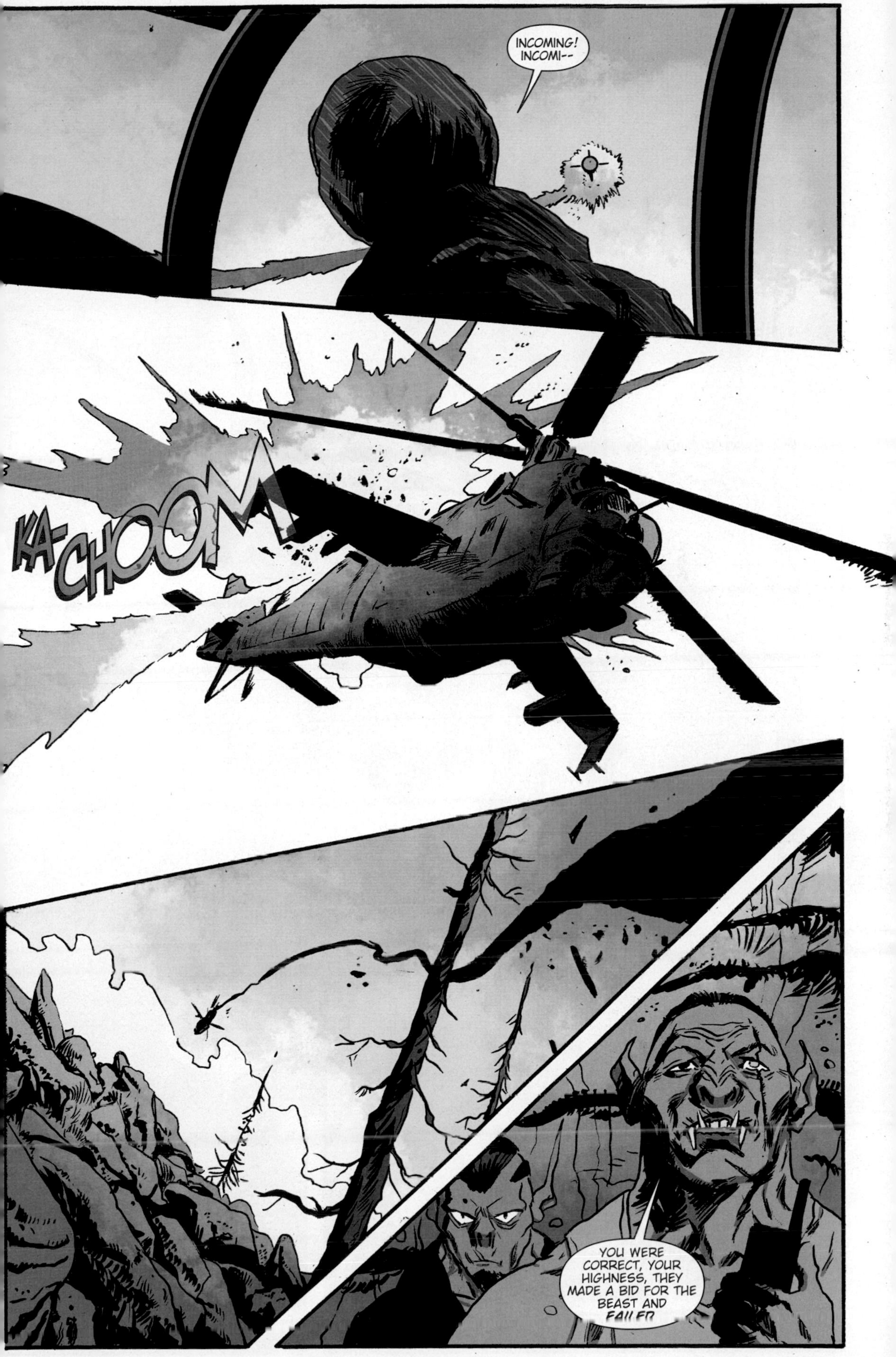
INCOMING! INCOMI--
KA-CHOOM
YOU WERE CORRECT, YOUR HIGHNESS, THEY MADE A BID FOR THE BEAST AND FAILED

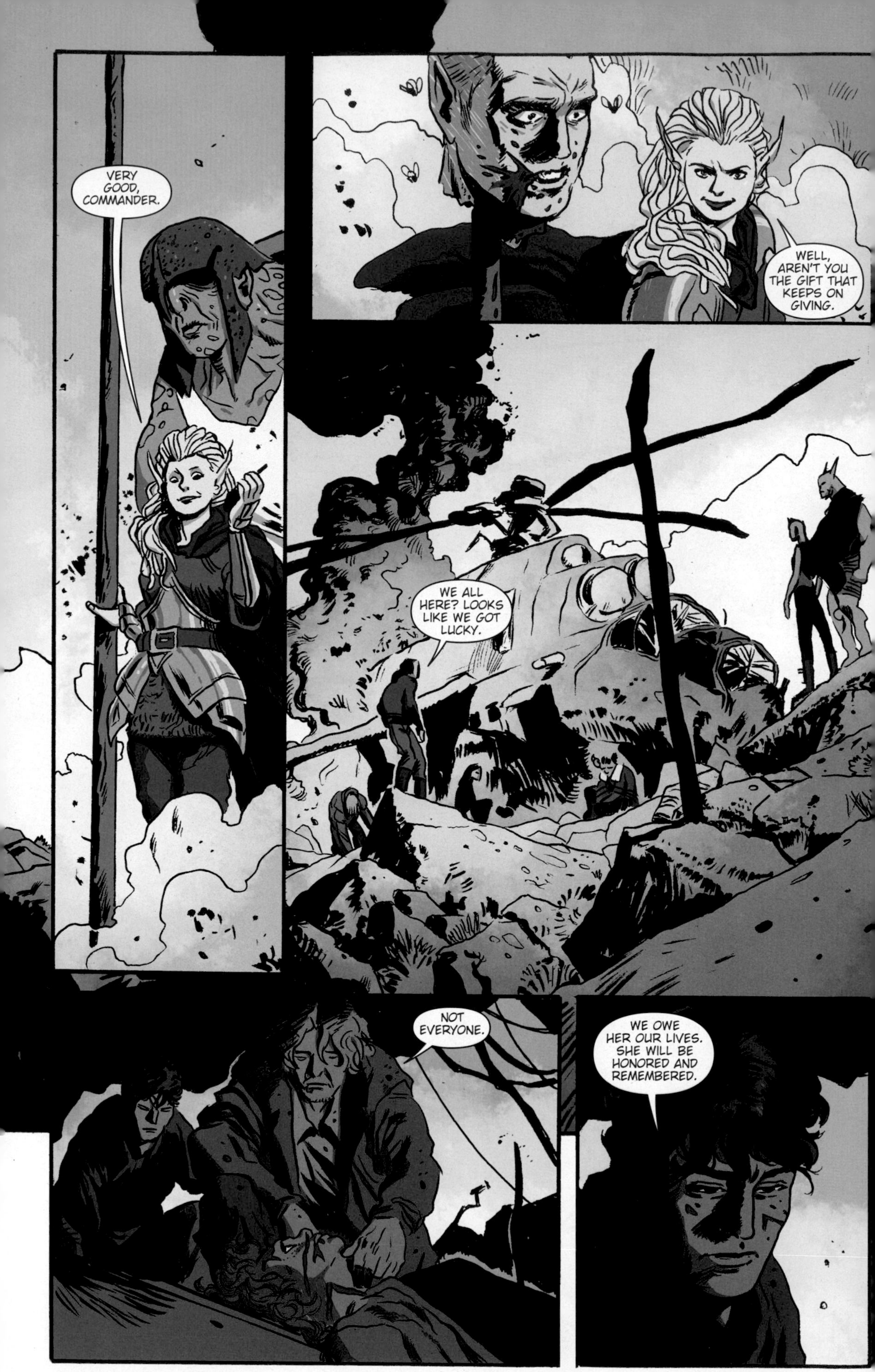
VERY GOOD, COMMANDER.
WELL, AREN'T YOU THE GIFT THAT KEEPS ON GIVING.
WE ALL HERE? LOOKS LIKE WE GOT LUCKY.
NOT EVERYONE.
WE OWE HER OUR LIVES. SHE WILL BE HONORED AND REMEMBERED.

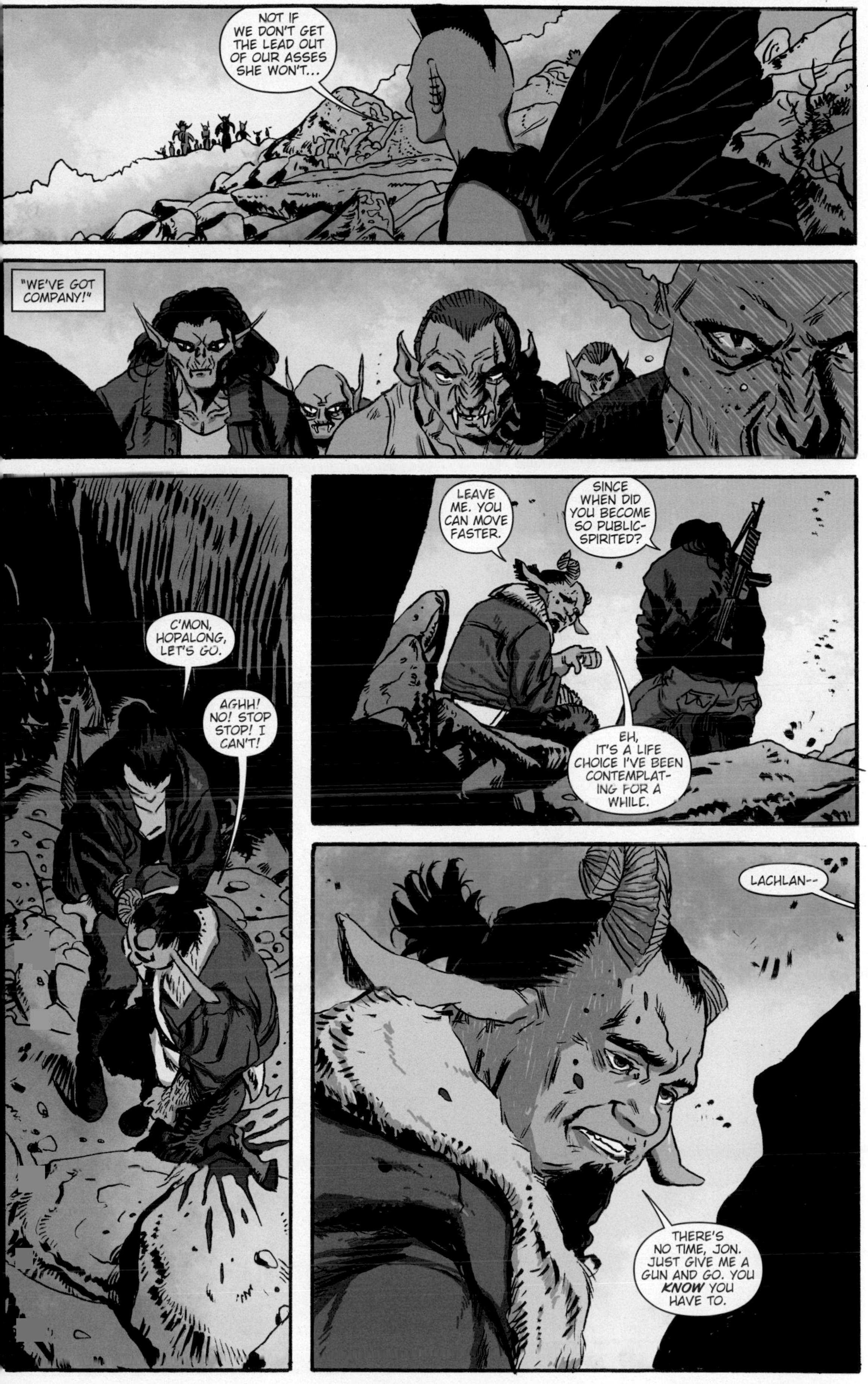
NOT IF WE DON'T GET THE LEAD OUT OF OUR ASSES SHE WON'T...
"WE'VE GOT COMPANY!"
C'MON, HOPALONG, LET'S GO.
AGHH! NO! STOP STOP! I CAN'T!
LEAVE ME. YOU CAN MOVE FASTER.
SINCE WHEN DID YOU BECOME SO PUBLIC-SPIRITED?
EH, IT'S A LIFE CHOICE I'VE BEEN CONTEMPLATING FOR A WHILE.
LACHLAN--
THERE'S NO TIME, JON. JUST GIVE ME A GUN AND GO. YOU KNOW YOU HAVE TO.

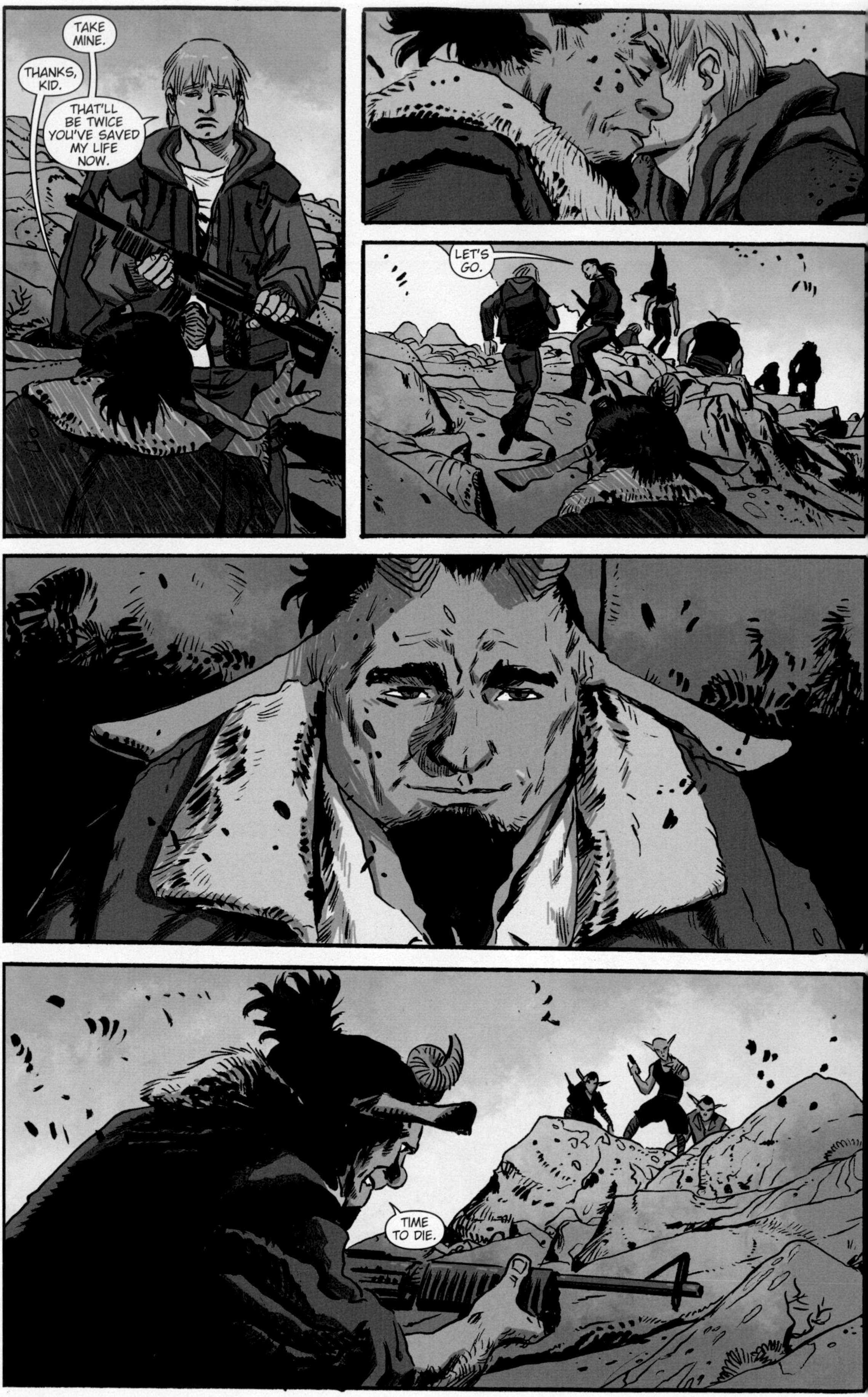
TAKE MINE.
THANKS, KID.
THAT'LL BE TWICE YOU'VE SAVED MY LIFE NOW.
LET'S GO.
TIME TO DIE.

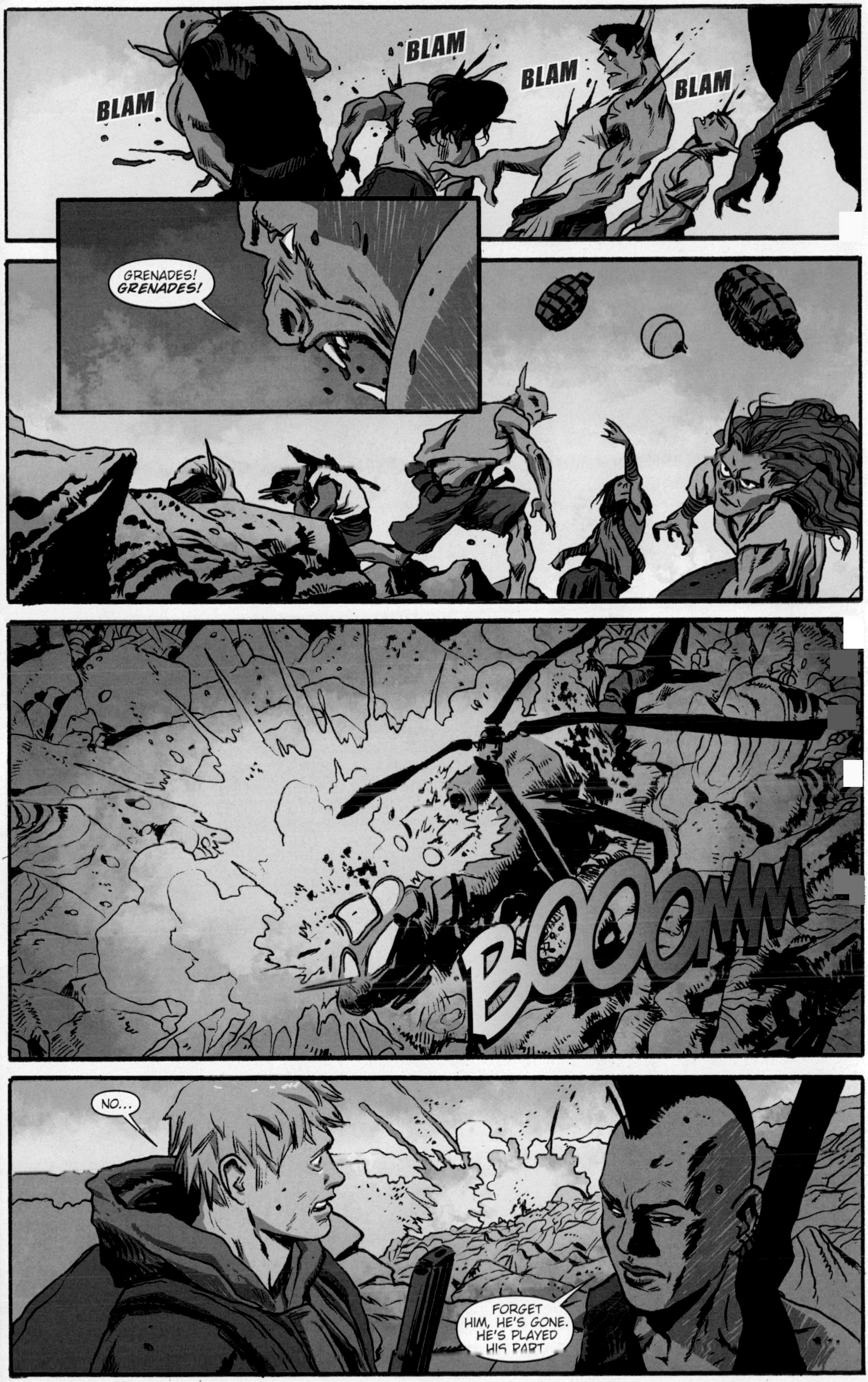
BLAM
BLAM
BLAM
BLAM
GRENADES! GRENADES!
BOOOMM
NO...
FORGET HIM, HE'S GONE. HE'S PLAYED HIS PART

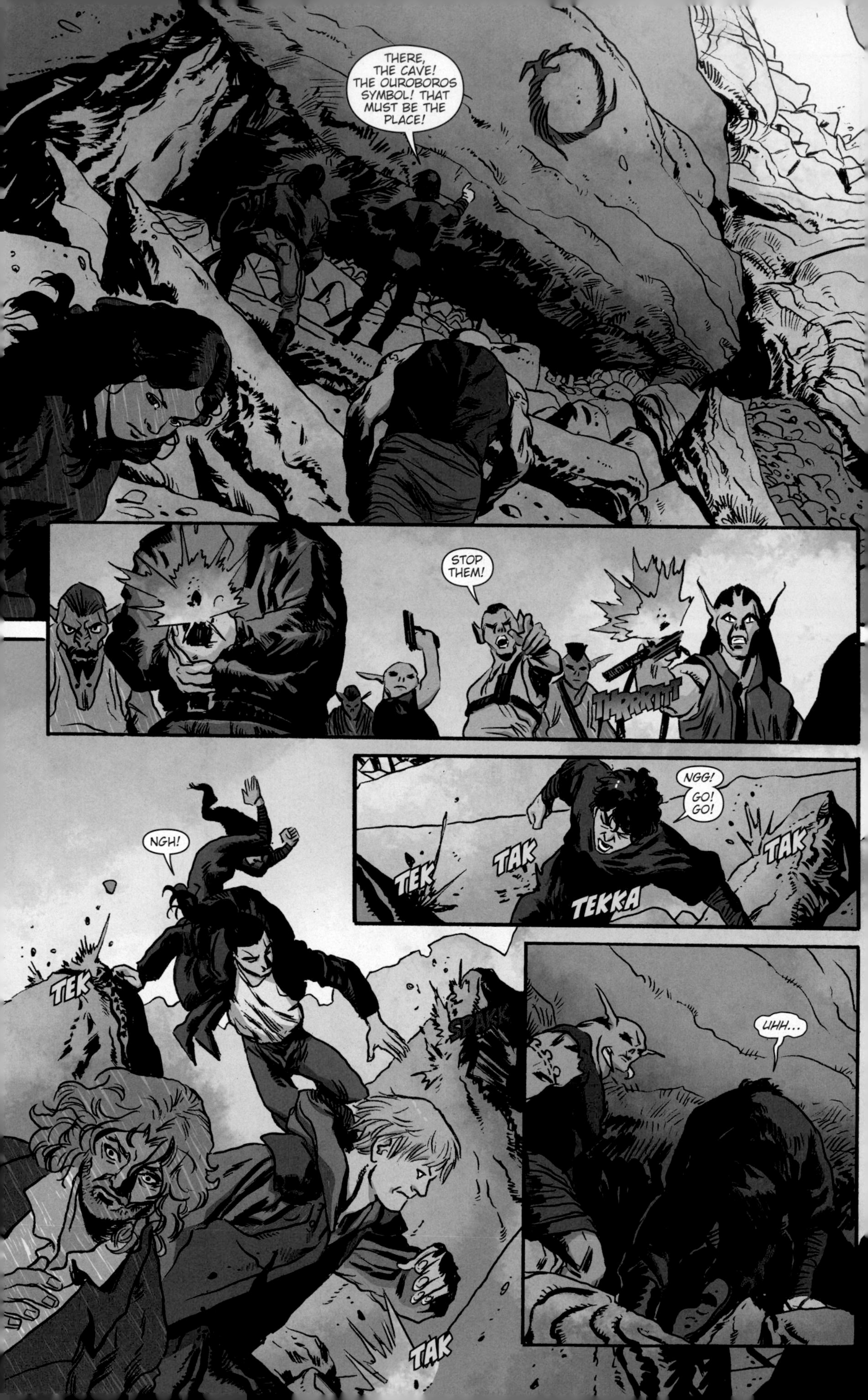
THERE, THE CAVE! THE OUROBOROS SYMBOL! THAT MUST BE THE PLACE!
STOP THEM!
THRRTTT
NGG! GO! GO!
TEK
TAK
TEKKA
TAK
NGH!
TEK
SPAKK
TAK
UHH...

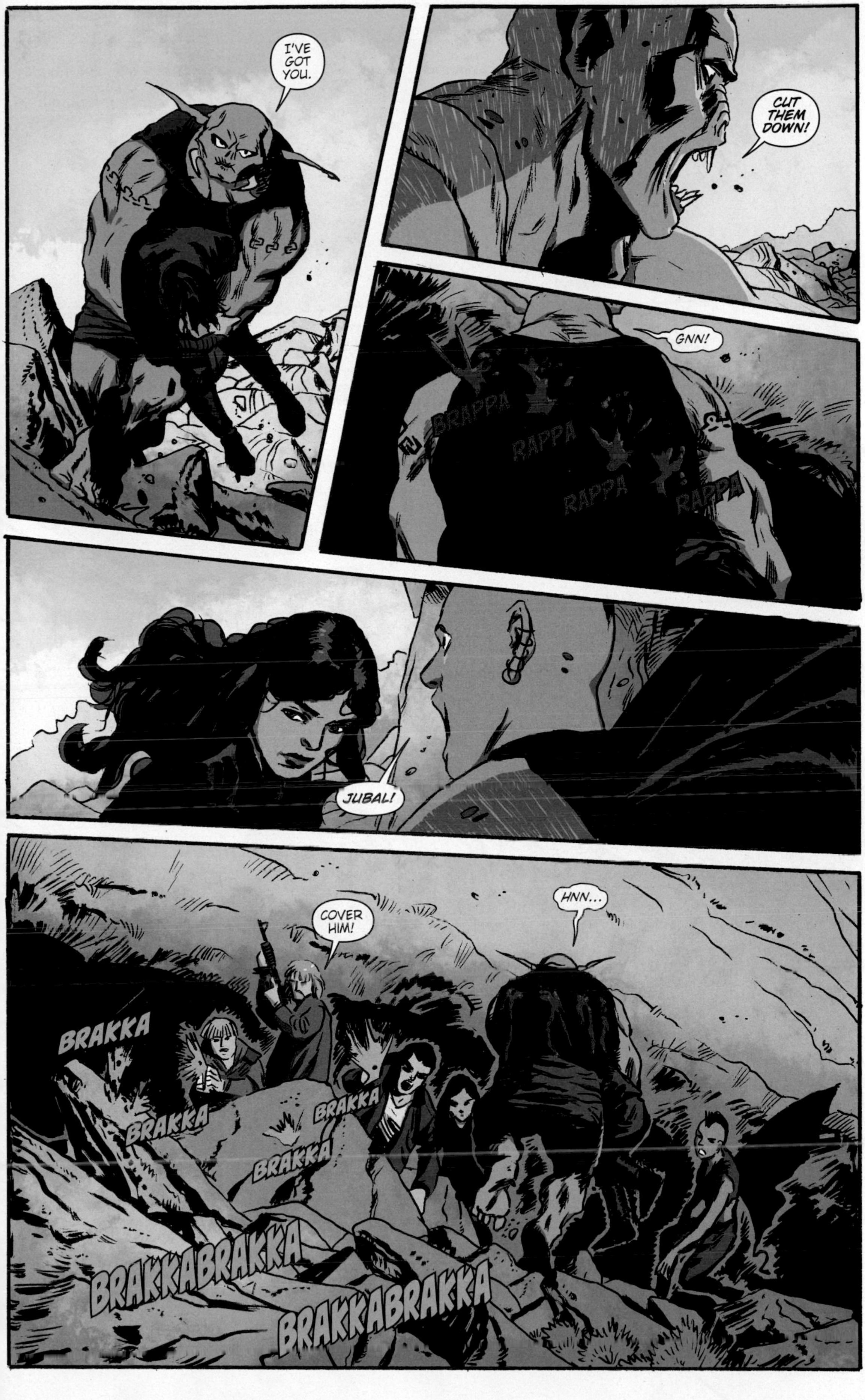
I'VE GOT YOU.
CUT THEM DOWN!
GNN!
BRAPPA
RAPPA
RAPPA
RAPPA
JUBAL!
COVER HIM!
HNN...
BRAKKA
BRAKKA
BRAKKA
BRAKKA
BRAKKABRAKKA
BRAKKABRAKKA

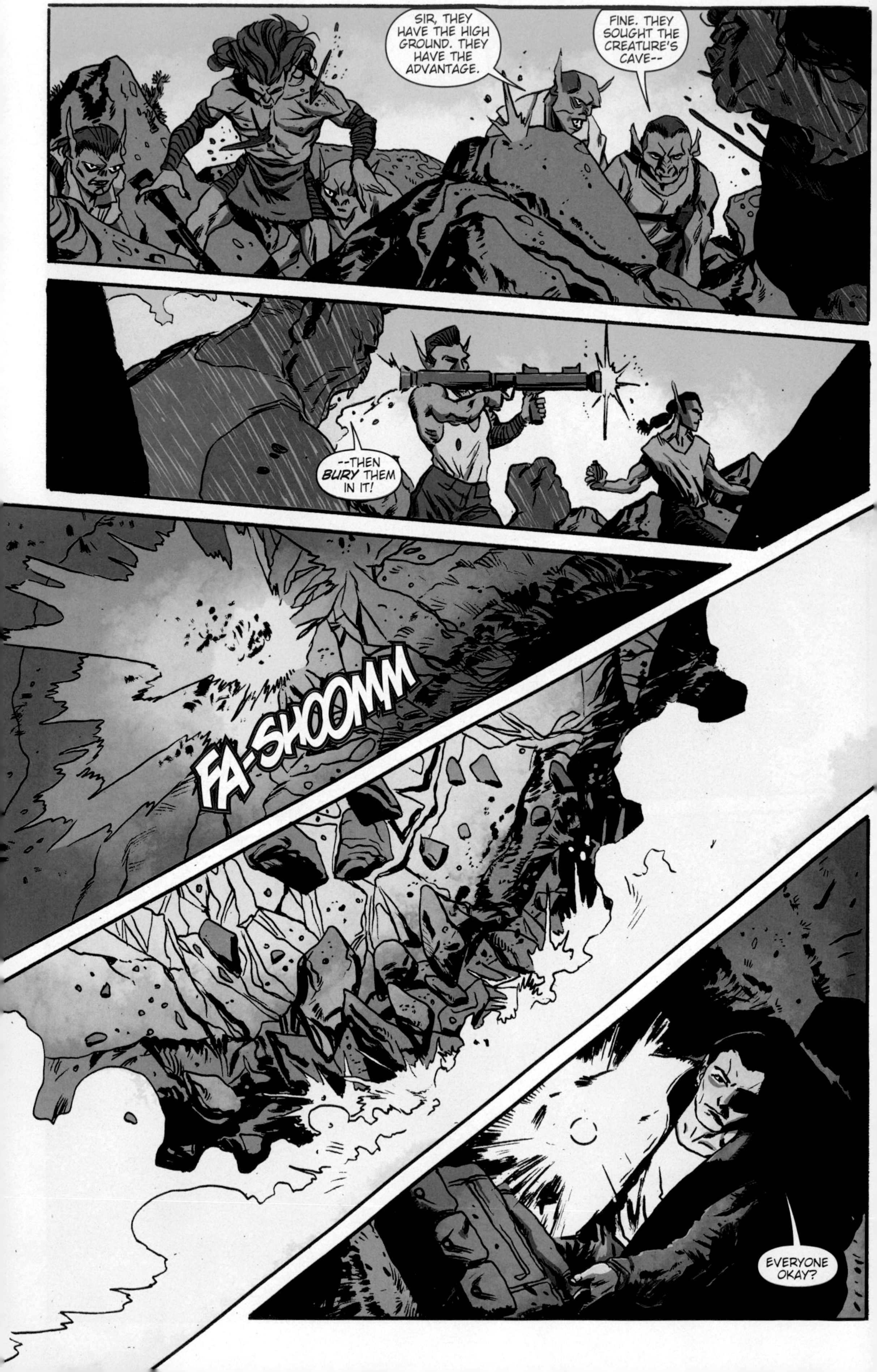
SIR, THEY HAVE THE HIGH GROUND. THEY HAVE THE ADVANTAGE.
FINE. THEY SOUGHT THE CREATURE'S CAVE--
--THEN *BURY* THEM IN IT!
FA-SHOOMM
EVERYONE OKAY?

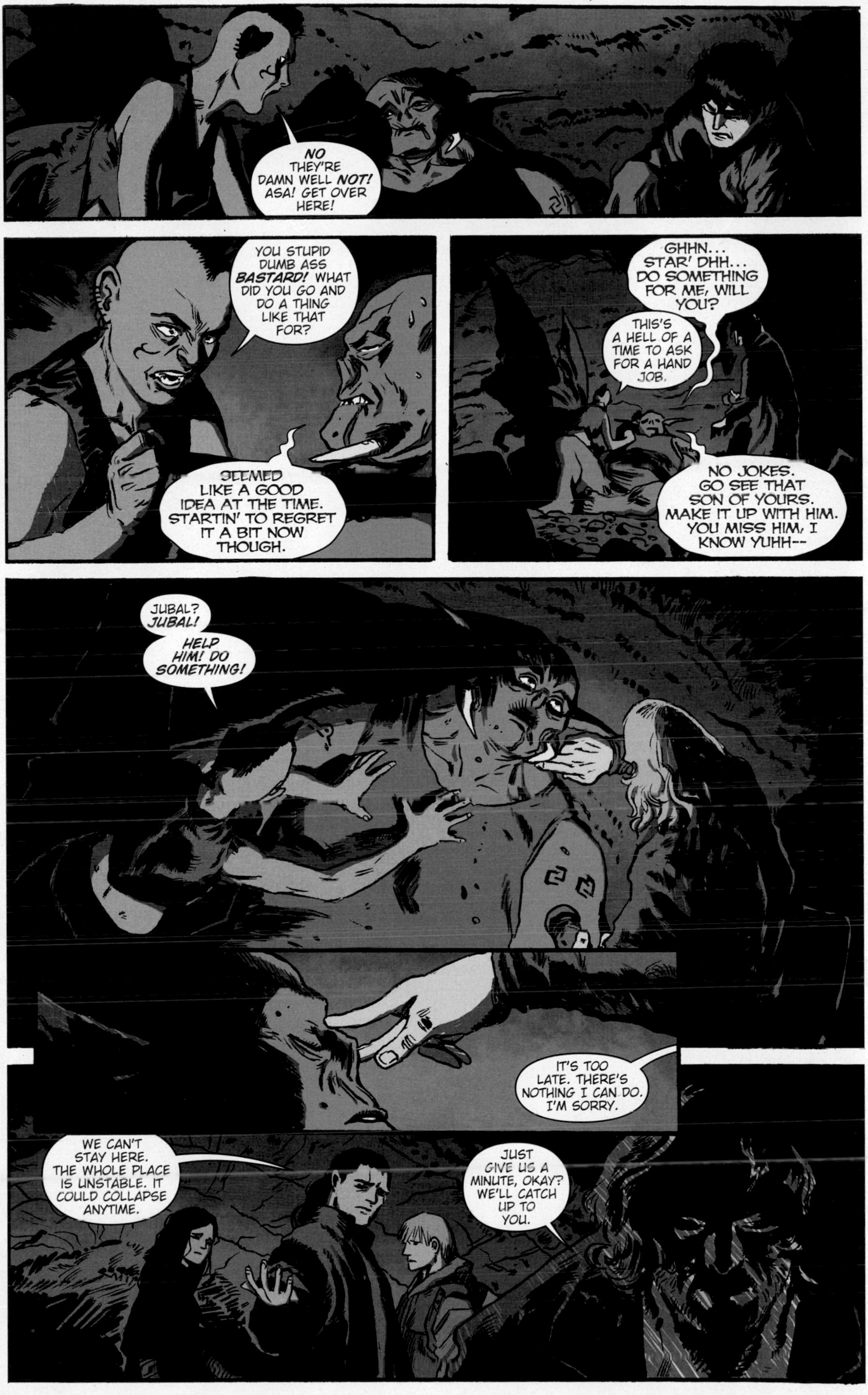
NO THEY'RE DAMN WELL NOT! ASA! GET OVER HERE!
YOU STUPID DUMB ASS BASTARD! WHAT DID YOU GO AND DO A THING LIKE THAT FOR?
SEEMED LIKE A GOOD IDEA AT THE TIME. STARTIN' TO REGRET IT A BIT NOW THOUGH.
GHHN... STAR' DHH... DO SOMETHING FOR ME, WILL YOU?
THIS'S A HELL OF A TIME TO ASK FOR A HAND JOB.
NO JOKES. GO SEE THAT SON OF YOURS. MAKE IT UP WITH HIM. YOU MISS HIM, I KNOW YUHH--
JUBAL? JUBAL!
HELP HIM! DO SOMETHING!
IT'S TOO LATE. THERE'S NOTHING I CAN DO. I'M SORRY.
WE CAN'T STAY HERE. THE WHOLE PLACE IS UNSTABLE. IT COULD COLLAPSE ANYTIME.
JUST GIVE US A MINUTE, OKAY? WE'LL CATCH UP TO YOU.

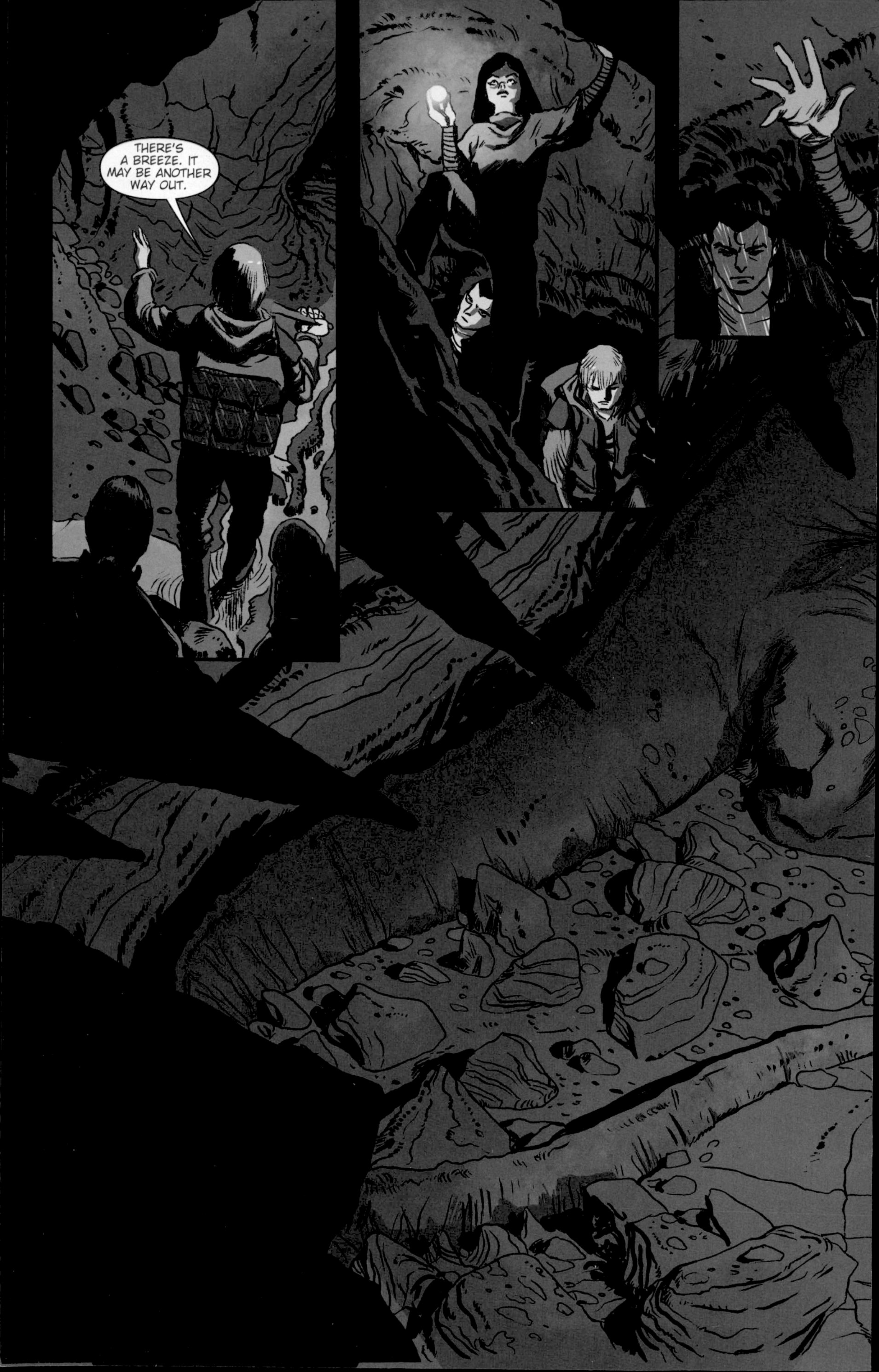
THERE'S A BREEZE. IT MAY BE ANOTHER WAY OUT.

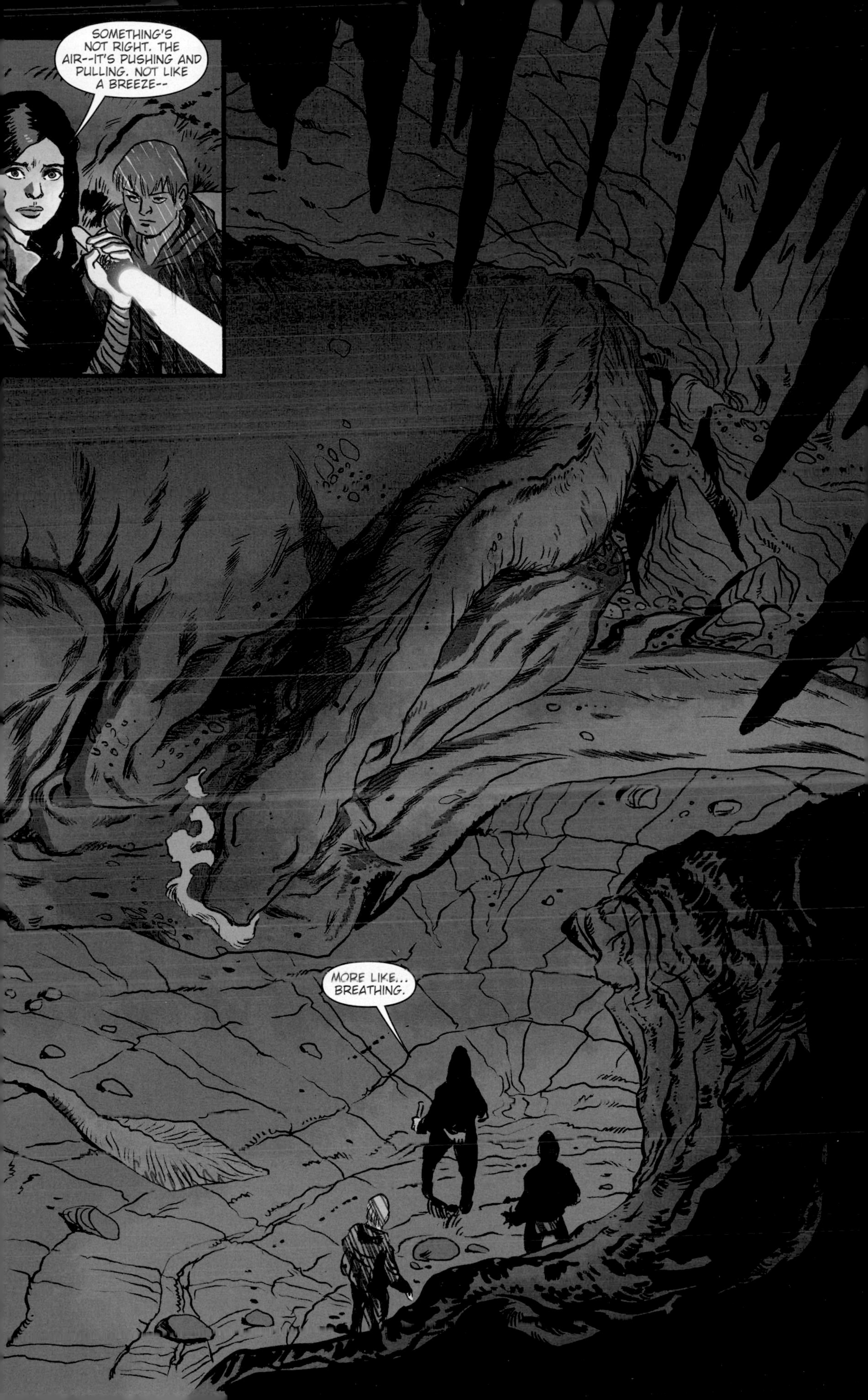
SOMETHING'S NOT RIGHT. THE AIR--IT'S PUSHING AND PULLING. NOT LIKE A BREEZE--
MORE LIKE... BREATHING.

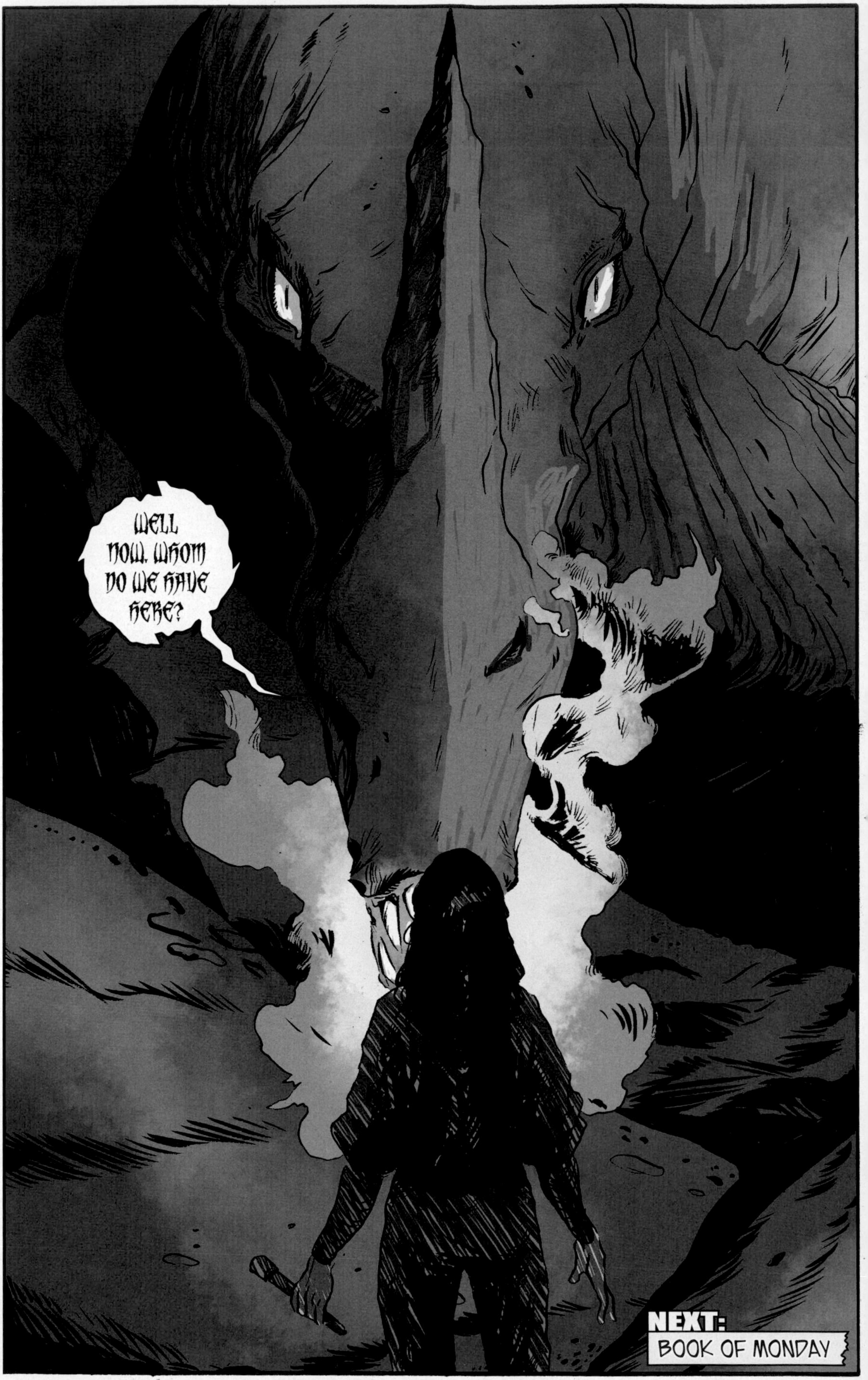
WELL NOW. WHOM DO WE HAVE HERE?
NEXT:
BOOK OF MONDAY

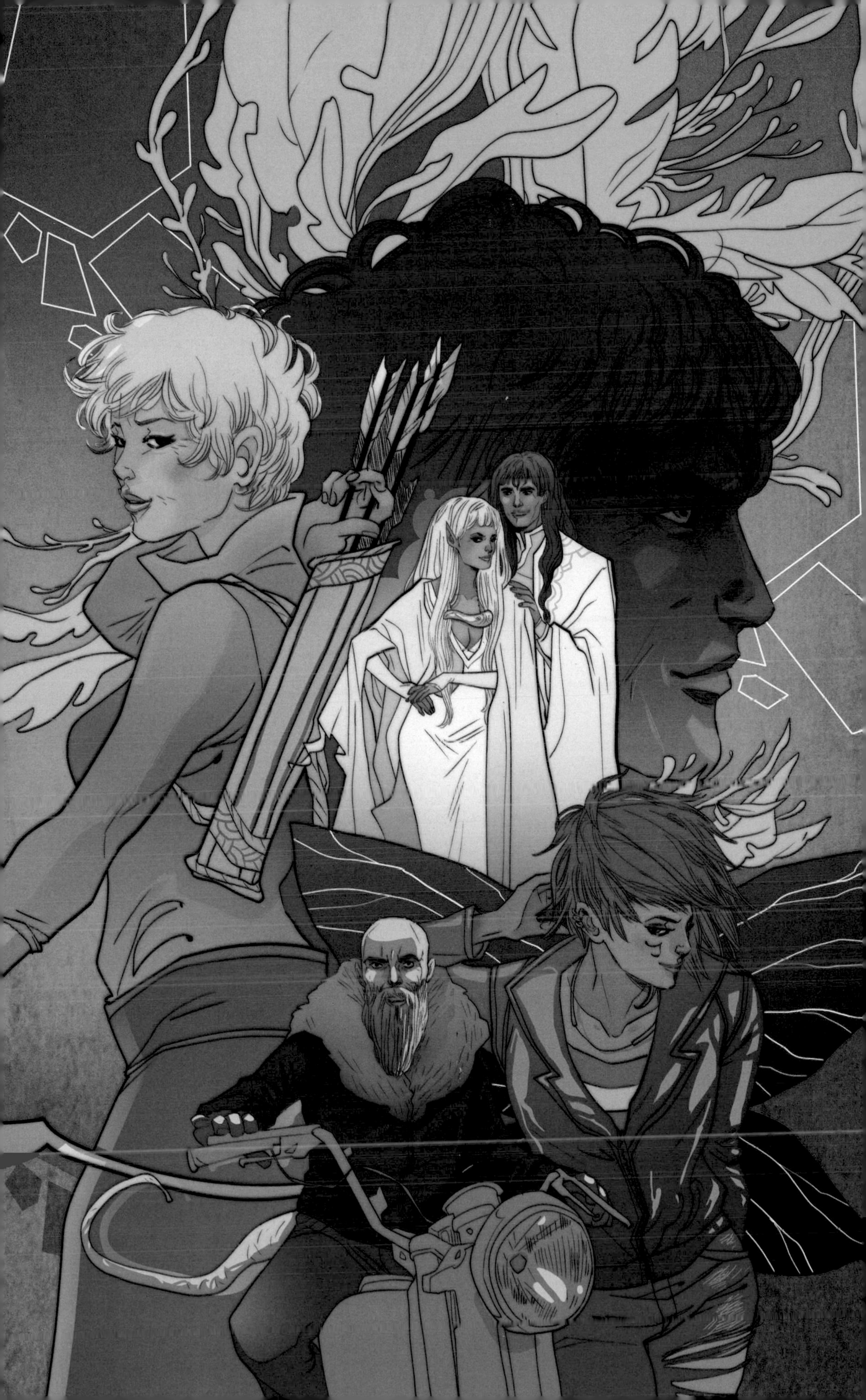

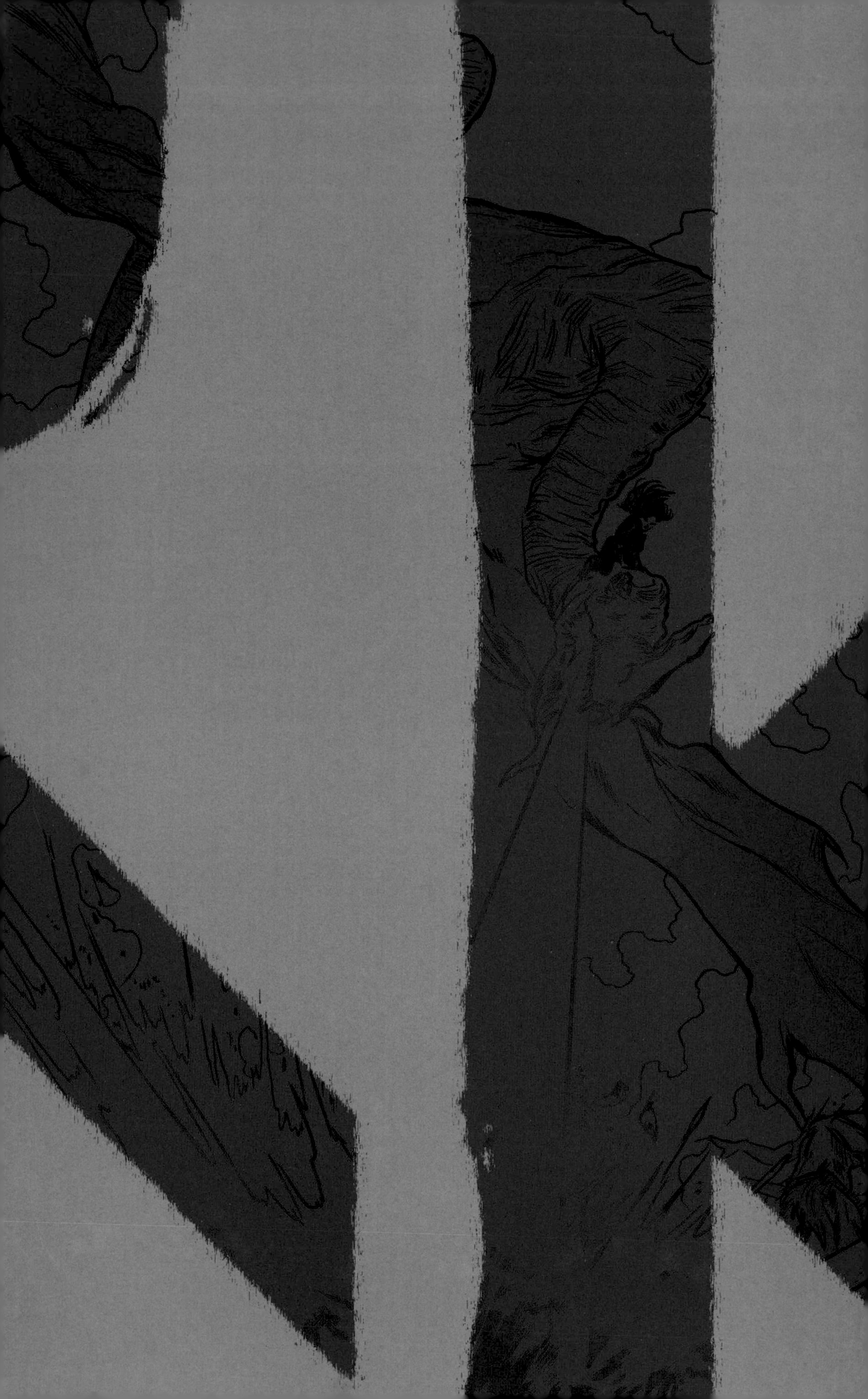

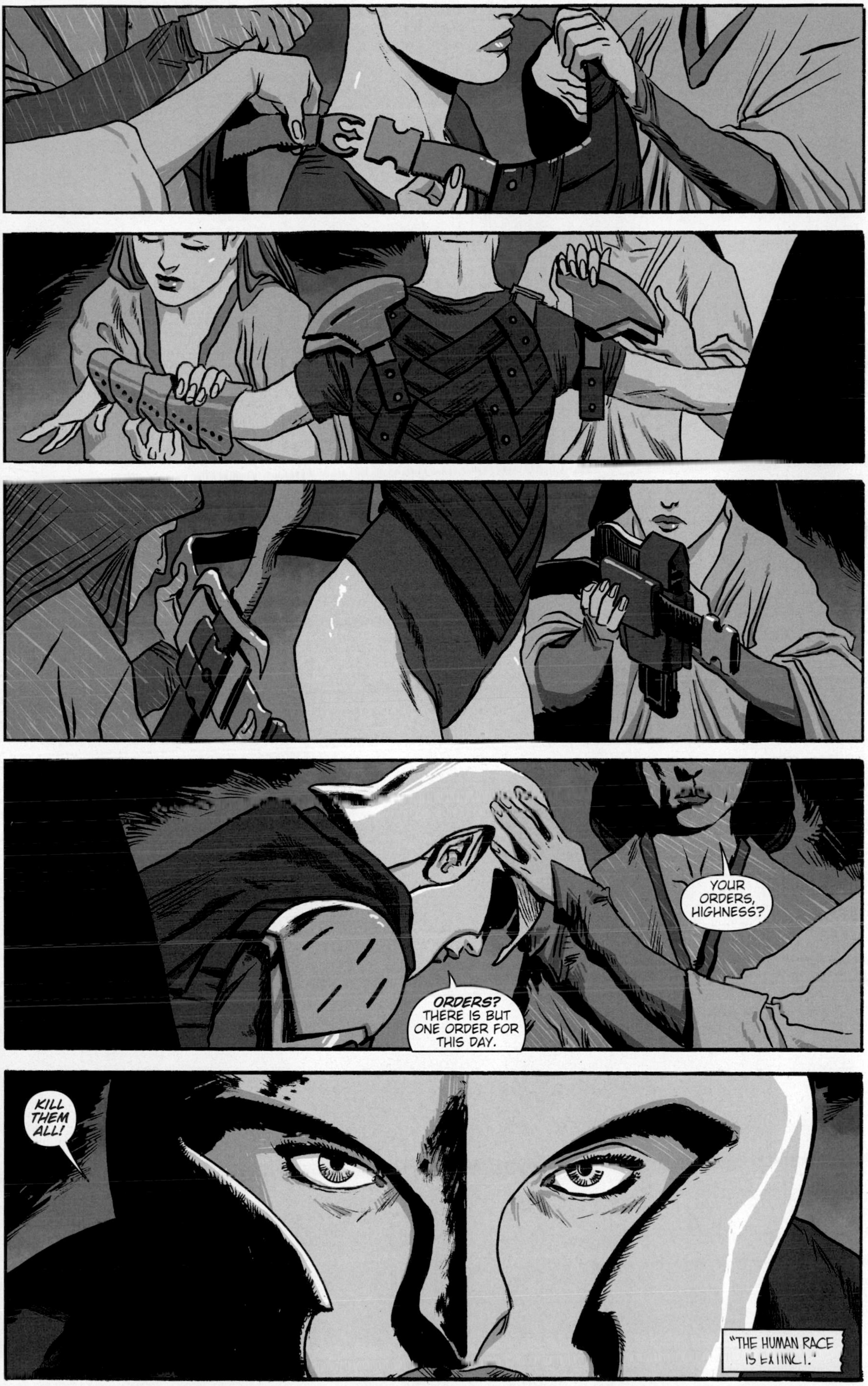
YOUR ORDERS, HIGHNESS?
ORDERS? THERE IS BUT ONE ORDER FOR THIS DAY.
KILL THEM ALL!
"THE HUMAN RACE IS EXTINCT."

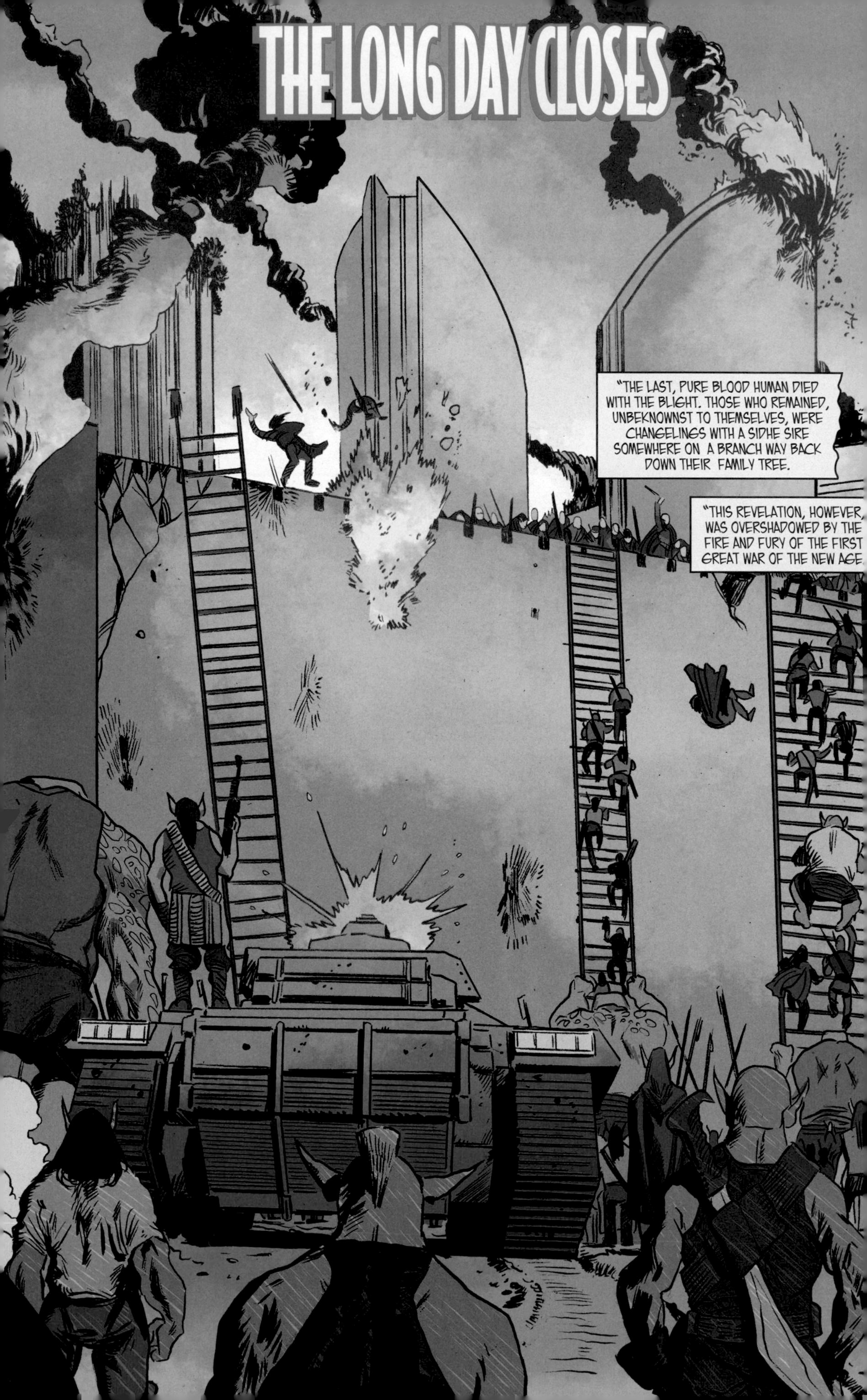
THE LONG DAY CLOSES
"THE LAST, PURE BLOOD HUMAN DIED WITH THE BLIGHT. THOSE WHO REMAINED, UNBEKNOWNST TO THEMSELVES, WERE CHANGELINGS WITH A SIDHE SIRE SOMEWHERE ON A BRANCH WAY BACK DOWN THEIR FAMILY TREE.
"THIS REVELATION, HOWEVER, WAS OVERSHADOWED BY THE FIRE AND FURY OF THE FIRST GREAT WAR OF THE NEW AGE.

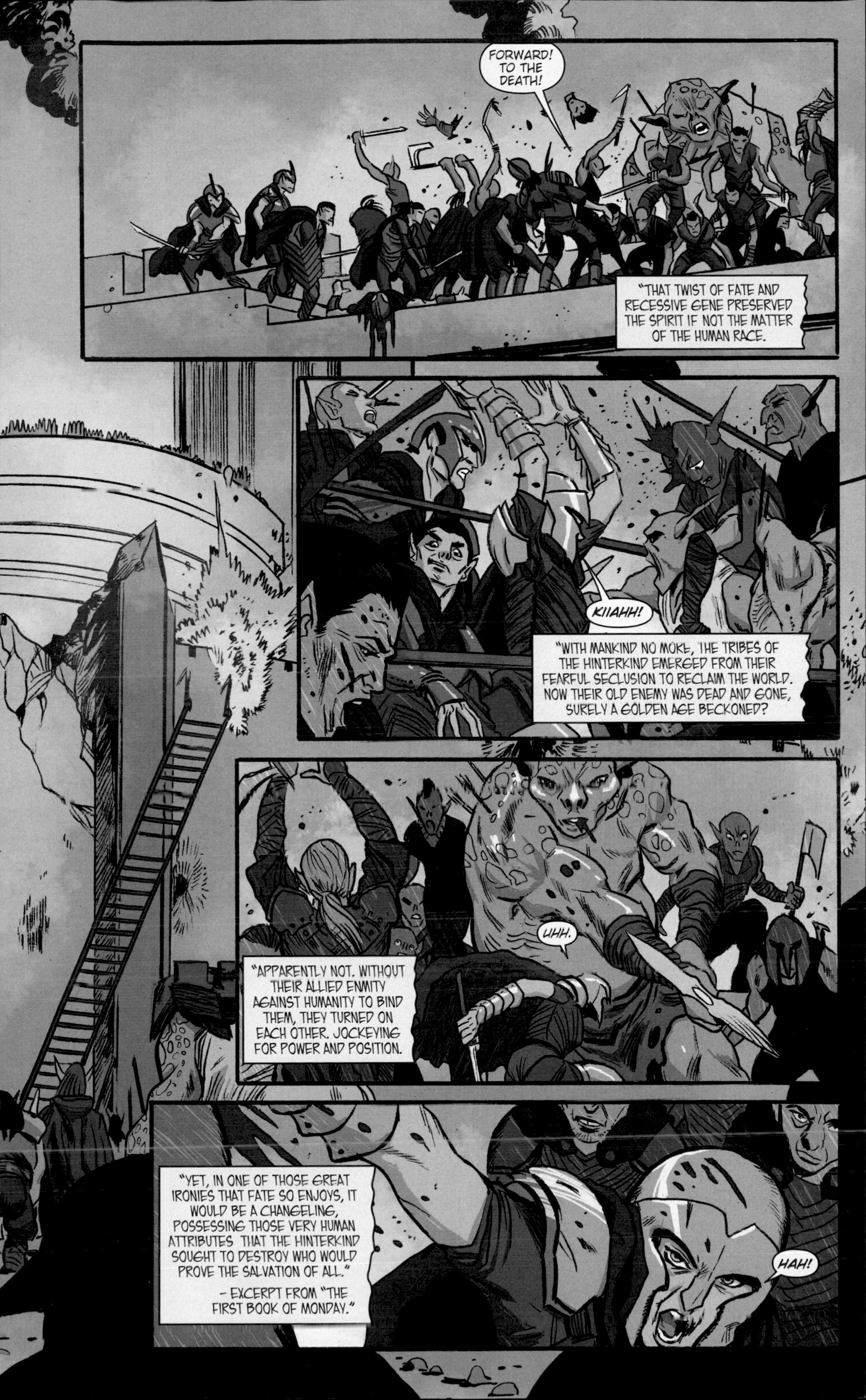
FORWARD! TO THE DEATH!
"THAT TWIST OF FATE AND RECESSIVE GENE PRESERVED THE SPIRIT IF NOT THE MATTER OF THE HUMAN RACE.
KIIAHH!
"WITH MANKIND NO MORE, THE TRIBES OF THE HINTERKIND EMERGED FROM THEIR FEARFUL SECLUSION TO RECLAIM THE WORLD. NOW THEIR OLD ENEMY WAS DEAD AND GONE, SURELY A GOLDEN AGE BECKONED?
UHH.
"APPARENTLY NOT. WITHOUT THEIR ALLIED ENMITY AGAINST HUMANITY TO BIND THEM, THEY TURNED ON EACH OTHER. JOCKEYING FOR POWER AND POSITION.
"YET, IN ONE OF THOSE GREAT IRONIES THAT FATE SO ENJOYS, IT WOULD BE A CHANGELING, POSSESSING THOSE VERY HUMAN ATTRIBUTES THAT THE HINTERKIND SOUGHT TO DESTROY WHO WOULD PROVE THE SALVATION OF ALL."
– EXCERPT FROM "THE FIRST BOOK OF MONDAY."
HAH!

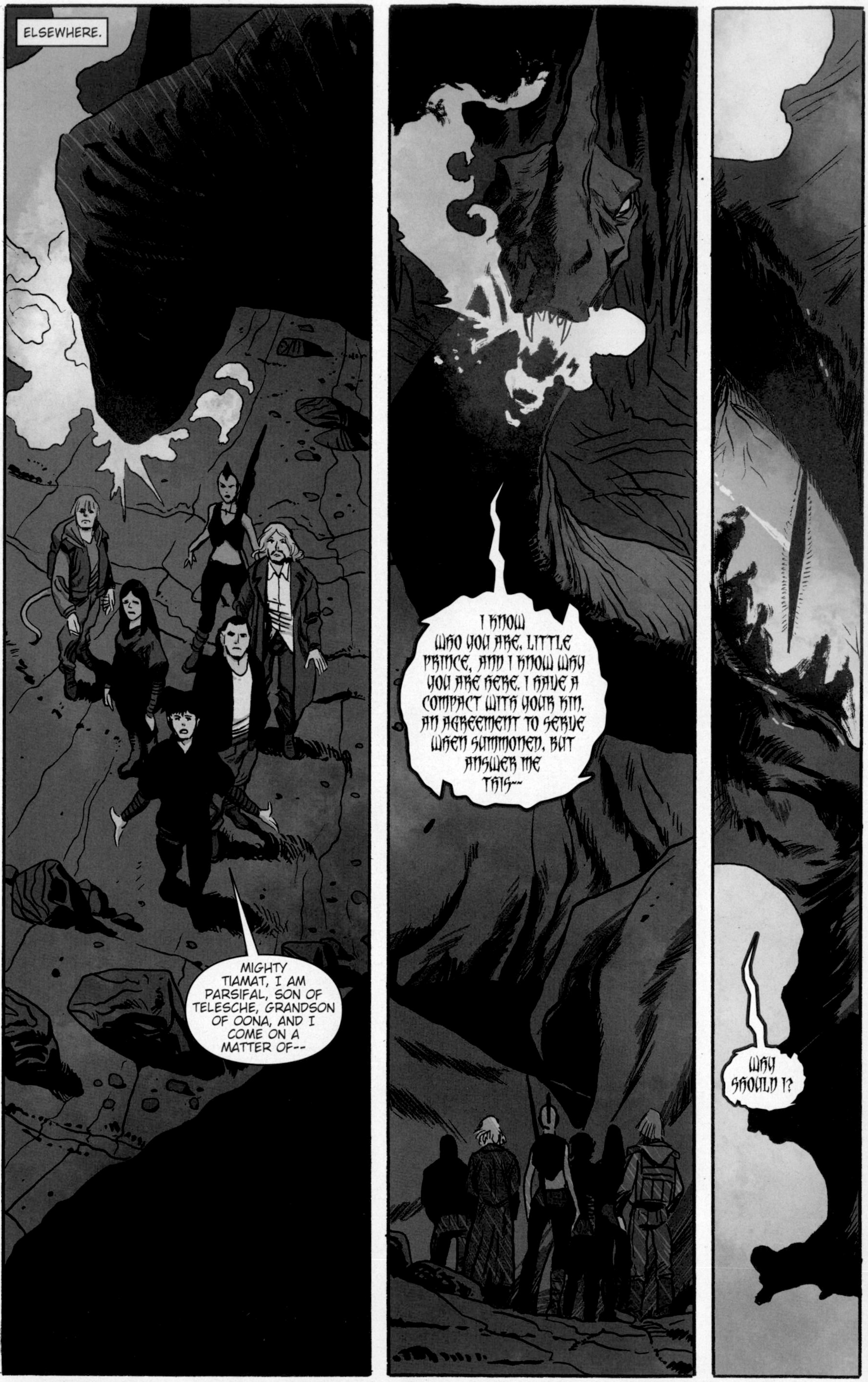
ELSEWHERE.
MIGHTY TIAMAT, I AM PARSIFAL, SON OF TELESCHE, GRANDSON OF OONA, AND I COME ON A MATTER OF--
I KNOW WHO YOU ARE, LITTLE PRINCE, AND I KNOW WHY YOU ARE HERE. I HAVE A COMPACT WITH YOUR KIN. AN AGREEMENT TO SERVE WHEN SUMMONED, BUT ANSWER ME THIS--
WHY SHOULD I?

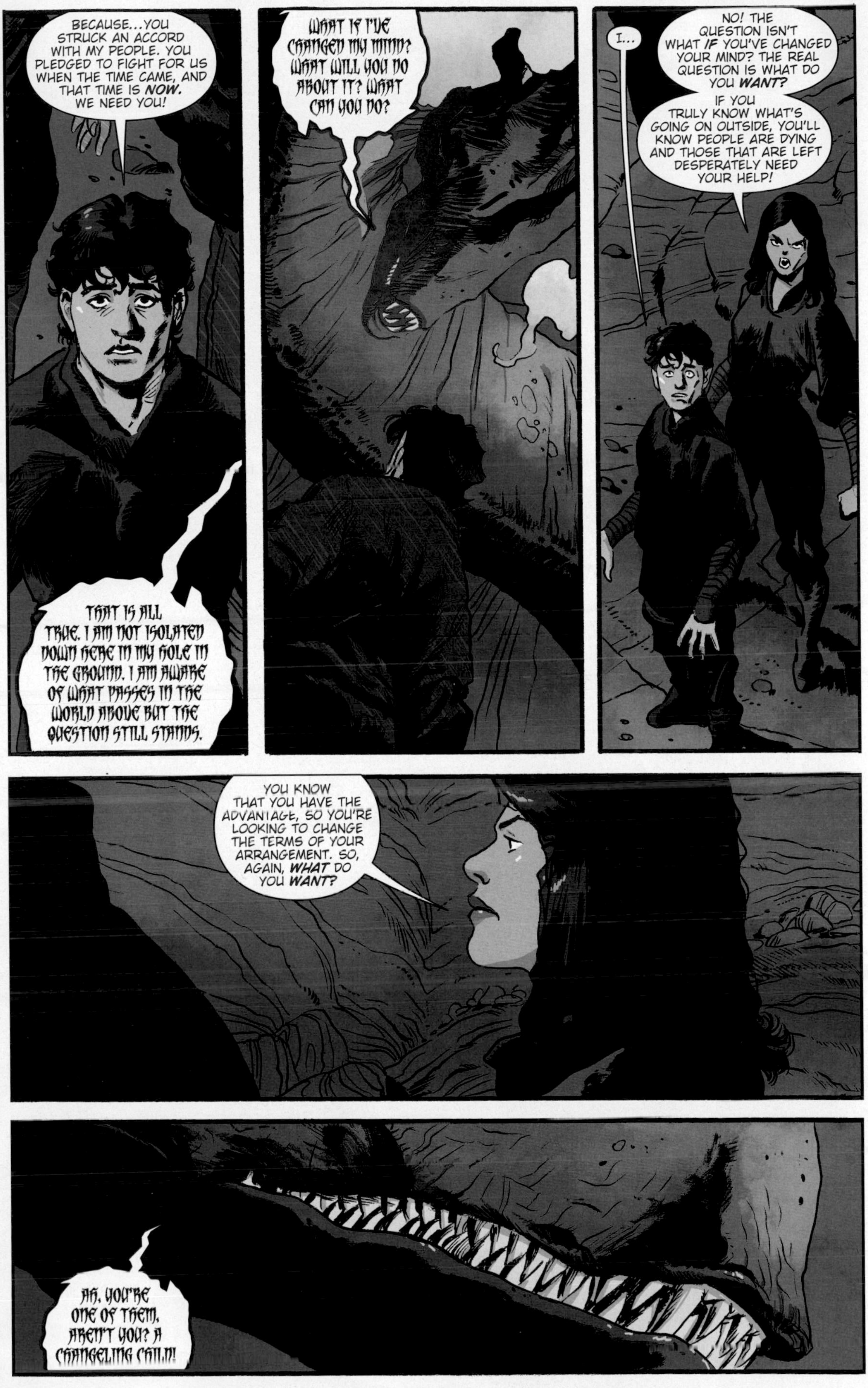
BECAUSE...YOU STRUCK AN ACCORD WITH MY PEOPLE. YOU PLEDGED TO FIGHT FOR US WHEN THE TIME CAME, AND THAT TIME IS NOW. WE NEED YOU!
THAT IS ALL TRUE. I AM NOT ISOLATED DOWN HERE IN MY HOLE IN THE GROUND. I AM AWARE OF WHAT PASSES IN THE WORLD ABOVE BUT THE QUESTION STILL STANDS.
WHAT IF I'VE CHANGED MY MIND? WHAT WILL YOU DO ABOUT IT? WHAT CAN YOU DO?
I...
NO! THE QUESTION ISN'T WHAT IF YOU'VE CHANGED YOUR MIND? THE REAL QUESTION IS WHAT DO YOU WANT?
IF YOU TRULY KNOW WHAT'S GOING ON OUTSIDE, YOU'LL KNOW PEOPLE ARE DYING AND THOSE THAT ARE LEFT DESPERATELY NEED YOUR HELP!
YOU KNOW THAT YOU HAVE THE ADVANTAGE, SO YOU'RE LOOKING TO CHANGE THE TERMS OF YOUR ARRANGEMENT. SO, AGAIN, WHAT DO YOU WANT?
AH, YOU'RE ONE OF THEM, AREN'T YOU? A CHANGELING CHILD!

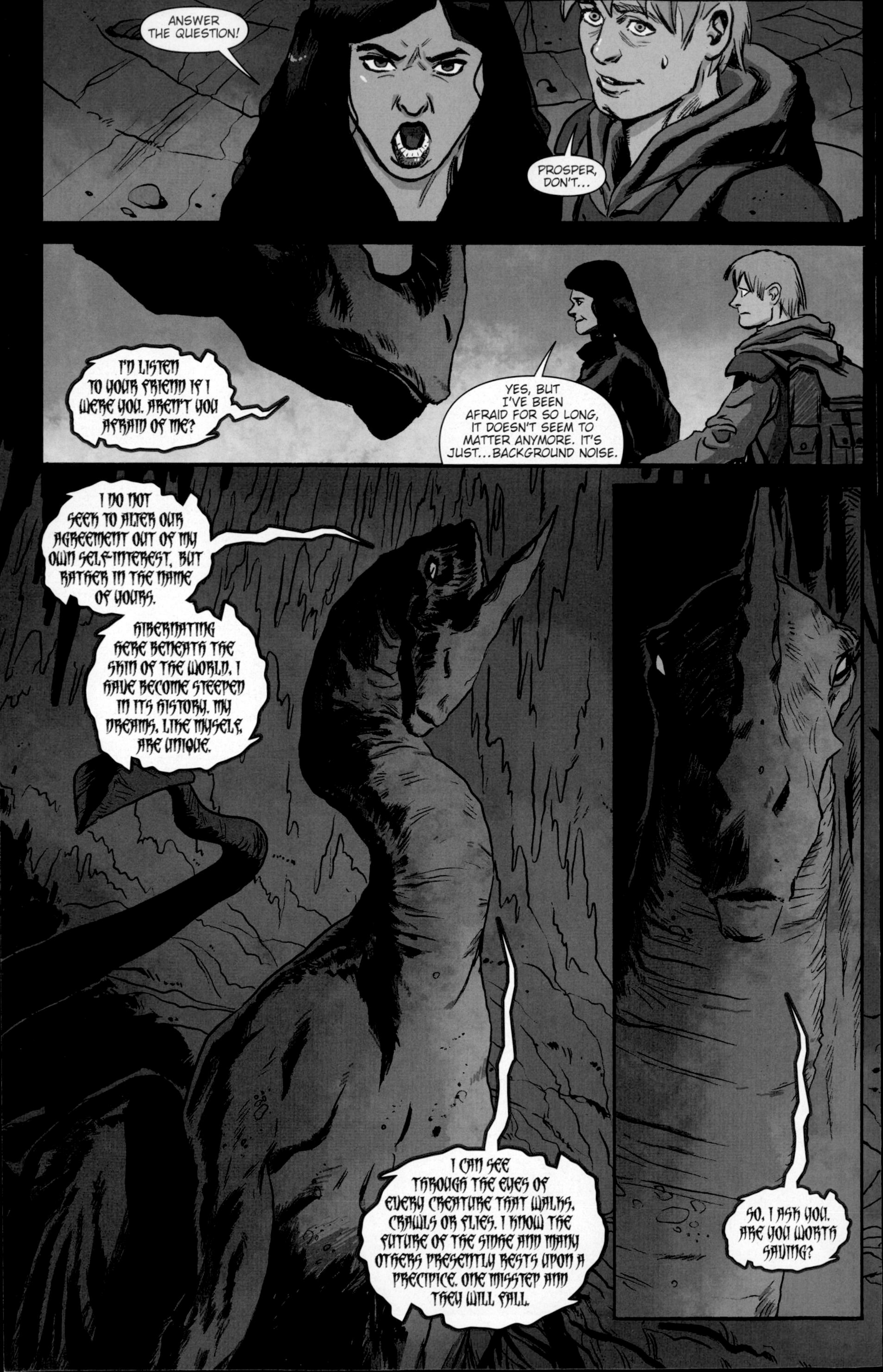
ANSWER THE QUESTION!
PROSPER, DON'T...
I'D LISTEN TO YOUR FRIEND IF I WERE YOU. AREN'T YOU AFRAID OF ME?
YES, BUT I'VE BEEN AFRAID FOR SO LONG, IT DOESN'T SEEM TO MATTER ANYMORE. IT'S JUST...BACKGROUND NOISE.
I DO NOT SEEK TO ALTER OUR AGREEMENT OUT OF MY OWN SELF-INTEREST, BUT RATHER IN THE NAME OF YOURS.
HIBERNATING HERE BENEATH THE SKIN OF THE WORLD, I HAVE BECOME STEEPED IN ITS HISTORY. MY DREAMS, LIKE MYSELF, ARE UNIQUE.
I CAN SEE THROUGH THE EYES OF EVERY CREATURE THAT WALKS, CRAWLS OR FLIES. I KNOW THE FUTURE OF THE SIDHE AND MANY OTHERS PRESENTLY RESTS UPON A PRECIPICE. ONE MISSTEP AND THEY WILL FALL.
SO, I ASK YOU. ARE YOU WORTH SAVING?

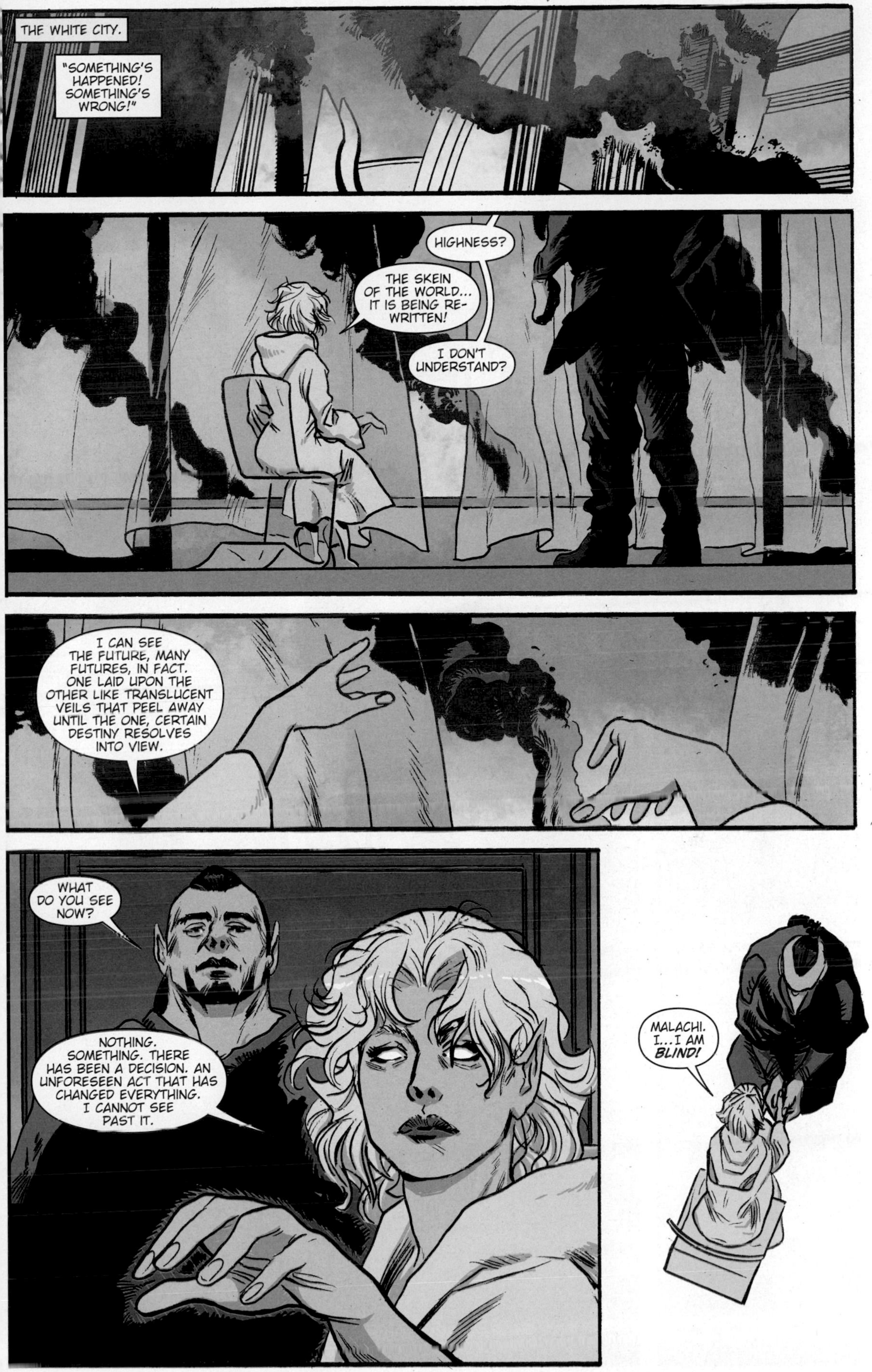
THE WHITE CITY.
"SOMETHING'S HAPPENED! SOMETHING'S WRONG!"
HIGHNESS?
THE SKEIN OF THE WORLD... IT IS BEING RE-WRITTEN!
I DON'T UNDERSTAND?
I CAN SEE THE FUTURE, MANY FUTURES, IN FACT. ONE LAID UPON THE OTHER LIKE TRANSLUCENT VEILS THAT PEEL AWAY UNTIL THE ONE, CERTAIN DESTINY RESOLVES INTO VIEW.
WHAT DO YOU SEE NOW?
NOTHING. SOMETHING. THERE HAS BEEN A DECISION. AN UNFORESEEN ACT THAT HAS CHANGED EVERYTHING. I CANNOT SEE PAST IT.
MALACHI. I...I AM *BLIND!*

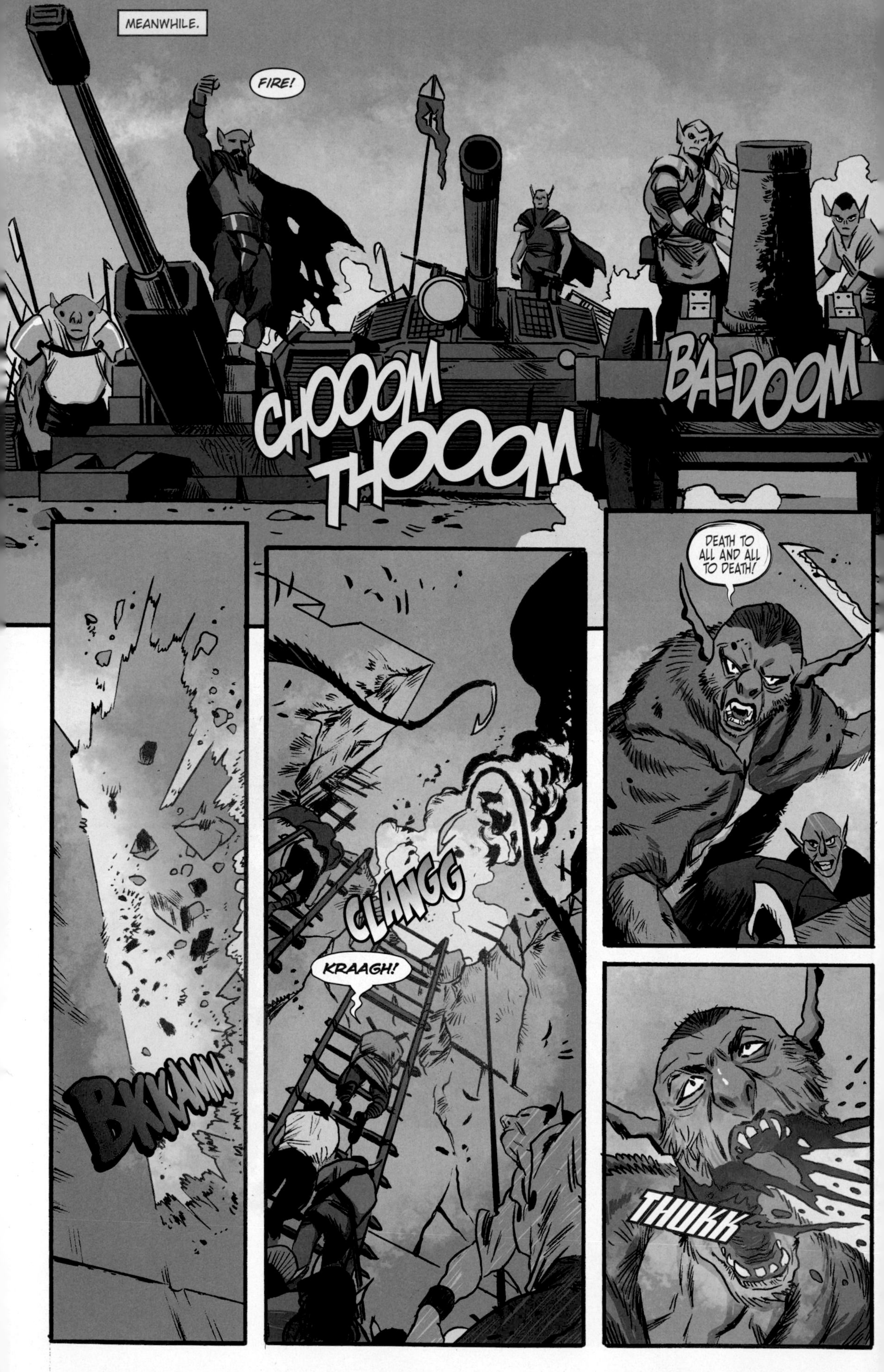
MEANWHILE.
FIRE!
CHOOOM
THOOOM
BA-DOOM
BKKAMM
CLANGG
KRAAGH!
DEATH TO ALL AND ALL TO DEATH!
THUKK

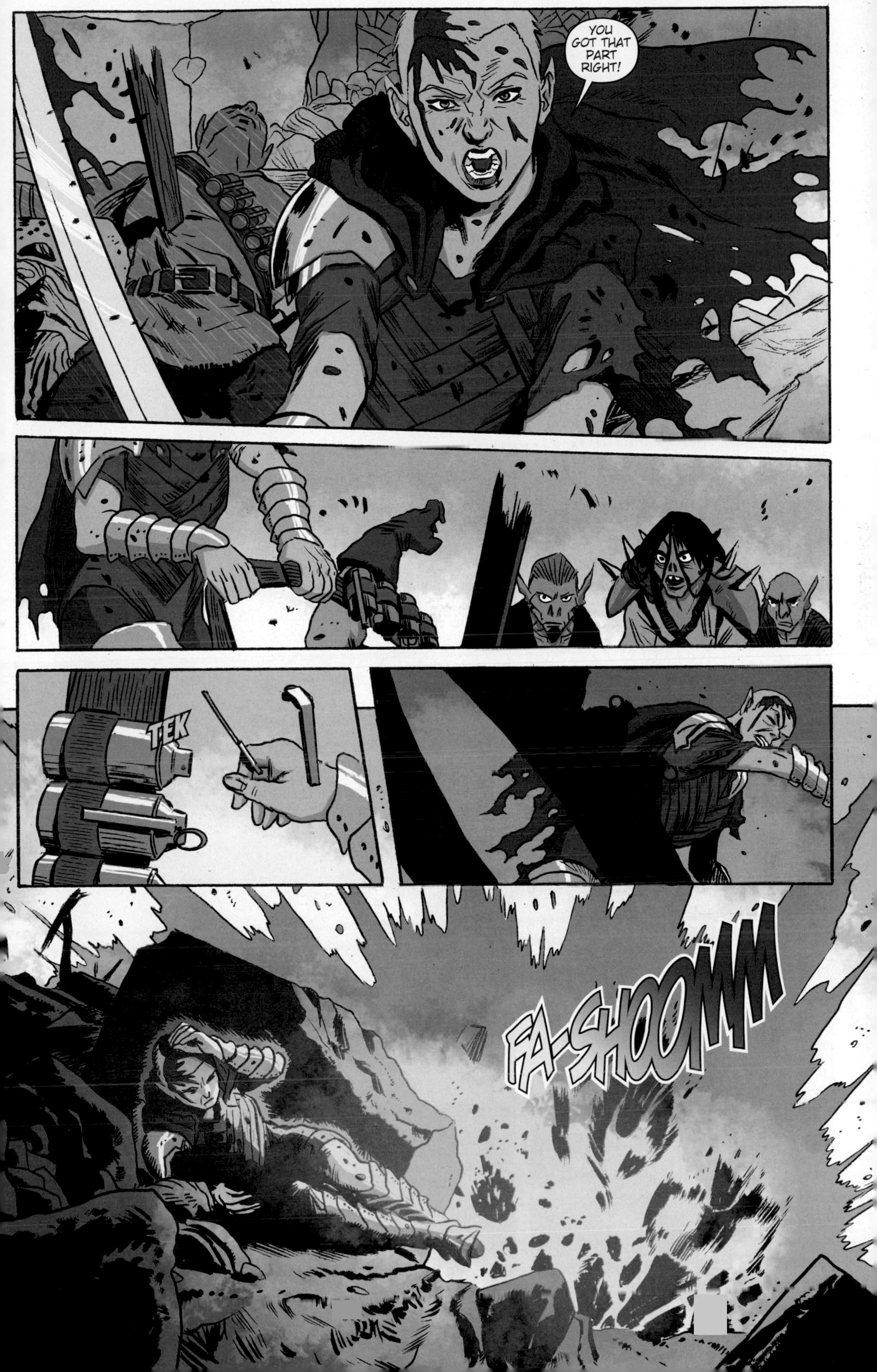
YOU GOT THAT PART RIGHT!
TEK
FA-SHOOMM

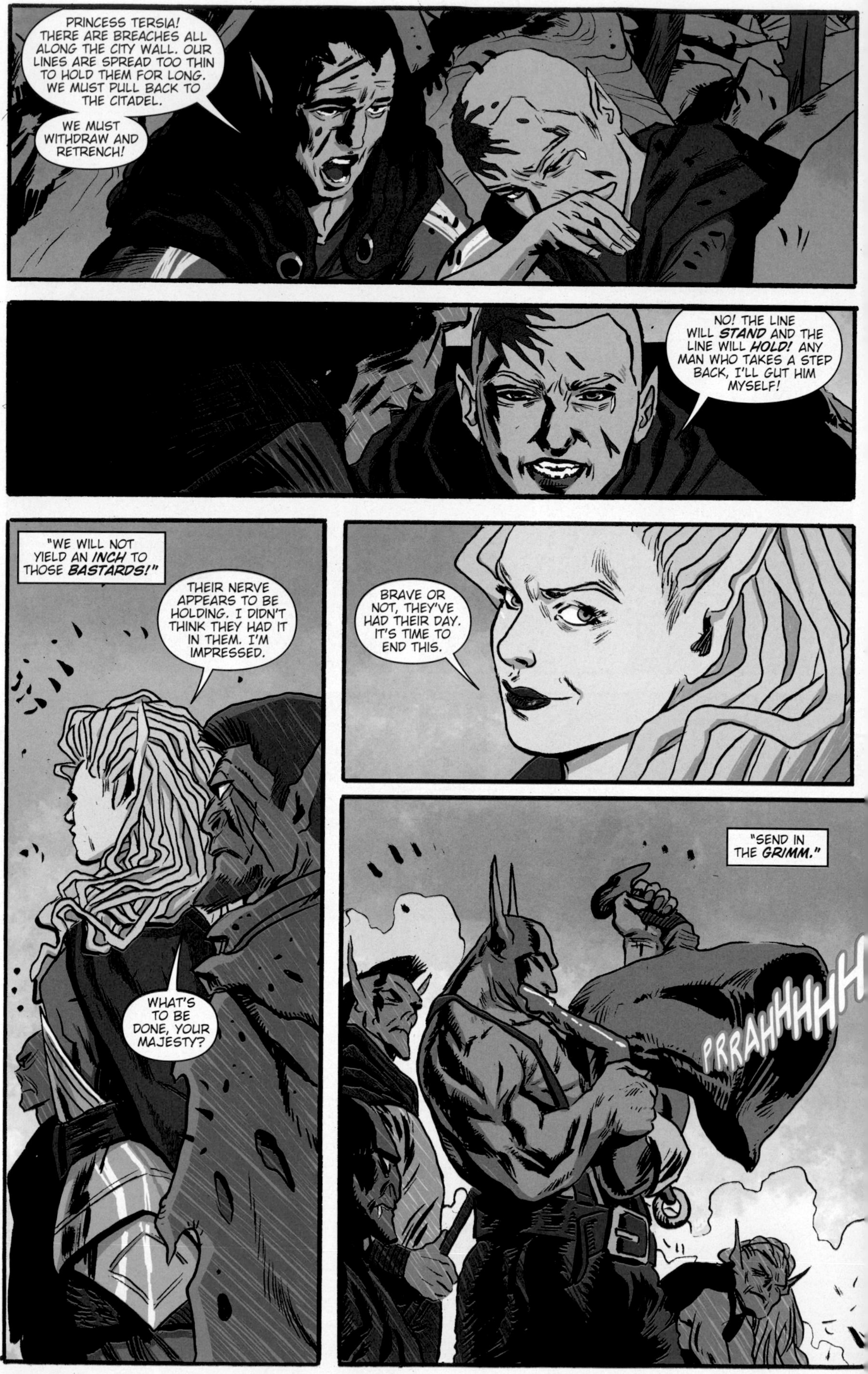
PRINCESS TERSIA! THERE ARE BREACHES ALL ALONG THE CITY WALL. OUR LINES ARE SPREAD TOO THIN TO HOLD THEM FOR LONG. WE MUST PULL BACK TO THE CITADEL.
WE MUST WITHDRAW AND RETRENCH!
NO! THE LINE WILL STAND AND THE LINE WILL HOLD! ANY MAN WHO TAKES A STEP BACK, I'LL GUT HIM MYSELF!
"WE WILL NOT YIELD AN INCH TO THOSE BASTARDS!"
THEIR NERVE APPEARS TO BE HOLDING. I DIDN'T THINK THEY HAD IT IN THEM. I'M IMPRESSED.
WHAT'S TO BE DONE, YOUR MAJESTY?
BRAVE OR NOT, THEY'VE HAD THEIR DAY. IT'S TIME TO END THIS.
"SEND IN THE GRIMM."
PRRAHHHHHH

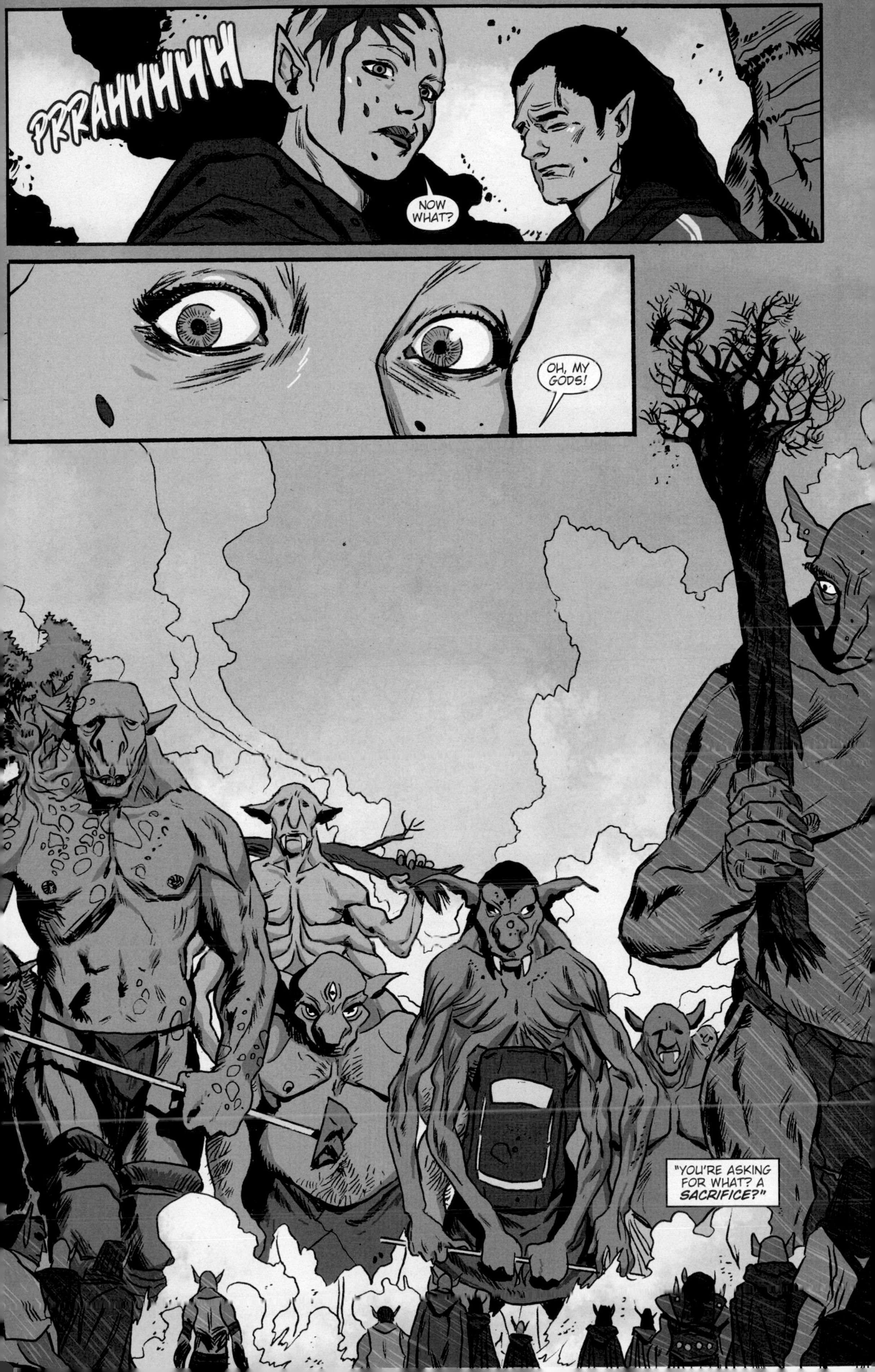
PRRAHHHHHH
NOW WHAT?
OH, MY GODS!
"YOU'RE ASKING FOR WHAT? A SACRIFICE?"

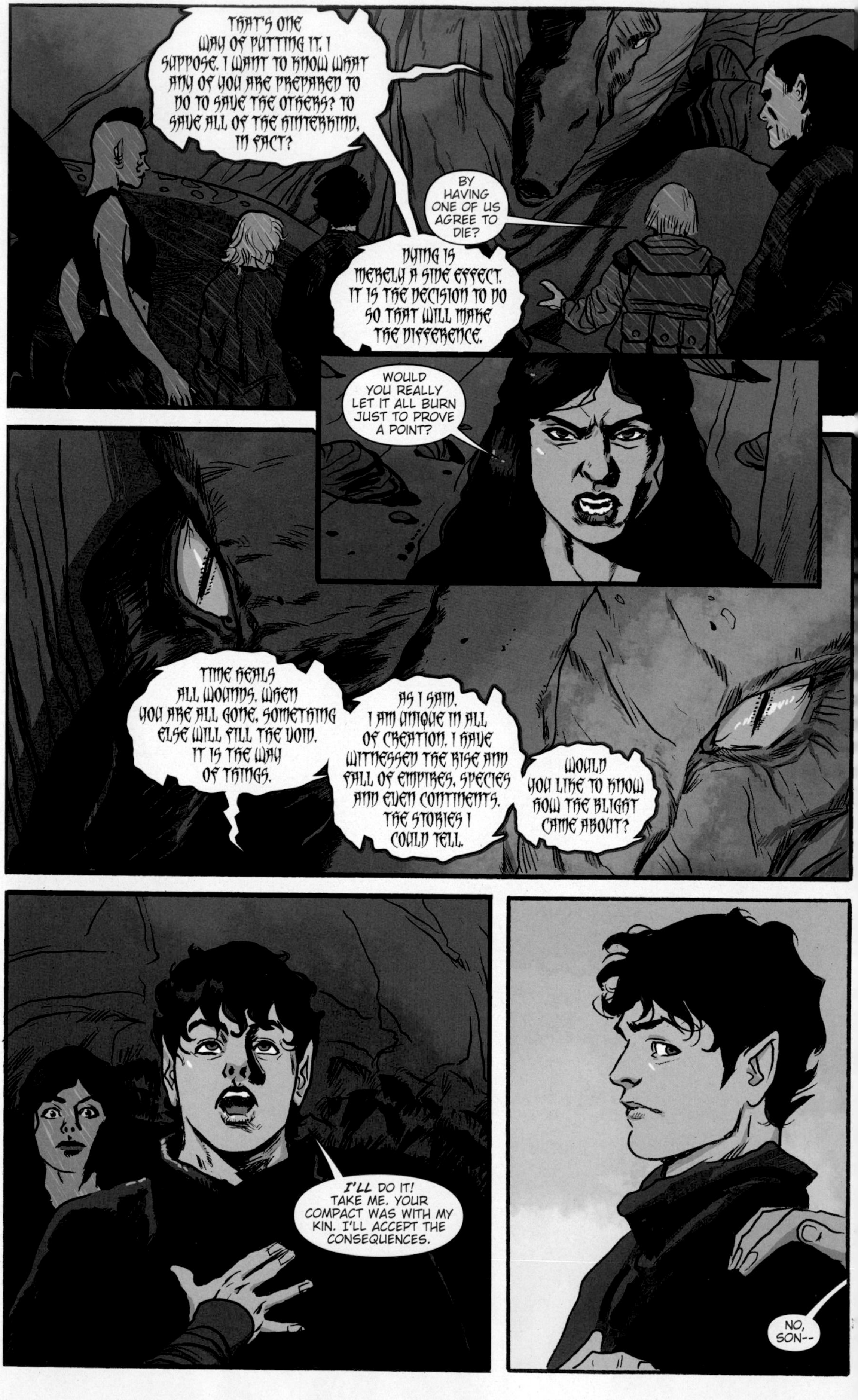
THAT'S ONE WAY OF PUTTING IT, I SUPPOSE. I WANT TO KNOW WHAT ANY OF YOU ARE PREPARED TO DO TO SAVE THE OTHERS? TO SAVE ALL OF THE HINTERKIND, IN FACT?
BY HAVING ONE OF US AGREE TO DIE?
DYING IS MERELY A SIDE EFFECT. IT IS THE DECISION TO DO SO THAT WILL MAKE THE DIFFERENCE.
WOULD YOU REALLY LET IT ALL BURN JUST TO PROVE A POINT?
TIME HEALS ALL WOUNDS. WHEN YOU ARE ALL GONE, SOMETHING ELSE WILL FILL THE VOID. IT IS THE WAY OF THINGS.
AS I SAID, I AM UNIQUE IN ALL OF CREATION. I HAVE WITNESSED THE RISE AND FALL OF EMPIRES, SPECIES AND EVEN CONTINENTS. THE STORIES I COULD TELL.
WOULD YOU LIKE TO KNOW HOW THE BLIGHT CAME ABOUT?
I'LL DO IT! TAKE ME. YOUR COMPACT WAS WITH MY KIN. I'LL ACCEPT THE CONSEQUENCES.
NO, SON--

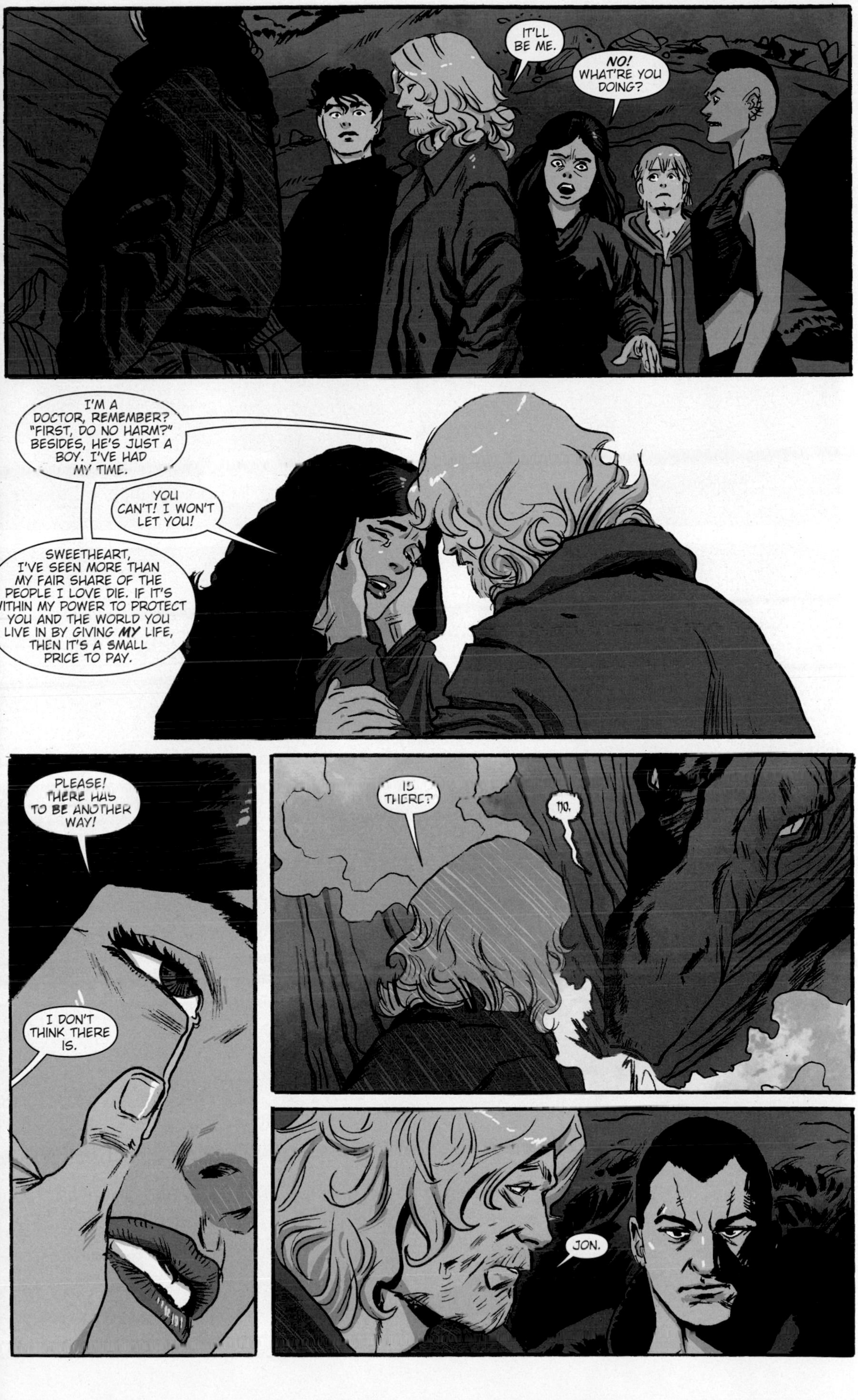
IT'LL BE ME.
NO! WHAT'RE YOU DOING?
I'M A DOCTOR, REMEMBER? "FIRST, DO NO HARM?" BESIDES, HE'S JUST A BOY. I'VE HAD MY TIME.
YOU CAN'T! I WON'T LET YOU!
SWEETHEART, I'VE SEEN MORE THAN MY FAIR SHARE OF THE PEOPLE I LOVE DIE. IF IT'S WITHIN MY POWER TO PROTECT YOU AND THE WORLD YOU LIVE IN BY GIVING MY LIFE, THEN IT'S A SMALL PRICE TO PAY.
PLEASE! THERE HAS TO BE ANOTHER WAY!
I DON'T THINK THERE IS.
IS THERE?
NO.
JON.

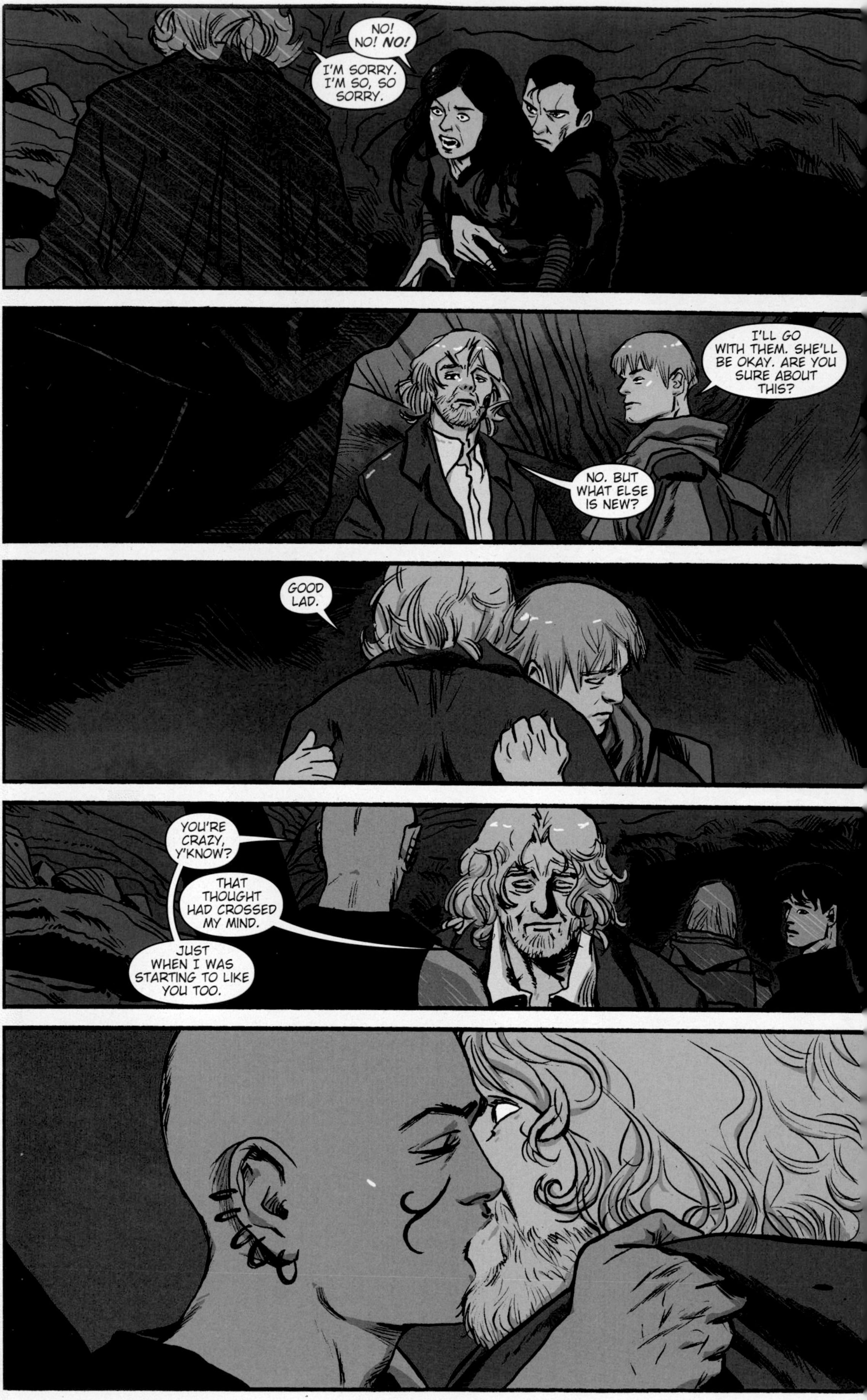
NO! NO! NO!
I'M SORRY. I'M SO, SO SORRY.
I'LL GO WITH THEM. SHE'LL BE OKAY. ARE YOU SURE ABOUT THIS?
NO. BUT WHAT ELSE IS NEW?
GOOD LAD.
YOU'RE CRAZY, Y'KNOW?
THAT THOUGHT HAD CROSSED MY MIND.
JUST WHEN I WAS STARTING TO LIKE YOU TOO.

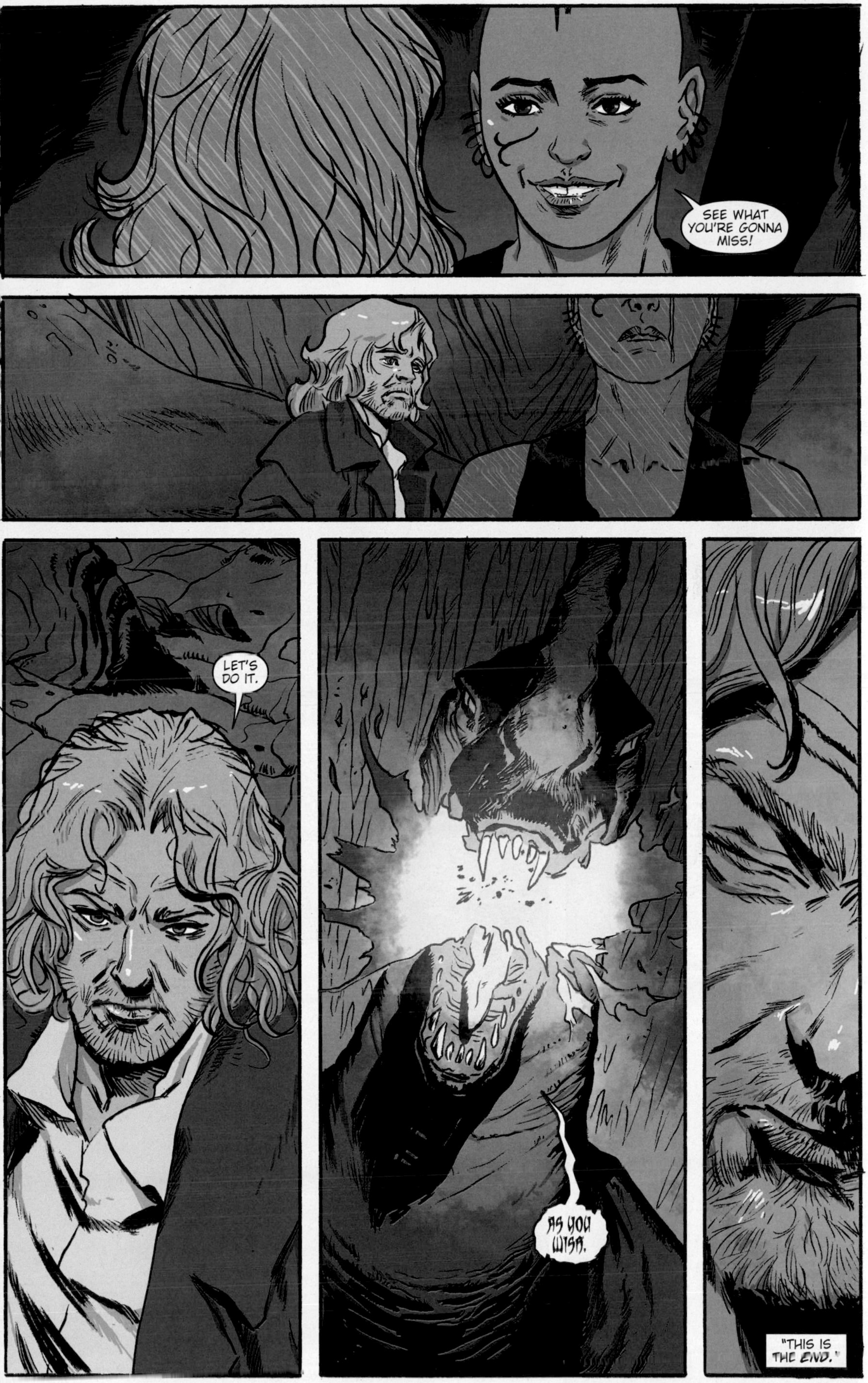
SEE WHAT YOU'RE GONNA MISS!
LET'S DO IT.
AS YOU WISH.
"THIS IS THE END."

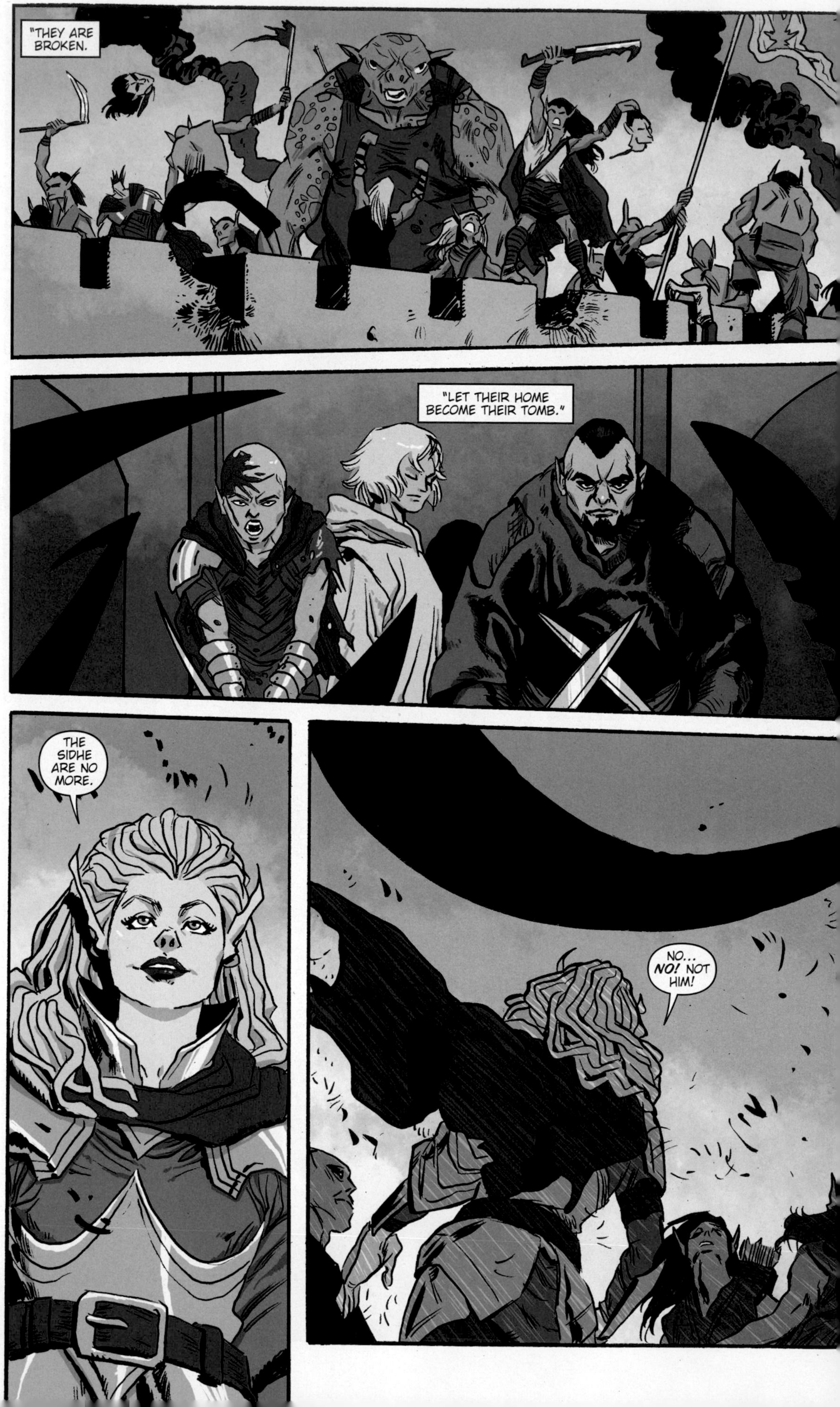
"THEY ARE BROKEN.
"LET THEIR HOME BECOME THEIR TOMB."
THE SIDHE ARE NO MORE.
NO... NO! NOT HIM!

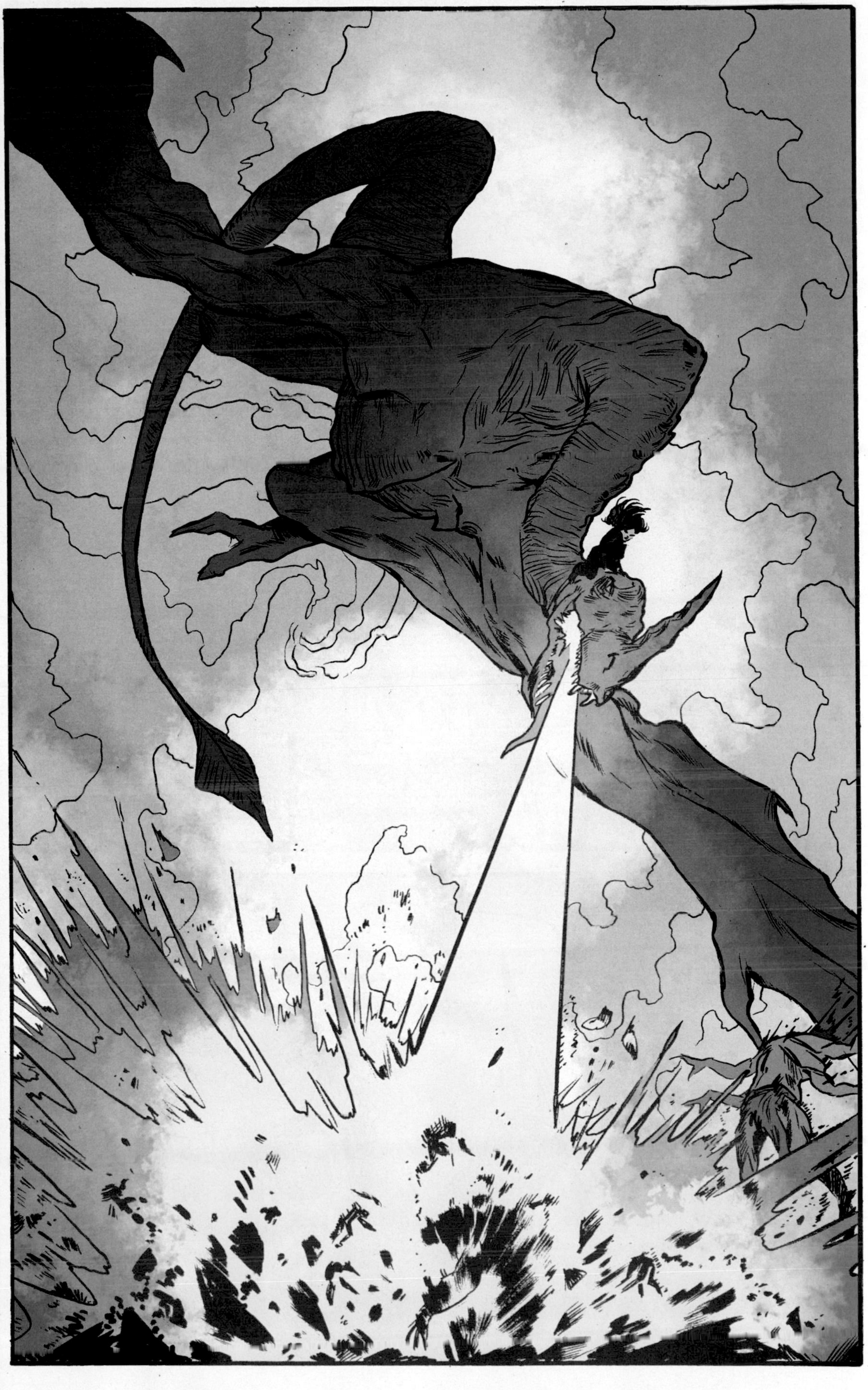

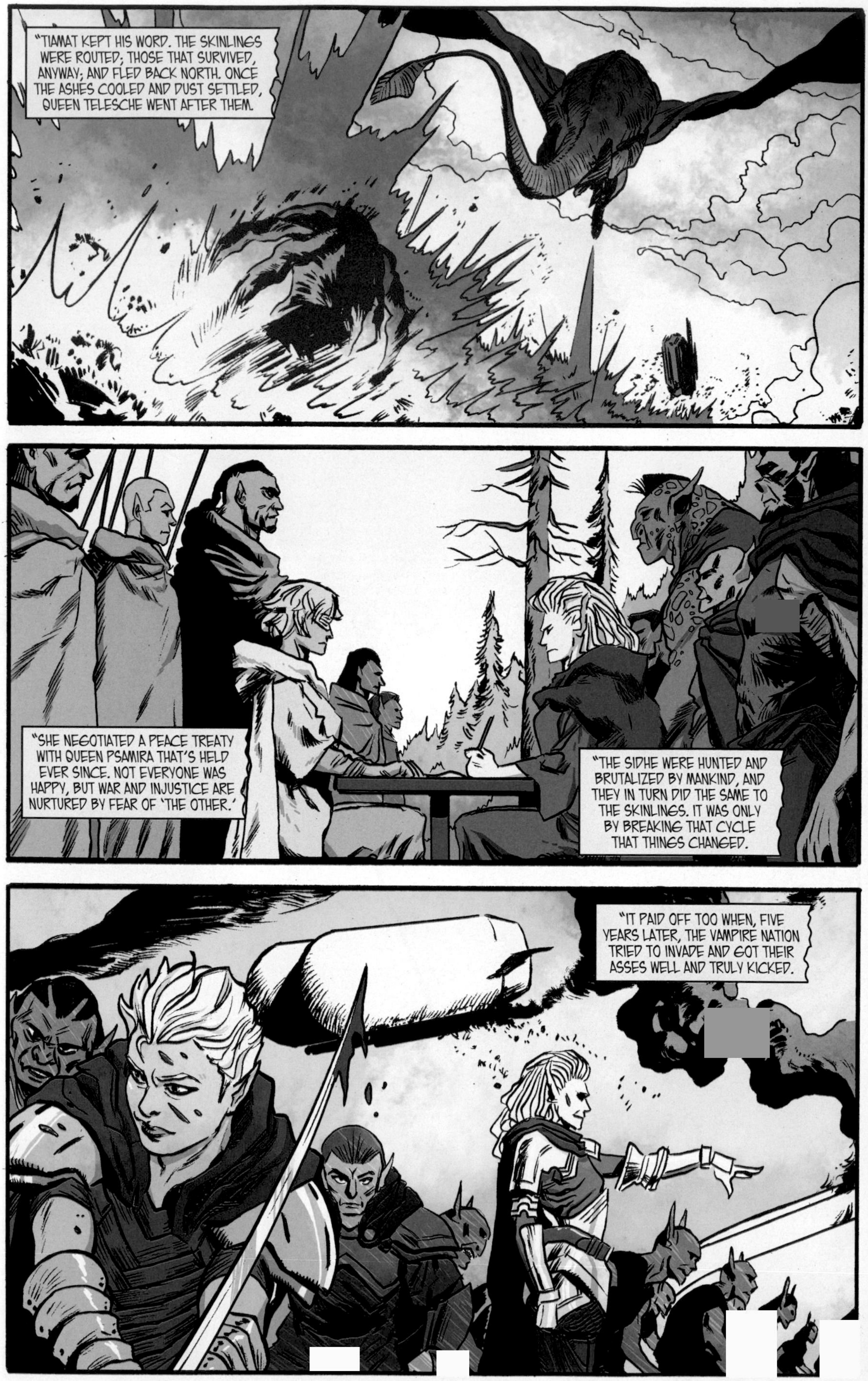
"TIAMAT KEPT HIS WORD. THE SKINLINGS WERE ROUTED; THOSE THAT SURVIVED, ANYWAY; AND FLED BACK NORTH. ONCE THE ASHES COOLED AND DUST SETTLED, QUEEN TELESCHE WENT AFTER THEM.
"SHE NEGOTIATED A PEACE TREATY WITH QUEEN PSAMIRA THAT'S HELD EVER SINCE. NOT EVERYONE WAS HAPPY, BUT WAR AND INJUSTICE ARE NURTURED BY FEAR OF 'THE OTHER.'
"THE SIDHE WERE HUNTED AND BRUTALIZED BY MANKIND, AND THEY IN TURN DID THE SAME TO THE SKINLINGS. IT WAS ONLY BY BREAKING THAT CYCLE THAT THINGS CHANGED.
"IT PAID OFF TOO WHEN, FIVE YEARS LATER, THE VAMPIRE NATION TRIED TO INVADE AND GOT THEIR ASSES WELL AND TRULY KICKED.

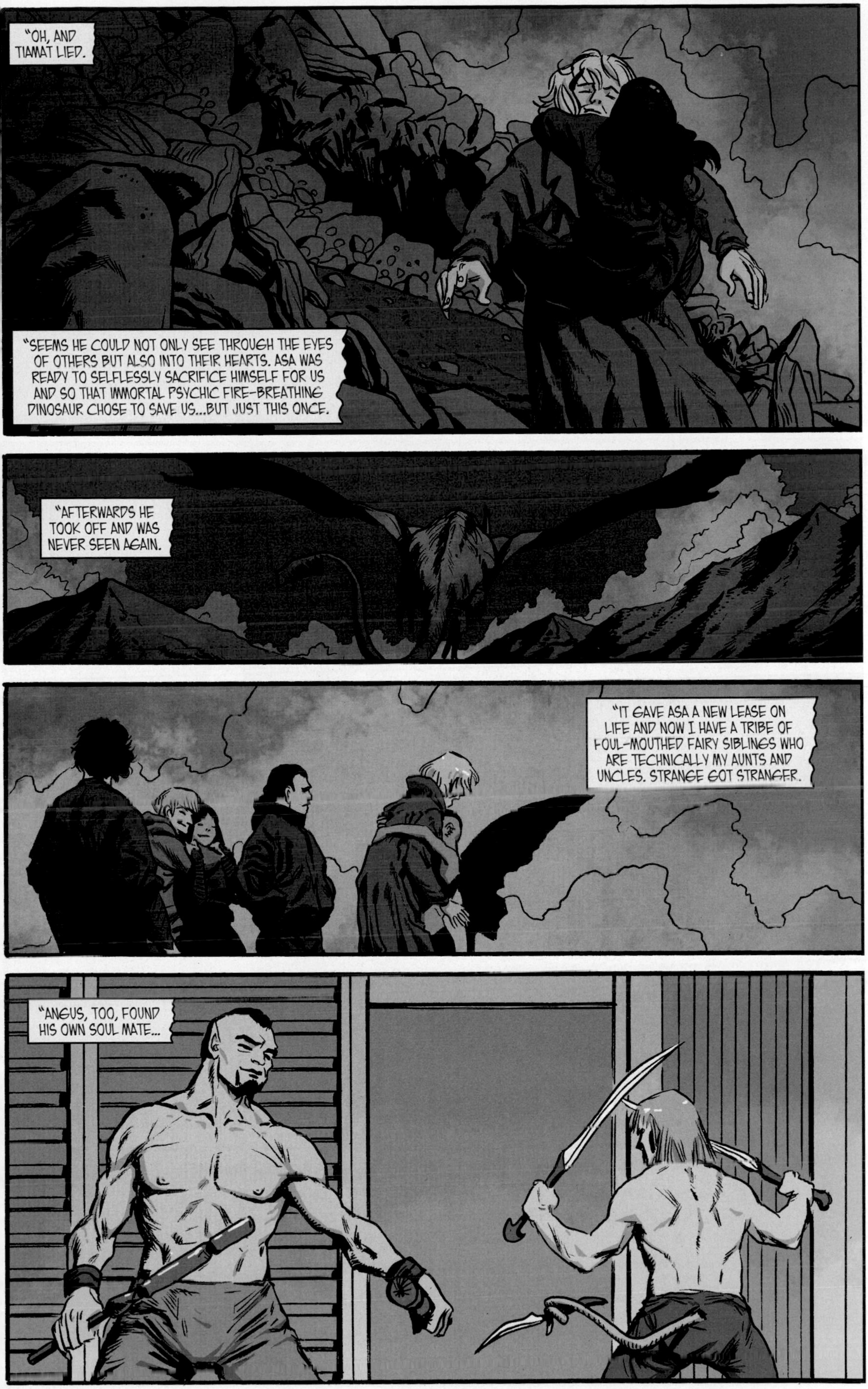
"OH, AND TIAMAT LIED.
"SEEMS HE COULD NOT ONLY SEE THROUGH THE EYES OF OTHERS BUT ALSO INTO THEIR HEARTS. ASA WAS READY TO SELFLESSLY SACRIFICE HIMSELF FOR US AND SO THAT IMMORTAL PSYCHIC FIRE-BREATHING DINOSAUR CHOSE TO SAVE US...BUT JUST THIS ONCE.
"AFTERWARDS HE TOOK OFF AND WAS NEVER SEEN AGAIN.
"IT GAVE ASA A NEW LEASE ON LIFE AND NOW I HAVE A TRIBE OF FOUL-MOUTHED FAIRY SIBLINGS WHO ARE TECHNICALLY MY AUNTS AND UNCLES. STRANGE GOT STRANGER.
"ANGUS, TOO, FOUND HIS OWN SOUL MATE...

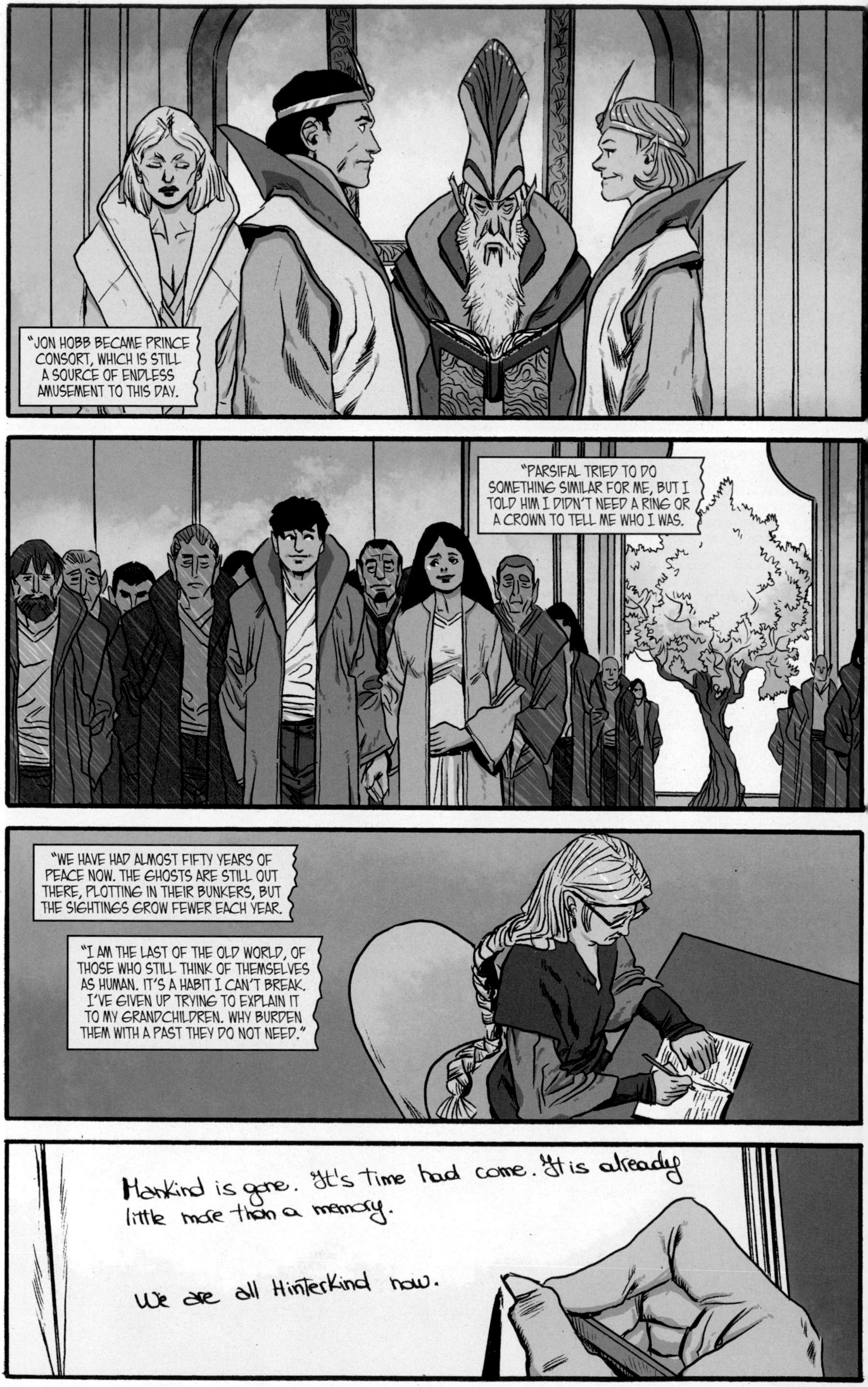
"JON HOBB BECAME PRINCE CONSORT, WHICH IS STILL A SOURCE OF ENDLESS AMUSEMENT TO THIS DAY.
"PARSIFAL TRIED TO DO SOMETHING SIMILAR FOR ME, BUT I TOLD HIM I DIDN'T NEED A RING OR A CROWN TO TELL ME WHO I WAS.
"WE HAVE HAD ALMOST FIFTY YEARS OF PEACE NOW. THE GHOSTS ARE STILL OUT THERE, PLOTTING IN THEIR BUNKERS, BUT THE SIGHTINGS GROW FEWER EACH YEAR.
"I AM THE LAST OF THE OLD WORLD, OF THOSE WHO STILL THINK OF THEMSELVES AS HUMAN. IT'S A HABIT I CAN'T BREAK. I'VE GIVEN UP TRYING TO EXPLAIN IT TO MY GRANDCHILDREN. WHY BURDEN THEM WITH A PAST THEY DO NOT NEED."
Mankind is gone. It's time had come. It is already little more than a memory.
We are all Hinterkind now.

THE END

ZONE COVERAGE

Thumbnail Layouts by Francesco Trifogli

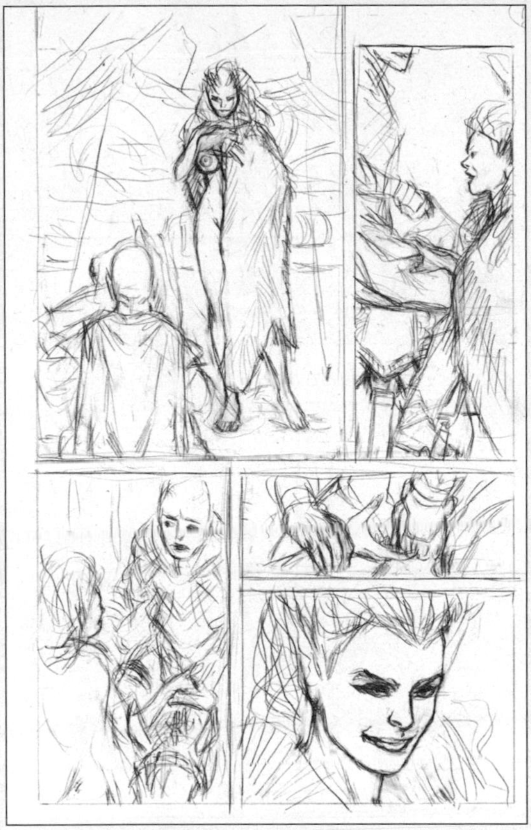

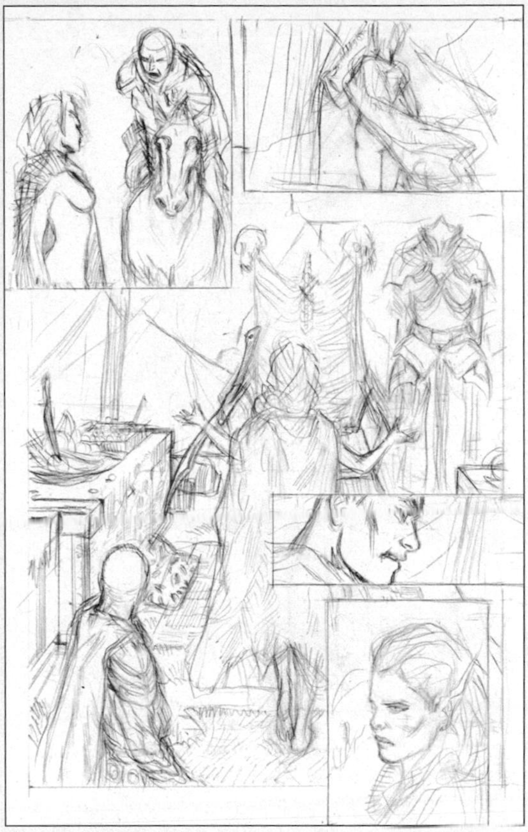

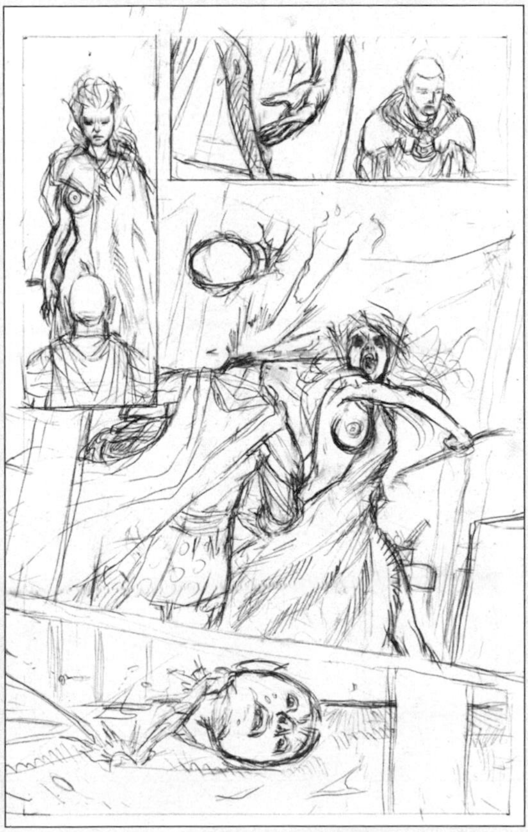

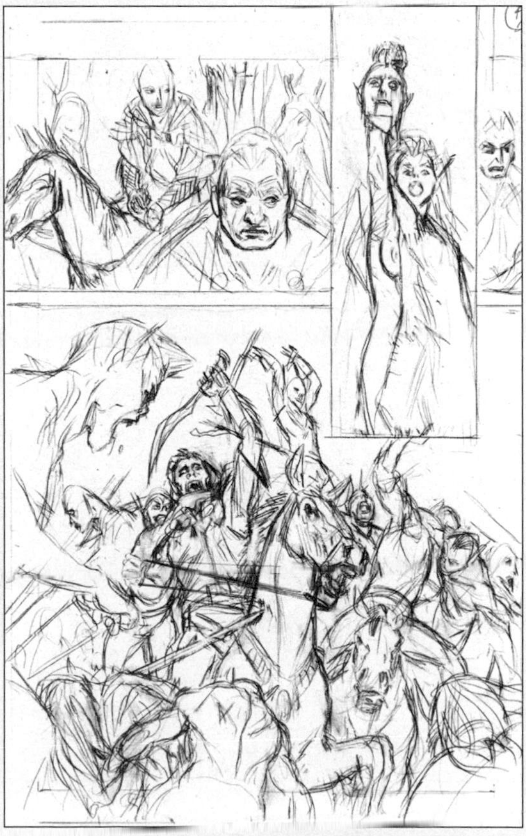

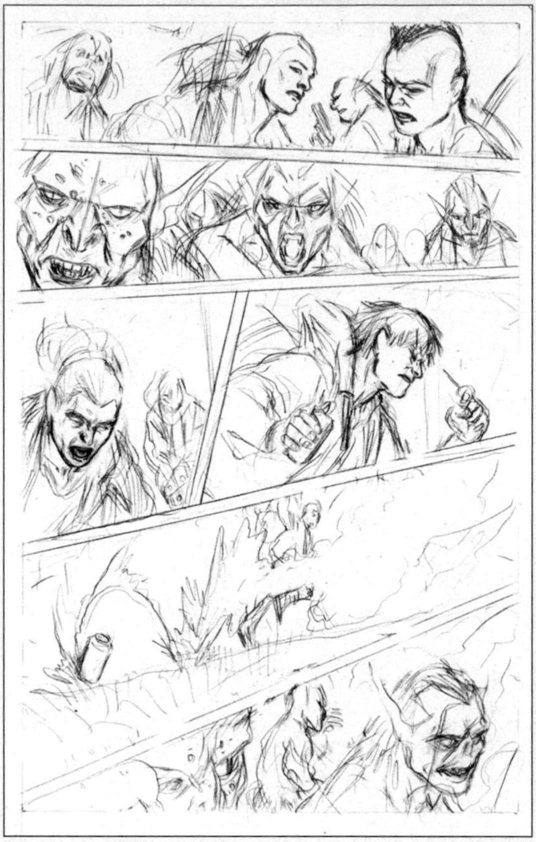
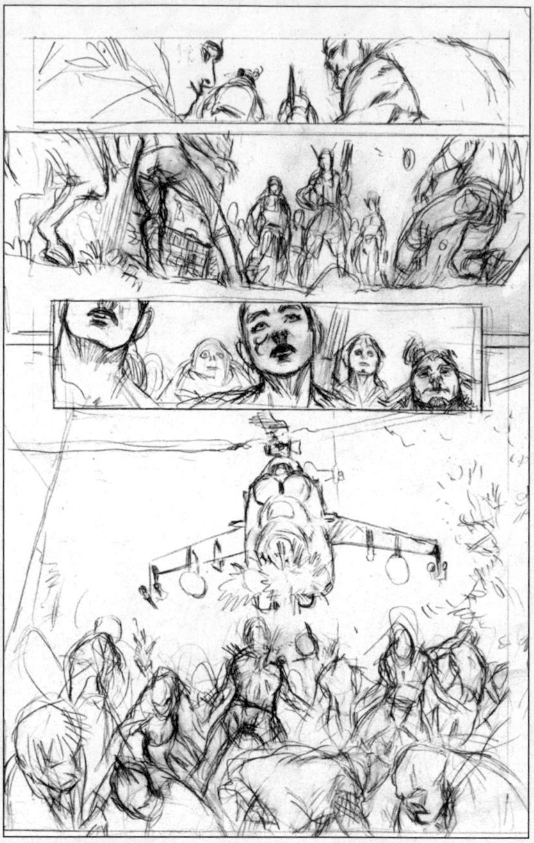
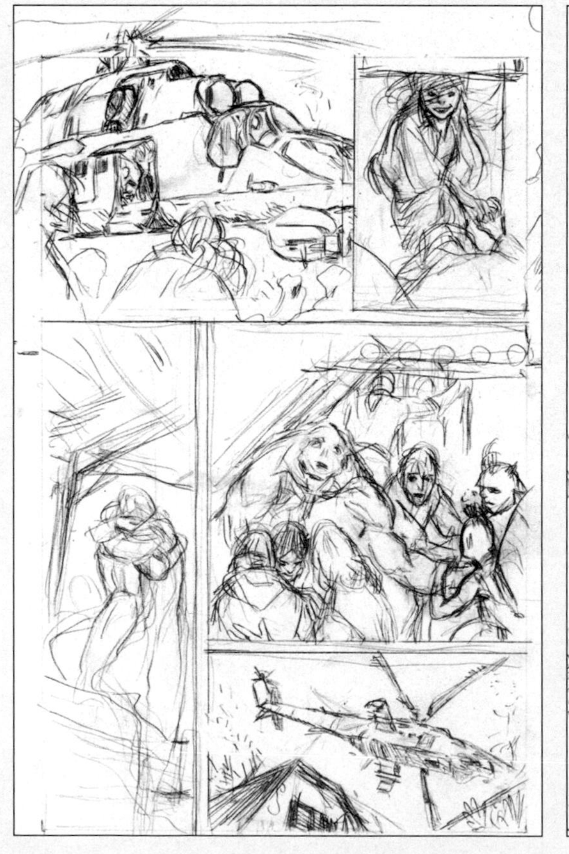
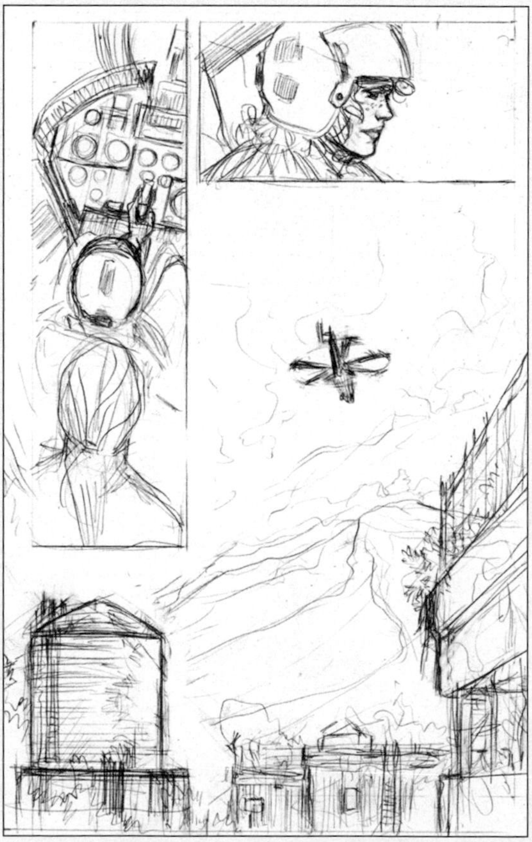

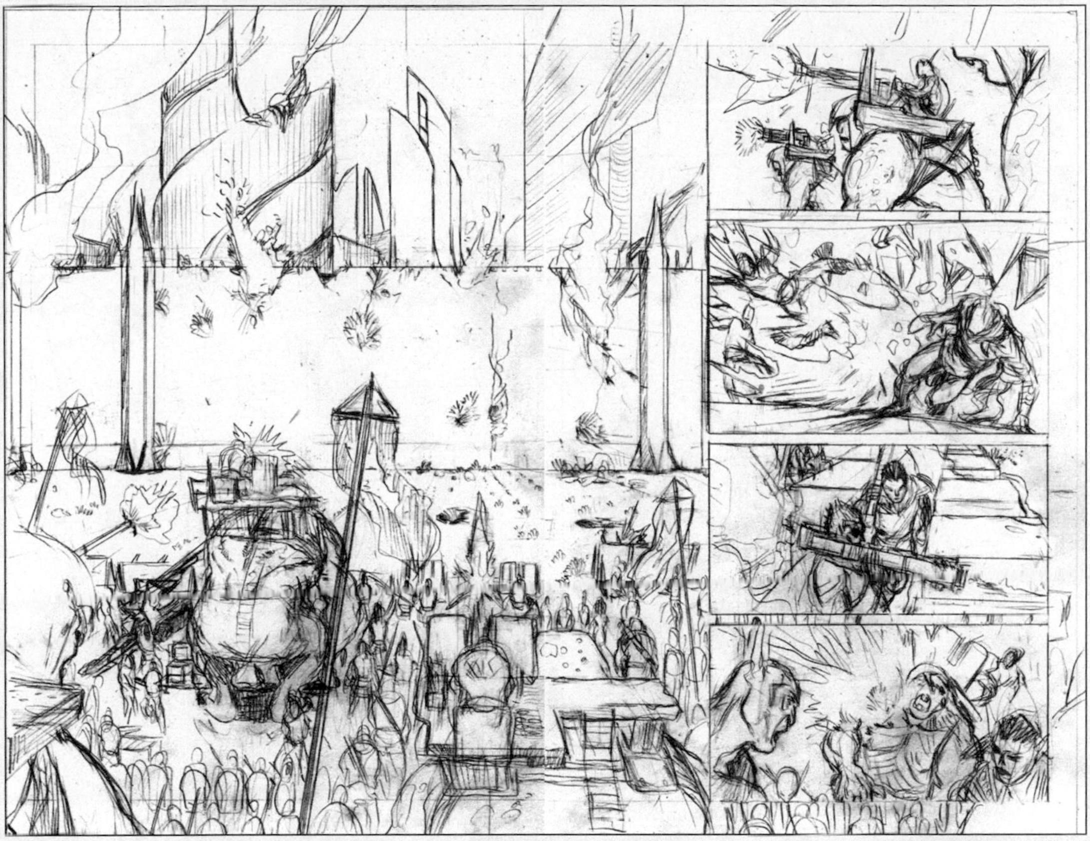

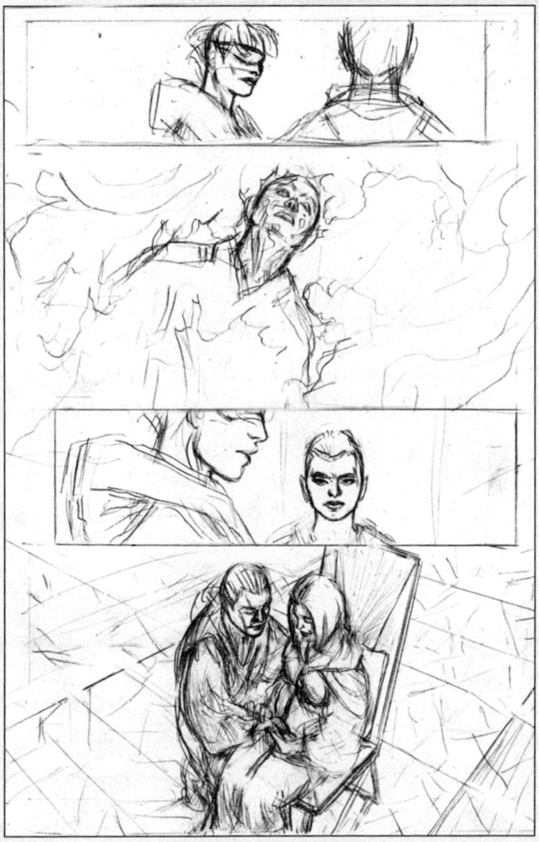

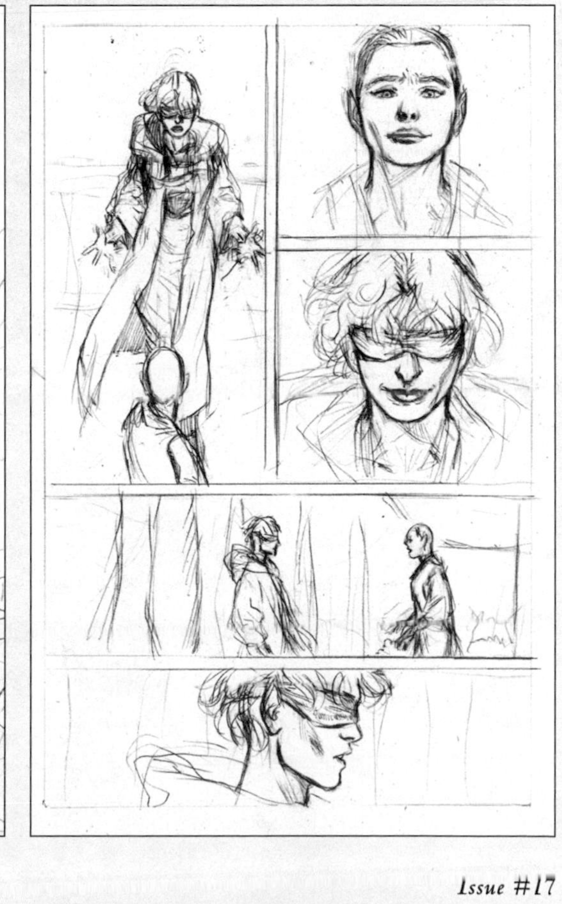

Issue #17

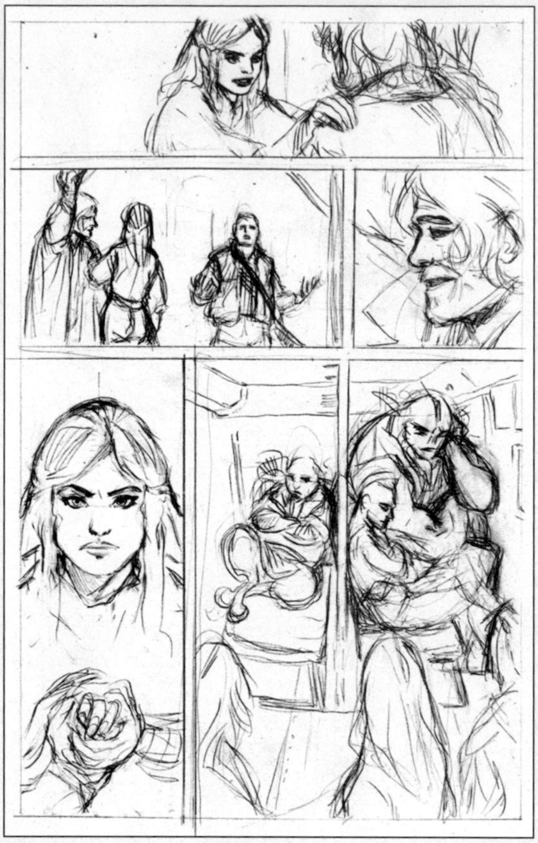
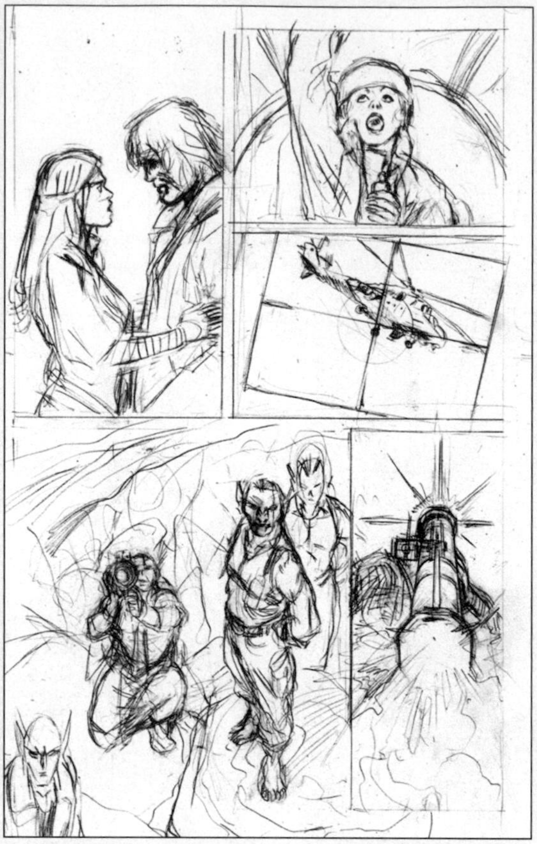
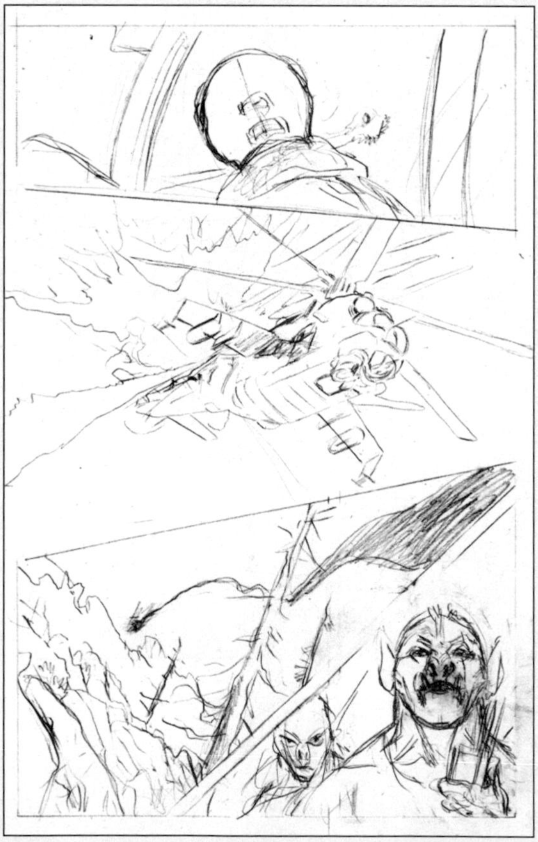
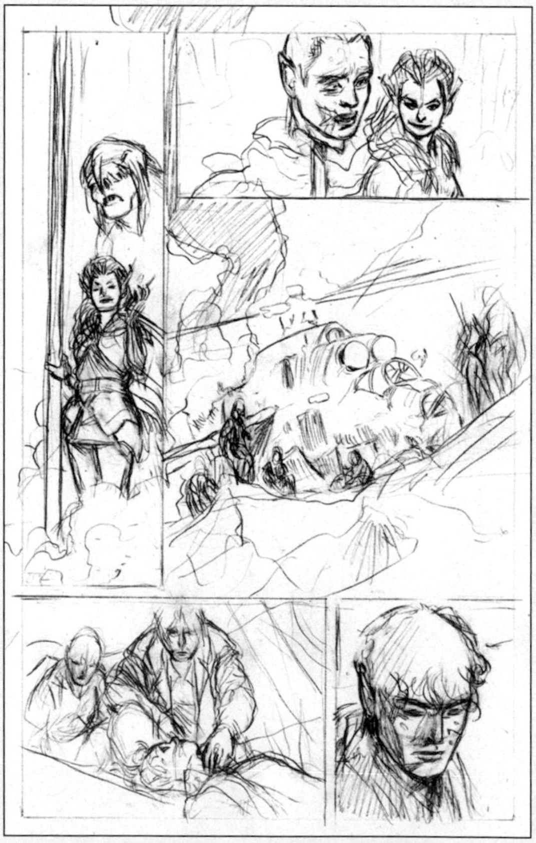

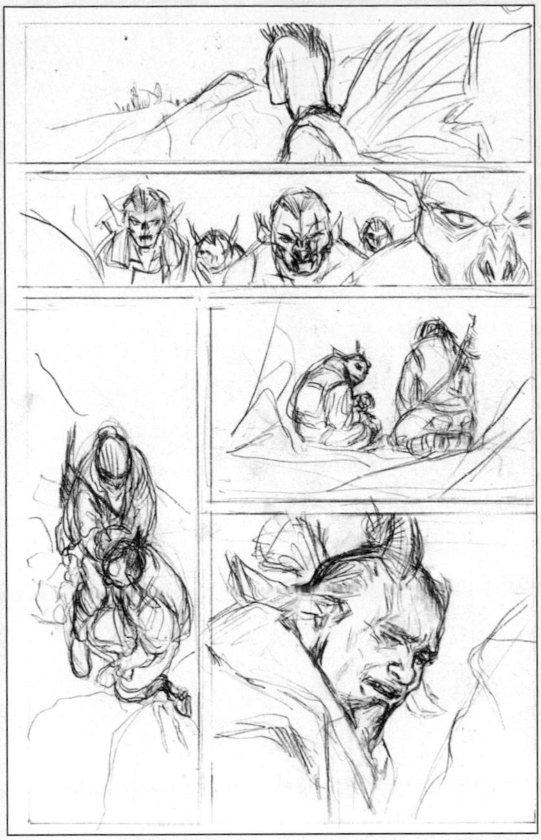
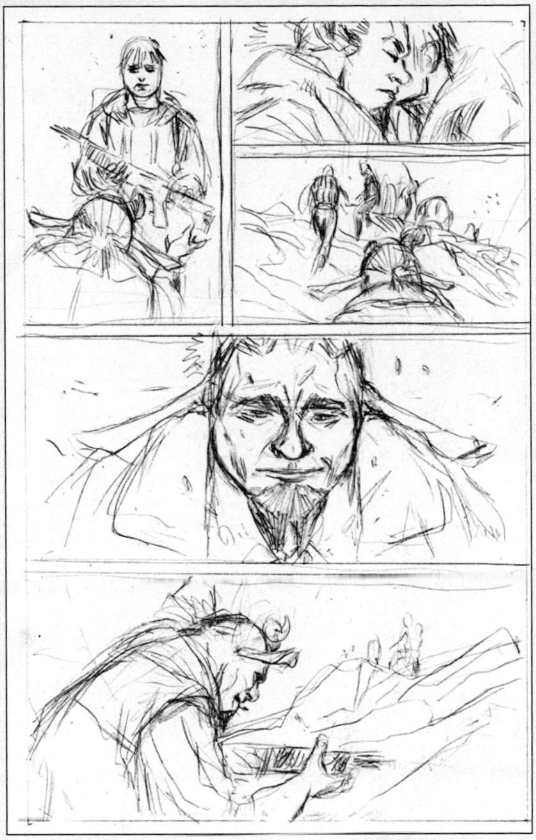
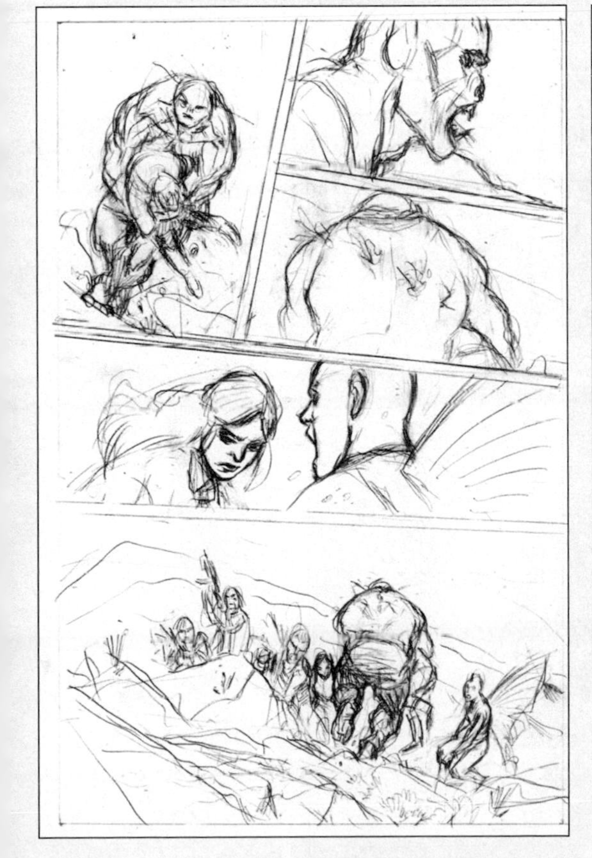
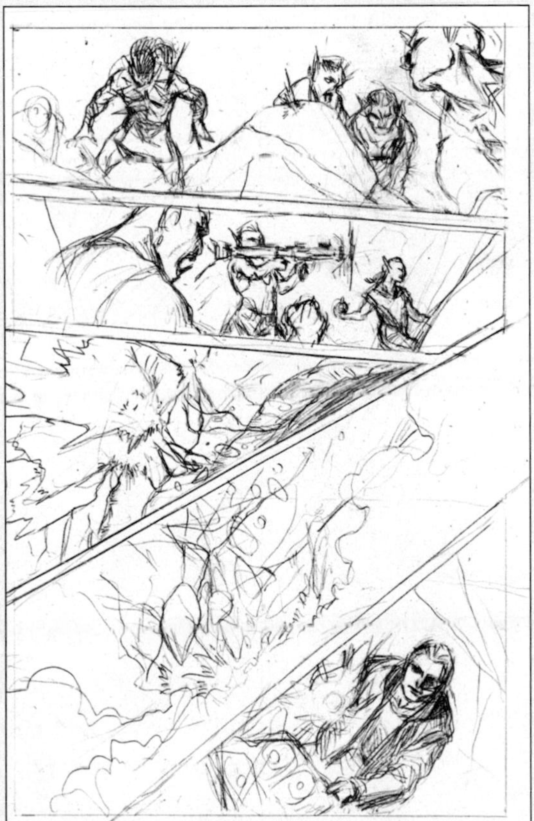

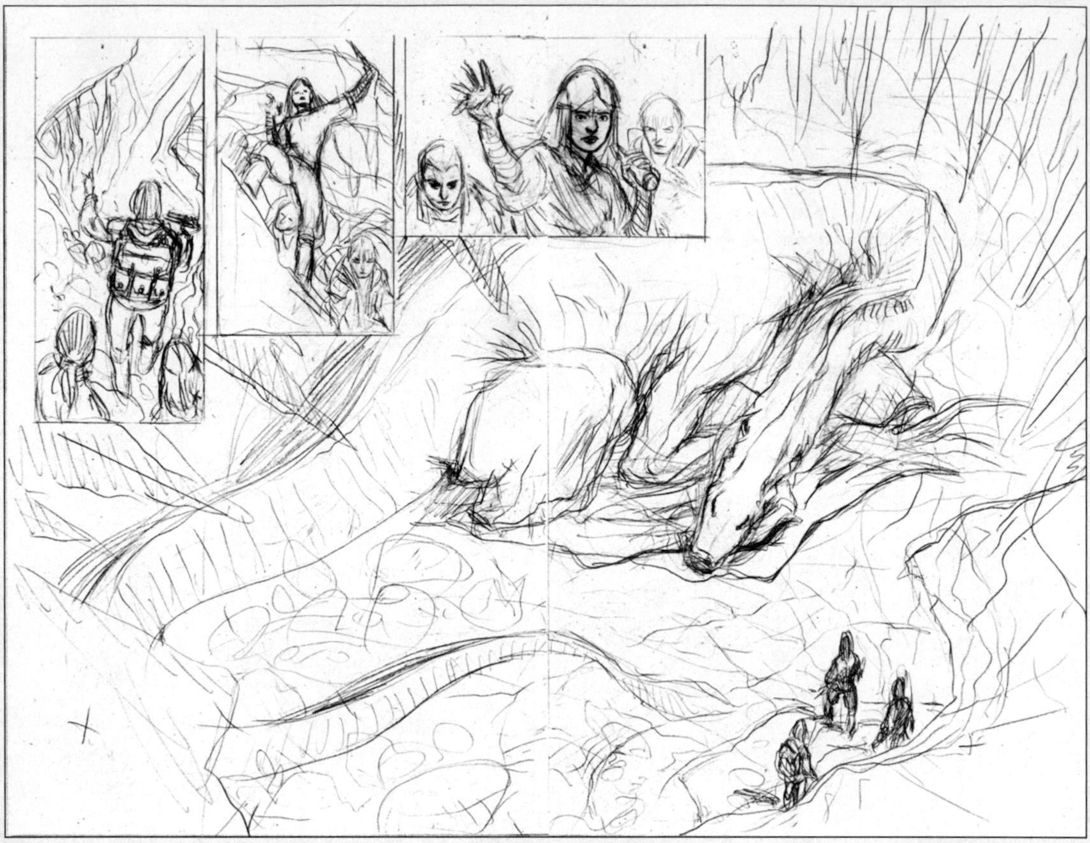
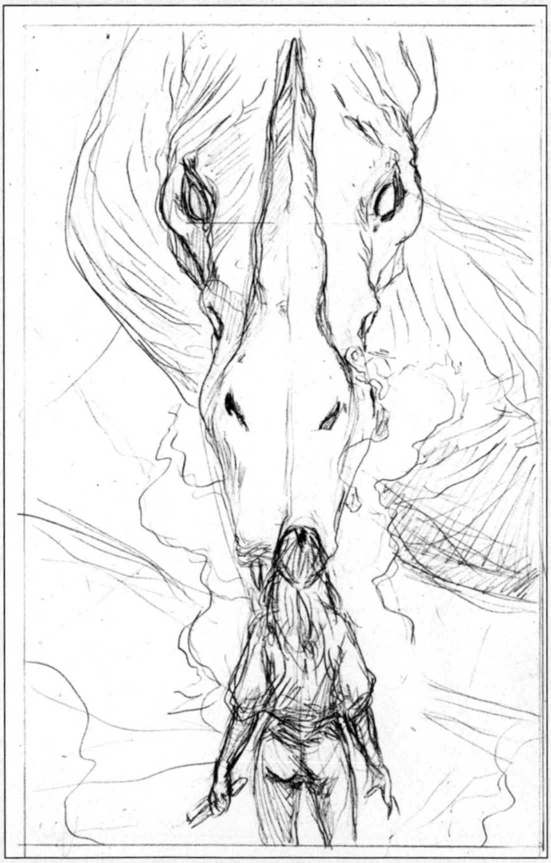

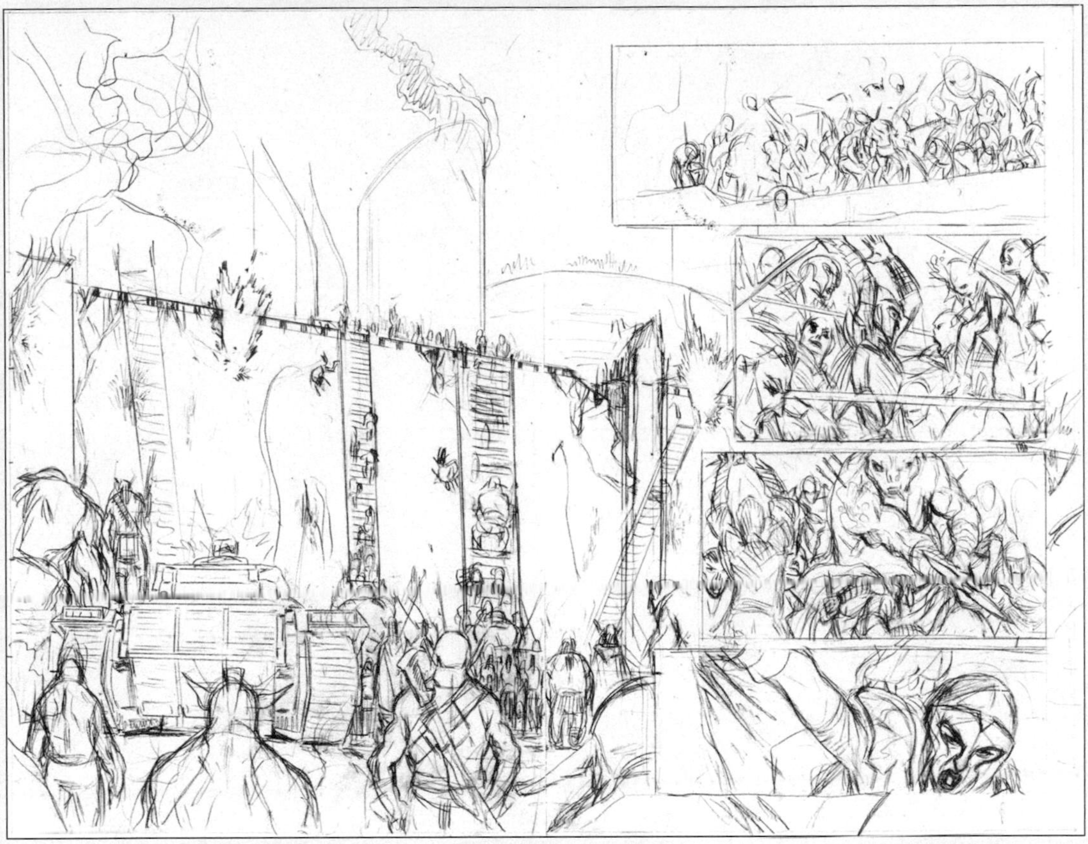

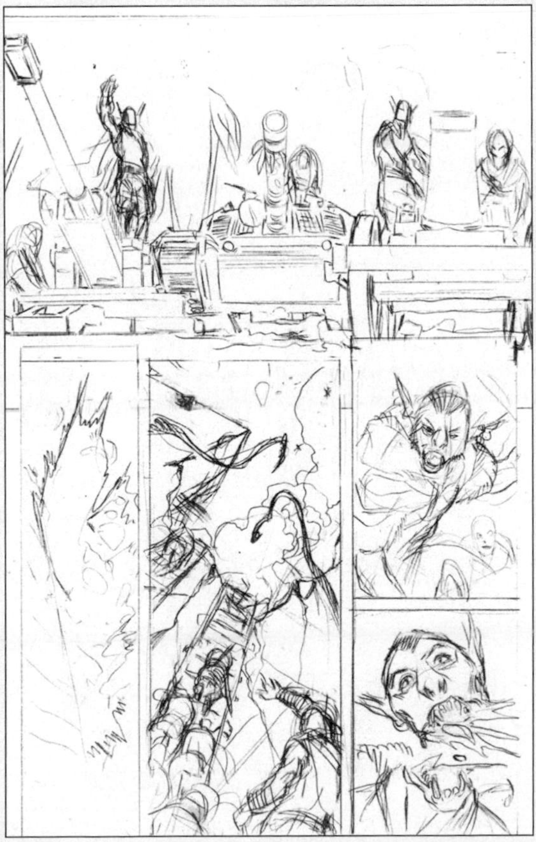

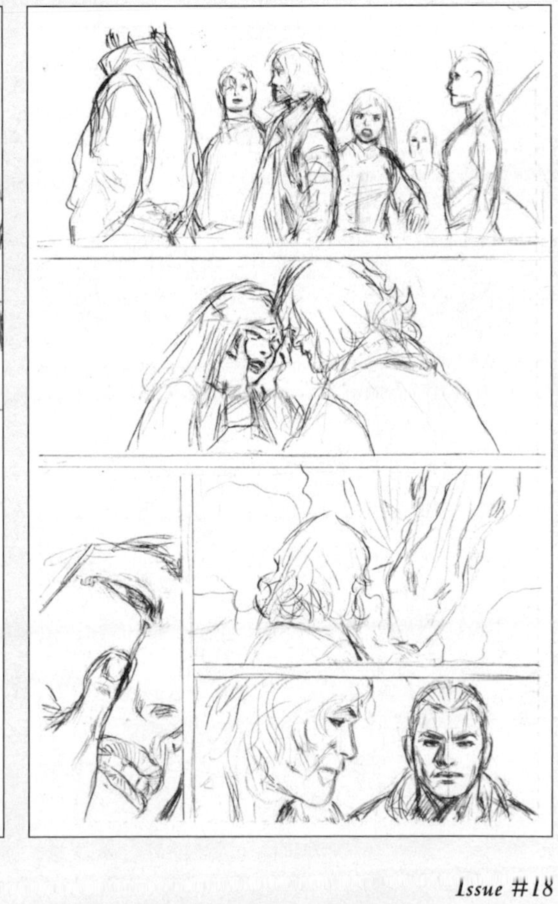

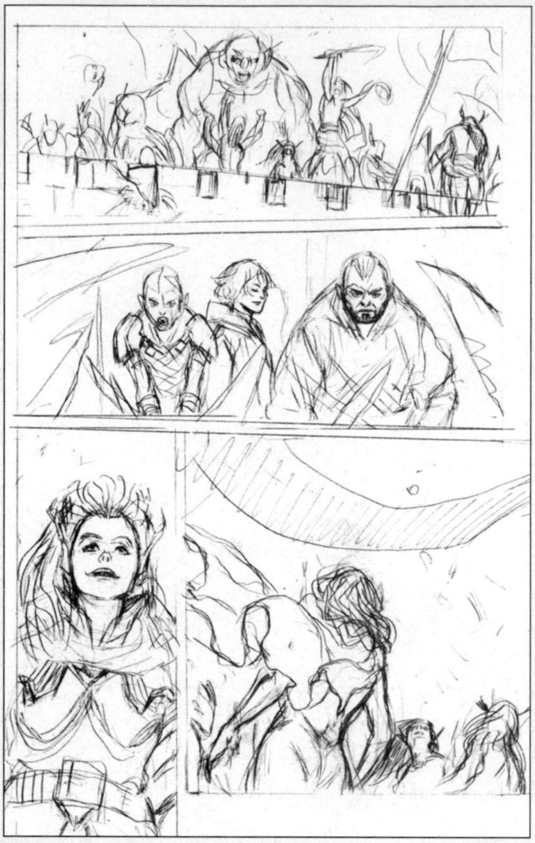
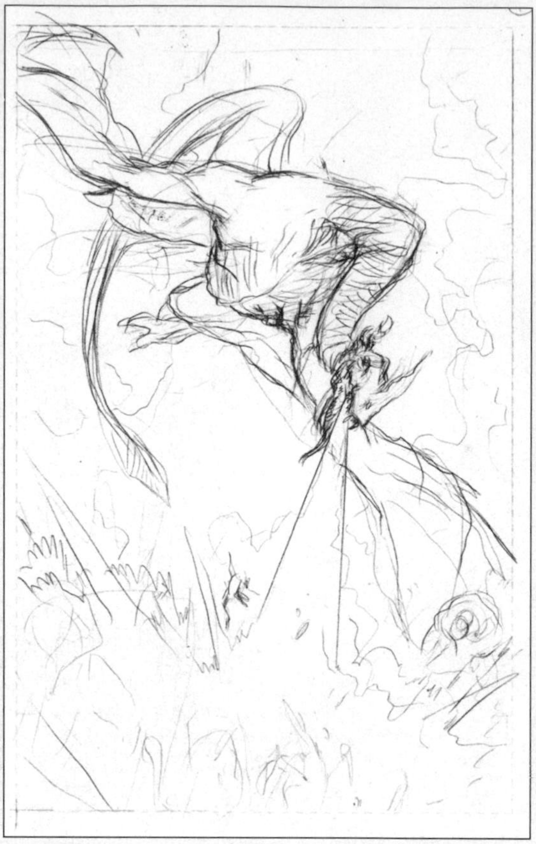
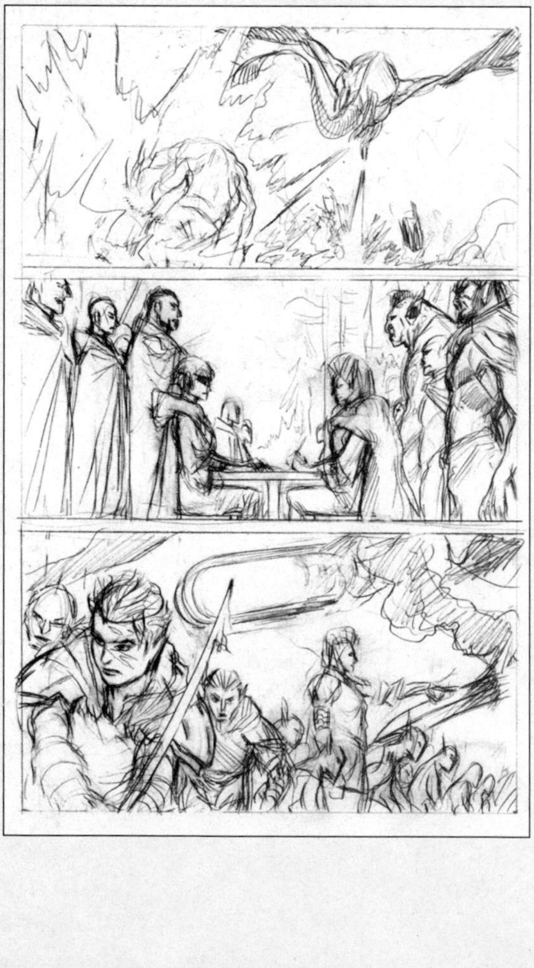
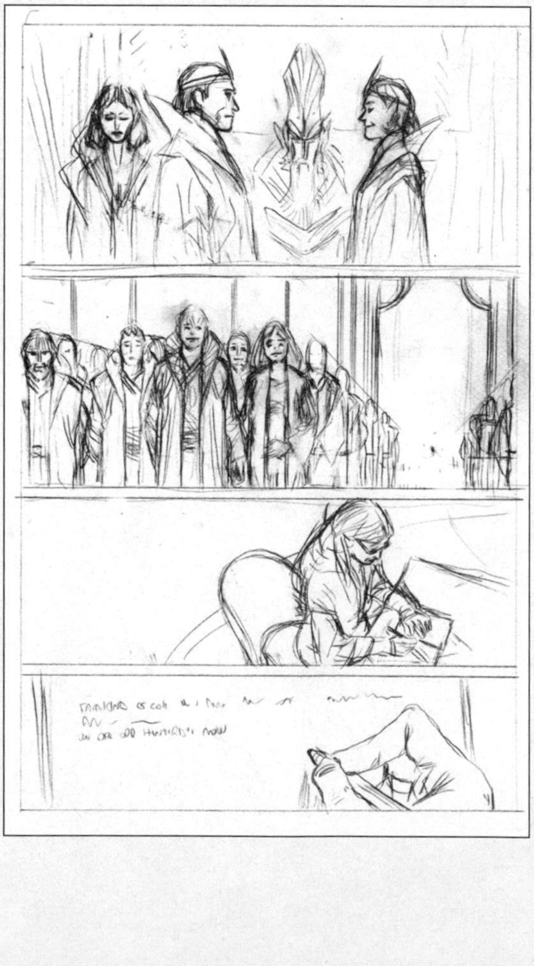